THE MISS-ADVENTURES OF AN IRREVERENT REVEREND

A Spirit-ed Guide for Rebels and Renegades

Rev. Stephanie Clarke

Rev. Stephanie Clarke
www.TimelessTransitions.net

Published by: TW Publishers, South Africa
www.publishingabook.co.za

ISBN: **978-0-9567716-3-6 (CreateSpace POD)**

Limits of Liability and Disclaimer of Warranty
The author and publisher shall not be liable for your misuse of this material. This book is strictly for informational and educational purposes.

Warning – Disclaimer
The purpose of this book is to educate and entertain. The author and/or publisher do not guarantee that anyone following these techniques, suggestions, tips, ideas, or strategies will become successful. The author and/or publisher shall have neither liability nor responsibility to anyone with respect to any loss or damage caused, or alleged to be caused, directly or indirectly by the information contained in this book.

TESTIMONIALS

A true citizen of the world, demonstrating the one-ness of us all.
Rev. Bob Grabowski, San Diego, USA

One counselling session with Rev Stephanie literally changed my life, as she uncovered the Truth for me. She set me on a path of discovery and study that gave life new meaning. I am forever grateful to this amazing teacher.
Melanie Hall RScP- School Teacher & Librarian, Johannesburg, S. Africa

Rev Stephanie Clarke is truly a Great Teacher, Inspirational Spiritual Leader, counsellor and friend. She embodies all that is Love, Joy and Peace. Her passion and enthusiasm towards teaching her students goes far beyond the call of duty. I am so blessed to have been taught and touched by this Beautiful Generous Spirit. Rev. Steph, thank you for allowing Spirit to move through you and as you. You taught me that IT IS ALL GOD and ALL GOOD!
Miriam Nunes, AiAfrica Travel, Cape Town, South Africa

Rev. Stephanie Clarke is a brilliant teacher, extraordinary minister and inspiring speaker. She is also delightful, charming and witty! But what I really wanted to talk about is how sexy she is, so full of "IT" and with a twinkle in her eye, and an appetite for life that this one lifetime cannot possibly satisfy.....
Rev. Nancy Zala, ordained New Thought minister at the Agape International Spiritual Center, and author of 'The Joy of Affirmative Prayer,' LA, CA, USA

Rev. Stephanie was one of my first teachers of New Thought, her authenticity and straight forwardness is what inspired me to take on the mantle of counsellor and teacher myself.
Rev. Ron Blair, (Agape) LA, CA, USA

Rev. Stephanie is amazing: a true world citizen and spiritual light who travels the globe bringing insight, wisdom and healing to all she meets.
Rev. Alice Bandy, The Heart of Teaching Center, Encinitas, CA, USA

Rev. Stephanie Clarke never fails to amaze me! Her creative spirit, enthusiasm and big loving heart are some of her exquisite qualities I have learnt to cherish so much. I feel fortunate, indeed, for the opportunity to have been one of her students. I enjoy her wonderful gift of creating meaningful and deeply touching ceremonies for many different occasions. Her ability to teach spiritual topics is phenomenal, especially with regard to getting her students involved in processes, discovering transformational tools, liberating us from being stuck in worn-out thinking patterns and moving us with ease and understanding into the freedom to make choices that serve the higher and greater good of all. I am grateful for her presence in my life and for the bright light emanating from her being.
Rev. Gerd Pontow, International Spiritual Director, Soul Home, S. Africa

ACKNOWLEDGEMENTS

I would like to acknowledge:

The Lords and Masters of the Akashic Records for being there to inspire my writing.

My spiritual teachers on both sides of the veil: Rev. Gladys Harrison in South Africa 1985-1989, Rev. Dr. Michael Beckwith, Rev. Carole Traylor, Rev. Joan Steadman and Rev. Nirvana Gayle at the Agape International Center of Truth, LA, 1992-1999. Also Zuriel Amadis, a student of Joel Goldsmith and The Infinite Way, who made his transition in 2004 but who extended himself as a teacher from 1996 up until his last breath.

My students and clients who have trusted me with their most secret and sacred selves and especially my 3 beloved practitioner students in South Africa who led the Soul Home community in my absence from 2005 - 2015: Rev. Gerd Pontow, Anka Daly, RScP (now retired) and Penelope Gottlieb, RScP.

All my dear reviewers: Di Arthur, Sally Edge, Laura Musgrave, Kathy Juline RScP, Carolina Unsain and Linda Ogden. Thank you for saying 'Yes!' to my request for help and for all your insightful comments and suggestions. Also J. Holmes and Chris Tyler – my technology angels.

My dedicated proof-readers: Carol Barker, Robert Maddison and my mum.

My editor: Nicolette Bosman who delivered magnificently and on time despite extreme happiness in her personal life.

My publisher: Webster Tsenase (TW Publishers) who is patient, kind, flexible, understanding and generous.

Sander Feinberg – for 11th hour consulting

T.G.M. who saw my spirit and loved Her.

Rev. Harriet Hawkins who held this book in prayer.

Lorene Belisama, former Director of the Agape Prayer Ministry, who is luminous and prayerful and enjoys a good cackle.

Dr. Martin Luther King, Jr., Mahatma Ghandi and Nelson Mandela and all those who live inside the possibility of a non-violent world.

Donna Kozik for creating the 'Write Your Book in a Weekend' workshop - the gentle boot and the clear guidance I needed to move me from dreaming to accomplishing. Bless you.

You, dear Reader, who wanted this book enough for me to write it.

This book is dedicated to

My Mother
Who loved me fiercely through it all

Please go to

<u>www.TimelessTransitions.net</u>

to download your FREE e-book

"7 STEPS

TO CREATING A HEALING MEMORIAL SERVICE

FOR A LOVED ONE"

Table of Contents

INTRODUCTION

In the Beginning....

One balmy, jasmine-suffused, January summer's evening in 1986, I crept in late to my first-ever Science of Mind class in Westdene. In those days Westdene was a "white" suburb of Johannesburg, South Africa, located on the border of the sprawling black township of Soweto. In her whitewashed garage that had been converted to a classroom, I heard Reverend Gladys Harrison give a metaphysical interpretation of the *Sermon on the Mount* from the *New Testament.* In that moment, I knew I had come home. My ongoing search for a spiritual teacher and teaching had ended; the conscious search for my personal connection with the Divine had just begun.

In hindsight, it all makes sense to me. *Apartheid*, the Dutch word meaning "separateness", was then the order of the day. It was the term used for the system of political separation between blacks and whites practised in South Africa. It was also a perfect mirror, however, for the sense of separation I harboured within myself - separation from God and my True Self. That sense of disconnectedness gave rise to my two constant questions:

1. What is wrong with me?
2. Who will fix it?

Both questions were fatally flawed and, therefore, unable to elicit a satisfying answer.

The "Word" According to Rev. Steph

This book is all about my personal exploration of my spiritual path and my first forays into the world of ministry, my oh-so-human mistake-making faculty as well as some of the lessons I learnt along the way. It is about the pain and confusion I experienced as a child, the experiences which kick-started my spiritual journey. And it is about my yearning for freedom that caused me to break rules, to flout convention and to run a million miles from any whiff of commitment or discipline! It is about synchronicity, providence and miracles—the gracious acts of a Higher Hand, orchestrating meetings and "God-incidences," opening doors to the Unknown and the Unexpected, shining Its Light on the path ahead. It is about the Infinite Love of the Divine that patiently waits for all of us to change our minds and expand our vision to see ourselves as We truly Are and Life as It truly Is.

It is Written Thus

Each chapter begins with a Biblical quote, followed by a metaphysical explanation and a personal story to illustrate the message or principle. Don't be concerned if you are new to metaphysics or, indeed, to the Bible. I have provided some short definitions of terminology for your reference in this Introduction.

Please do not take my metaphysical interpretations of the Bible as gospel! I offer you my best understanding, based on the level of consciousness I had attained at the time of this writing. It could all change tomorrow as all learning is ongoing. Besides, I believe that in the end, we all have to discover and devise our own individual theologies.
This can be annoying!

Religion and/or Spirituality?

Just so that I can reassure you that I am not "holier than thou," let me tell you that often, after a wedding or a memorial service conducted during my ministry in South Africa, guests approached me with an apologetic demeanour and sheepishly said, as if they were afraid I would judge them:
"You know I have never been very religious but...."
I would interrupt them and say:
"No, nor have I."
Invariably, they looked shocked. They'd had a false assumption that I must have had a Christian upbringing and been a "believer" for years before embarking on this ministerial mission. Nothing could be further from the truth!

In actual fact, I grew up in a non-religious family. This meant that I was subjected to very little overt religious conditioning, for which I am extremely grateful. As far as I am concerned, this meant that less inner work was required on my part to clear out the layers of painful and limiting man-made beliefs and religious concepts that could have blocked the Universal Good in my experience. Nevertheless, I believe I absorbed a veritable abundance of subliminal guilt, perfectionism and the tendency to self-flagellate from the northern European "Christian" culture in which I chose to begin this particular wheel of incarnation. Fortunately, I was not burdened with an extra helping of dogma-theology from a religious family of origin.

Given my lack of religious background, I must admit that I was astounded by my inexplicable familiarity with the Bible when I started my training as a Metaphysical Minister. Somehow I just "knew" the famous sayings of Jesus and other oft-quoted verses from the Bible, which can only have come down to me from Religious Instruction classes in my childhood. This was deeply gratifying because I had expected to feel like a heathen impostor at Ministerial School. I need not have worried. Academically, it turned out, I was quite competent. It was in my moral development that my heathen tendencies were lurking. However, you will be pleased to learn that in the first term of Ministerial School, I was impressed from Above with a radical insight:
"Now that I am training to be a minister, perhaps I should give up having affairs with married men?"
I remember beaming with pride at my new moral resolve.

Your own Calling?
And now, Reader, if you should ever have entertained any teensy-weensy, persistent, nagging thoughts such as:

"I want to be a minister," but are still in denial and trying to reverse rapidly away from your calling, we should consider it no accident that this book has found its way into your hands. Perhaps you are not quite ready to leave your comfort zone? Or you think you are not worthy enough spiritually? Or you are not educated enough religiously? Or you quake at the very thought of public speaking? Or you dread having to lead a moral life inside a fish bowl? But, if upon reading this book you start thinking:
"Hell, if she can do it, so can I!"
Then a piece of this book's mission will have been accomplished.

Regardless of your religious background, training or lack of it, I want to reassure you to "Fear not, little flock." *(Fear not, little flock; for it is your Father's good pleasure to give you the kingdom. Ref.: Luke 12:32.)* The important thing is that you and I have reached this point together. I wrote this book at the perfect time for me. You are reading it at the perfect time for you.

A Choice

Dear Reader, you have reached a fork in the road. The following few sections are an overview of metaphysics and the New Thought/Ancient Wisdom teachings. If this is already a familiar field to you, you can fast track to Chapter 1. Otherwise, read on to learn more.

What exactly is Metaphysics?

The word "metaphysics" originates from the Greek. "Meta" means "after/beyond" and "physics" means "nature." In traditional philosophy, metaphysics refers to the branch of philosophy that attempts to understand the ultimate nature of reality, both visible and invisible. However, the current meaning of metaphysics is more closely related to the world of mysticism and, in particular, to the experiences of oneness with the All.

New Thought Religions

The New Thought religions developed in the U.S.A. in the late 19th century. Mary Baker Eddy, who founded the Christian Science Church, was one of the forerunners of the movement. She taught Emma Curtis Hopkins, who in turn taught Charles and Myrtle Fillmore, Nona Brooks and Ernest Holmes. These bold teachers respectively founded the three New Thought religions: Unity, Divine Science and Religious Science.

There is a tendency today to refer to this movement as "New Thought/Ancient Wisdom" for, although it was only formalised in the late 19th and early 20th centuries, the tenets of the teaching are the salient truths central to every major world religion, spiritual tradition and ancient philosophy.

All of the metaphysical groups which emerged in the late 19th century represented a radical breakaway from the traditional Christian faith of their time. This was a time in which people were seen as "sinners" or "worms in the dust, God was a judgemental male autocrat in the sky, Hell was a serious spewer of fire and brimstone and the the Devil was patiently licking his lips, waiting to perpetually torture sinners as soon as they crossed over to the next world.

These New Thought teachers discovered that the Divine Power actually lay within themselves and that, through the conscious application of their thoughts along the lines of spiritual Truth, they could heal any condition of mind, body or "body of affairs" i.e. human experience. For preaching this "heresy," i.e. for taking the power out of the hands of the Church and putting it back into the minds and hearts of the people, these brave spirits stood the risk of being jailed. (Reader, if you want to know more about the history of New Thought, please refer to *Spirits in Rebellion* by Charles S. Braden.)

Religious Science and the Science of Mind

The spiritual philosophy taught in the Religious Science churches is called the Science of Mind. The Religious Science Church organisation, founded in 1927, divided into two separate factions in the 1950s. One was named the "United Church of Religious Science" (UCRS) while the other was named "Religious Science International" (RSI.)

UCRS changed its name in September 2006 to "United Centers for Spiritual Living," abbreviated to "UCSL." At the same time, RSI changed its name to "International Centers for Spiritual Living," "ICSL" for short.

In 2012, after operating apart for more than fifty years, the two organisations merged and are now operating together under one name: "Centers for Spiritual Living," or "CSL."

The philosophy is now more popularly termed the "Science of Mind and Spirit." I refer mostly to the church as "UCRS" throughout this book, because that was its name when I was training and leading my ministry.

Is the Religious Science Movement a Cult?

No.

If Religious Science was a cult, this would mean that the members of the study groups and churches would not be permitted to rise higher in consciousness than the leader of the organisation. In a typical cult situation, members who want to think independently, become too powerful or try to break away from the cult, are usually stopped and even punished. Ernest Holmes, the founder of Science of Mind, stated emphatically that Religious Scientists are "open at the top." He knew that spiritual leaders would come along who would be able to embody and convey a greater level of consciousness than he could attain in his lifetime. The "open at the top" approach, means that students are *expected* to achieve a higher consciousness than that of their teacher or leader. Not only that, this is encouraged and applauded. Everyone benefits from this more evolved consciousness, not just the Religious Science students but the whole world, as we are all part of the One Mind. Jesus said *"And I, if I be lifted up from the earth, will draw all men unto me." (Ref.: John 12:32.)*

Is the Church of Religious Science related to the Church of Scientology?
No.

New Thought Philosophy
The following is an overview of the New Thought philosophy. As you go through this book, you will note that I use capital letters for words that are synonyms for God, e.g. Love, Law, Life, Power, Idea, Word, etc. I also prefer to use the pronoun "It" instead of He/Him in order to divest myself of the old idea that God is a male person. Sometimes I even refer to God as "She." Now that is a lovely new thought, is it not?

a) **One Power**
Basic New Thought philosophy maintains that there is only One Power, which some people choose to call God. This Power is Omnipotent, Omniscient and Omnipresent, i.e. there is nothing outside this Power and nothing other than this Power. The Power is fundamentally good; not good as in the opposite of "bad," but good as in "whole" or "holy." This Power is creative; It made/is making the entire universe out of Itself. Its invisible Thought, Word or Idea became and is forever becoming material substance. Spiritual ideas or "seed thoughts" i.e. "ideas that come from God" eventually manifest in physical form. This is the Process of Creation; thoughts become things.

b) **The Creative Process and the Law**
This Power made us in "Its image and likeness" *(Then God said, "Let Us make man in our image, after our likeness." Ref.: Genesis 1:26)* meaning that we have creative powers too. Our creative

power rests in our thoughts and our language. But what aspect of the Power makes our seed ideas show up as form? We call it the Universal Law. The Law is like the soil. Whatever you plant in it grows. For example, a tomato seed contains within itself the potential to become a fully grown perfect tomato. The soil unquestioningly accepts any seed we choose to plant (or the seeds which birds and insects scatter randomly), nurtures it and allows it to develop until it is ready to emerge into physical manifestation and its fully grown form as a tomato, a flower or whatever the picture on the seed packet depicts.

But now let's talk about sex, which I love to do, especially in a spiritual context. Strict Catholics might have you believe that sex is merely a process for the purpose of procreation, but I say that sex is also for the purpose of *explaining* the Process of Creation. Ha! Now that is another new thought. The male seed fertilises the female egg and impregnates the female womb. Just like the Law, the womb nurtures the embryo until it is a fully developed baby ready to be birthed in tangible and visible form.

This Law works as all the known laws of the physical universe do in that it is one hundred percent consistent, impersonal and will not fall out of integrity with itself. For example, gravity never changes. It doesn't care who you are. If you jump off a high building, you will probably go splat! Gravity will never apologise. Even if you and I think we are special, the Universal Law treats everyone and their thoughts in the same manner. It creates for us what we deeply believe and think about most of the time, in the form of people, places and things in our world of experience. Remember the soil and the womb. They do not argue with what we plant in them and they do not have the power to change the germinating seed into something else.

c) **Human Conditioning**

So if we are gods, made in the image and likeness of the Divine and have been blessed with Infinite Creative Power to manifest every good thing, why aren't we living in Paradise on earth? Why are we fighting wars, locally and globally, but mostly in our own heads? Well, most of us have *not* been raised in the belief that we are whole and holy beings, connected to all of Life, conduits for Joy, Aliveness, Love, Abundance and full Self-Expression. On the contrary, we have been subjected to some insidious conditioning as part of our human journey of incarnation.

Most of us raised in a western culture have been unconsciously taught to believe that we are small, limited, separate humans, at the mercy of forces outside of ourselves. We have become attached to our human identity, believing that to be the truth about who we really are. And what is our human identity? It is simply a set of concepts relating to our:

- biological origins;
- ancestry;
- nationality;
- physical features;
- skin colour;
- culture;
- religion;
- habitat;
- geographical location;
- education;
- school achievements;
- IQ;
- qualifications;
- talents;
- abilities;
- friends;
- dress size;
- preferred designer labels;
- favourite music;
- opinions;
- political persuasions;

- experiences;
- beliefs, both personal and cultural;
- moral codes and
- decisions about who we are.

All of the above make up our little egoistic self and we will defend them all to the death. Please feel free to add to the list.

d) False Beliefs

In addition to inheriting a plethora of beliefs (many of them negative or limiting) from the culture we grew up in, we have also made "piles" of personal decisions about ourselves and about life based on the inaccurate interpretation of events in the days when we were pre-verbal. For example, most of us have had the experience as babies of screaming for food in our cots and not being fed immediately or not being heard and, therefore, not fed. This experience gives rise to decisions such as: "I am not worthy of love" or "I will never be heard" or "Life is cruel."

Although these beliefs are all lies, they appear to be true because we believe them and the Law is duty-bound to serve them up to us in the form of our experience. The more we experience the beliefs showing up in our world, the more we convince ourselves that we must be right about what we believe. Jesus Christ said to us "It is done unto you as you believe." (*And Jesus said unto the centurion, Go thy way; and as thou hast believed, so be it done unto thee. Ref.: Matthew 8:13.)*

For me, this is the cornerstone of the Science of Mind teachings. It has nothing to do with our theoretical beliefs about God or Jesus or Salvation. For example, some traditional Christians believe that Jesus was the only begotten Son of God who died for their sins and, because of that, they are "saved" and will go to heaven when they die. No, "It is done unto you as you believe" means that life will show up for you and me according to our dominant beliefs, attitudes, opinions, judgements and the old wiring that is contained in our consciousness. So, if we change our thinking and start to believe a new thought that is positive, uplifting and expansive, our experience will reflect that.

Consciousness then, is the sum total of our beliefs, attitudes and opinions. Our negative or false beliefs continue to dominate our existence until they are examined and cast out. Becoming aware of all the "lies" we have long believed that are based on a sense of a separation from the Whole, can open the mental prison bars to freedom. And one key way of changing these old beliefs and, thereby, the miserable effects they produce in our worlds, is through affirmative prayer.

e) **Prayer or Spiritual Mind Treatment**

The greatest gift that Ernest Holmes, author of the *Science of Mind* textbook and founder of the Church of Religious Science, brought to us was a scientific form of prayer known as *Spiritual Mind Treatment.* It is a five-step method of dismantling the lies in our minds and of claiming the Truth about our Divinity, thereby revealing the One Power within us and around us that is essentially good and that has already manifested the substance of our desires. As soon as the predominant body of thought shifts from falsehood to Truth within a group or individual, there is a corresponding shift in their outer experience. Some people call that a miracle; it is certainly not "lucky" or a "fluke." The German novelist, Johann Paul Richter said, "The miracles of Earth are the laws of Heaven."

f) **The Spiritual Evolution of Humanity**

As humanity evolves, the traditional notions of ourselves as victims, or "worms in the dust," with God as the external punishing or rewarding parental figure, are giving way to concepts of God as an Internal Source of Power and a Spiritual Partner. We are all on the journey of growing into spiritual maturity, taking personal responsibility and learning co-creativity, whereby we live out the privilege of our true Divine nature, expressing our love for the good of ourselves, everyone around us and the universe as a whole. Our planet is our cosmic playground where we carry out the magnificent experiment of incarnation into the physical realm and discover Who We Are as gods of unlimited power.

Ye are Gods!

The Master Teacher, Jesus the Christ, asked, *"Is it not so written in your law, I said, you are gods?" Ref.: John 10:34.)* Jesus taught that once we are in touch with our godhood, we can access our power to become the makers of miracles. *(He who believes in me shall do the works which I do; and even greater than these things he shall do. Ref.: John 14:12.)* In my opinion, this verse does not mean that we have to believe that Jesus existed or that he was the only begotten Son of God. It means we have to believe in our own inner Christhood, our own Spark of Divinity, and to live from that awareness. Jesus was the example, not the exception, instructing us to perform miracles too. *(Now go and do thou likewise. Ref.: Luke 10:37.)*

God aka...

Ernest Holmes freed me up hugely when he said that the word "God" was loaded with meanings, many of which were fear-based and might be counter-productive when attempting to create a personal relationship with the Indwelling Power. Holmes suggested that using other terminology, such as Universal Mind, Creative Power, Divine Love—in fact, any words we like that assist us to make or enhance our own unique inner connection, opens this concept up.

The George Lamsa Bible

The Bible quotes in this book are chiefly taken from the *George Lamsa Bible*, which is a translation from Aramaic into English. Why this version? Aramaic was the language of Jesus. George Lamsa's family comes from the area in the Middle East where Aramaic is still spoken and where many customs and traditions have endured through the centuries. So I believe that this particular Bible version contains the most accurate translation available to us, even though we should bear in mind that sections of its original wording have been changed, deleted and unintentionally mistranslated.

Metaphysical Bible Interpretation

To understand the metaphysical approach to the Bible requires that we think of it as the story of the development of our spiritual consciousness, starting in the *Old Testament* and journeying through the *New Testament.* In our human development, we grow from selfish, immature children into wise loving adults (well, sometimes but not always!) So, too, in our spiritual development, we shift from the darkness of ignorance to the light of awareness and understanding. The metaphysical interpretation of the Bible can be our tour-guide on this journey through our own psycho-spiritual terrain. (Reader, please note, I have not structured this book according to the linear sequence of development referred to above; I allowed my right-brained, intuitive nature to guide the path.)

An Apology to Reverend Phil Quirke

One of my wonderful teachers at Santa Anita Ministerial School in California, Reverend Phil Quirke, taught an illuminating class on Bible Exegesis which means, "how to accurately explain and interpret biblical texts in order to reveal their significance and relevance." He invited us, the fledgling professional ministers, to take an academic approach and to interpret quotes from the Bible in context when teaching or preaching. He advised us not to just snatch random quotes and twist them to fit a moral lesson or a particular bias, as some preachers are wont to do.... Oh dear. Forgive me, Rev. Phil, for I have sinned. I have done exactly what you told us *not* to do in the coming pages.

(Before we go any further, Reader, I should tell you that the word "sin" comes from a Greek archery term meaning "to miss the mark." Isn't that liberating?)

My Story

The collection of stories in this book speak to my unfolding journey towards the conscious recognition of my own Divinity. You will see how I often did NOT *do likewise* as Jesus the Christ commanded us to. In fact, most of the time, I did the *exact opposite* while I learnt what did not work and then what worked based on the quality of my experiences.

My prayer for you, my Reader...

As the scroll unfurls, dear Reader, may you look with compassion upon your own cloak of humanhood. May your spark of Christhood be ignited more powerfully than ever before. And may we all join in remembering our common heritage and our divine destiny.

P.S. Oh yes, and may you enjoy multiple giggles along the way.

Part 1

CHILDHOOD
1958-1969

Chapter 1

Be as a Child

1. At that very hour the disciples came up to Jesus and said, Who is greatest in the kingdom of heaven?
2. So Jesus called a little child, and made him stand up in the midst of them.
3. And he said, Truly I say to you, Unless you change and become like little children, you shall not enter into the kingdom of heaven
4. Whoever therefore will humble himself like this little child, shall be great in the kingdom of heaven
5. And he who will welcome one like this little child in my name, welcomes me.

Matthew 18:1-5

Interpretation

A classic metaphysical technique for interpreting the Bible is to see the characters in a story as aspects of ourselves. So, in this story,

- The disciples represent the voice of our ego which is driven by a need for superiority and, in this case, spiritual one-upmanship;
- Jesus represents the Awakened Adult, or Christ Self, within everyone's consciousness. This awakened aspect of consciousness is free of ego and, therefore, unafraid of articulating Truth even if this very Truth causes the one speaking to appear mad or become unpopular in the eyes of the people in their world;
- The child who Jesus welcomes represents our inner Divine Child—the part of us that is essentially pure, innocent, playful, forgiving, present, loving, joyful, creative, sensitive and in touch with the subtle dimensions of existence.

In this Bible story, the disciples believed Heaven was a place they would go to after death and that God was the benign-but-judgemental, male authority figure whom they would meet upon arrival. They wanted to know who would be considered to be the most spiritual, who would be the most loved by God, who would have the greatest stature in the eyes of the Almighty, who would be regarded as a true holy man. Jesus shocked them all by answering: "a child."

What was Jesus' message here? Was he advocating that we act like undisciplined little kids and revert to being selfish, immature and irresponsible? No, not at all. He was attempting to point out that the Kingdom of Heaven is here and now and that children (or the essence of the Divine Child within you and me), who are not completely consumed by ego, still have the capacity to live in the Now and, therefore, have direct access to the Presence of God which indwells this present moment.

Interesting Footnote:
I saw the Dalai Lama being interviewed on TV recently. Clearly, he is a wise old soul, a man who has allowed his suffering to bear the fruit of deep compassion. He is disciplined in his daily practise of meditation, tireless in his embrace of all seekers who come to him for assistance and yet, at the same time, displays the carefree capacity to giggle and crack jokes with his interviewer, to be amused by the slightest of things. He seems to dwell in the Kingdom of Happiness, his Divine-child-self fully integrated within his adult being.

My Story
Look, I never grew up wanting to be a minister. Ask anyone. I wanted to be an ice-skater or a hairdresser. However, as you read this chapter, you will see that the seeds and the weeds of my destiny as a minister were clearly sown in my childhood. The seeds proved to be more powerful than the weeds but, nevertheless, I had some very good reasons for not wanting to become a woman of the cloth. See below.

Weeds
(some early contra-indications)

Bad Experience of the Christian Family Next Door
Life was not always rosy in the home of my childhood. In stark contrast to the regular bouts of screaming and crying, tension and torment, in our semi-detached house, the next-door neighbours, on the other side of the adjoining wall, led the life of saintly committed Christians. Religiously they went to church every Sunday, sang in the choir, attended bell-ringing practice and made gooseberry jam for the church fête. Through the eyes of seven-year old me, none of these religious activities served to make them particularly joyful, alive or loving. Thankfully, they did not evangelise. Possibly they saw the futility in trying to convert my family? They kept themselves to themselves in what seemed to be a very safe, predictable, do-good, martyr-ish, suppress-

your-unholy-urges-at-all-costs, kind of world. I suspect they silently judged us for being hopeless sinners.

In the years of holy war between the "righteous" and the "heathens," we—my parents, my two sisters and I—proved the Christian neighbours right about our fundamentally sinful nature by attacking them verbally from the safety of our trench behind that adjoining wall: we threw them to the lions of our ridicule; we stabbed them with our mockery; we pointed spears of contempt their way. They were sitting targets for our scathing attacks. Since the human me was made in my parents' image and likeness, *(Then God said, "Let Us make man in Our image, according to Our likeness" Ref.: Genesis 1:26)* it was easy to see why we attacked the neighbours: we were tough. Dysfunctional but tough. The neighbours were wimps. They tried so hard to be good—even perfect—just as they imagined their Father in Heaven would be and how they should be to get approval from Him. They reined their darker humanity into their tight bodies and their pinched, vacant faces. They preferred polite distance and saintly suppression, while they stood on the sidelines feeling righteous because we were everything un-Christian that they were trying so hard not to be.

Bad Experience of My Father

My father was a violent alcoholic, although no one understood that he had a disease at the time. We were all scared of his unpredictable Jekyll and Hyde character. Drunk or dry, his illness ravaged the family home in the form of a cruel, dark, brooding rage that stimulated fear and hurt in mum, my sisters and me. Alcohol is the great remover. It removes stains; it also removes health, sanity, trust, safety, love, dignity, stability and hope.

There were frequent loud fights between my parents, both verbal and physical. My mother fought for her own survival so that she could protect and raise her three daughters in the boxing ring of my father's alcoholism. Perhaps the neighbours were praying for us? Someone must have been because we all got out alive, except my father who died of his disease.

Bad Experience of Vicars and Churches

As a child, I did not grow up going to church except on special occasions. One such occasion, unforgettable for the pain it rendered, was my twin-sisters' Christening. After the ceremony the vicar was busy posing for a photo with a baby sister in each arm. I was only three at the time, far too little for him to notice, and he accidentally stood on my toe. Ouch! The first ever photo of me standing outside a church shows my face contorted in pain while the vicar smiled on, oblivious to his wounded flocklet. Not very auspicious.

When I was four, mum and dad took me to Auntie Margaret's wedding. Auntie Margaret was my godmother. I loved her. It should have been a joyful experience but I had to wear a stiff, starched, white dress that was very uncomfortable and itchy. A little white straw hat was tied firmly to my head with an itchy ribbon under my chin. My pain is very obvious on the wedding photos: I was squinting and frowning into the sun and could not wait to get that stupid dress off!

Once in the church, mum and dad were chatting while we sat in the pews and waited for the bride to walk up the aisle. I told them to be quiet because we were in church. By this stage in my life, I had been in church about twice so, of course, I knew the church etiquette inside out! Mum and dad were a little surprised to be reprimanded by their 4-year old daughter but they knew I was right and they obeyed. Ha! The power was luscious even then. The church was cold and smelled funny and the people were not having much fun. They even cried at the end of the wedding service.

Bad Experience of Sunday School

I never got on well at Sunday School. I didn't mind drawing the shepherds in their dressing gowns with a long handkerchief on their heads, but I could not get to grips with drawing sheep, cows and donkeys. They feature quite heavily in Bible stories and if you can't draw them, you feel stupid. Besides, at age six, I could not understand the connection between the stories about God in the Middle East hundreds of years ago and my life in the U.K. in 1963. Was I missing something? Yes, among other things, a mythology of misogyny. I am glad I missed it.

Bad Experience of Christmas Plays at School

Nor did I get to play the cool limelight roles of a leading angel or Mary in the nativity plays at school. Tall, sallow and painfully shy, I was neither cute nor could I act. The crowd scenes were my lot. I was usually cast in the role of a quiet, zero-personality, male shepherd because of my height. I also got to impersonate quite a few trees.

Bad Experience of Female Religious Role Models

There were no female religious role models in my early life—only the saints, like Joan of Arc, who, because of their outspoken faith, got themselves tortured by the kings and the bald men in long dresses. Then there were the nuns who had to shave their heads to make themselves sexless and get married to a God whom they could not see or touch or hold. And why did they have to shave their heads if they were going to cover them up anyway with their weird starchy pointy headgear?

There were certainly no female church leaders in middle-class, Christian Surrey. They simply hadn't been invented then. No, women were simply vicars' wives, a tireless adjunct to their husbands, managing the affairs of home and church behind the scenes while the glory went to God/husband. And Sundays, a sacred day of rest for most Christians, was the most hectic day of the week for the wives, dedicated to making tea and caring for the flock with no time off on Monday to recuperate.

Vicars' wives were not sexy. Ladies who churched were frumpy—as if religious devotion required an agreement to shut down on feminine beauty, sexuality and pleasure. God forbid they should be like the temptress, Eve, and cause the men in the parish to fall into sin. What sin? The sin of sex? No, I am referring to the traditional male sin of blaming the woman for their male erection and all activity that comes from it....

The American comedy show, *Saturday Night Live*, did a great send up of "Church Lady." Played by a tall male comedian, "she" was an ugly battle-axe, dressed in a conservative tweed suit, wearing sensible brogues, 1960s glasses, tightly permed short hair, no make-up and a supercilious frown. She was angry, sexually frustrated and sickeningly pious. Why would any young girl aspire to become that?

Where were the female role models in the religious education of my childhood? Well, I could grow up to be a sweet, saintly mother like Mary, which looked a bit boring and hard work, or a bad girl like Eve or Mary Magdalene. It should not take you too long to discern where my predisposition lay....

Bad Experience of the Patriarchy

The way it looked to me, God was a man and mostly angry – just like my dad. God's son, Jesus, was a man and his dad loved his son so much that he made his son suffer and bleed to death on the cross. But "God is Love," we are told. Hmmm. All the disciples were men – or so the male mythology of religion has traditionally informed us. They proved to be useless when Jesus was arrested. Moses was a man and most of the other biblical prophets were men. They did a lot of walking through the wilderness and sitting in the desert meditating. John the Baptist lived in the desert too. He ate locusts and wild honey. Not an enviable life-style. Well, eating honey is fine. Not sure about the locusts though....

Yes, when I was a child, church and organised religion were solely in the domain of men in those dark days before Feminism moved across the face of the deep.... *(And the earth was without form, and void; and darkness was upon the face of the deep. And the Spirit of God moved upon the face of the waters. Ref.: Genesis 1:2.)*

Thank Goddess for Feminism that saved young girls from the three fates of nurse, secretary or teacher before they got selected for the Marriage & Breeding cattle trucks. Yes, girls did not become ministers when I was a child, nor did they even dream of it. There were simply no precedents. (Ironically, I can see now that the job of female minister is a combination of the three fates of nurse, secretary and teacher with some Bible bits thrown in.)

Seeds
(some early positive indications)

Public Speaking

At age seven, Heaven smiled upon me in the form of my favourite Junior School teacher, Miss Carpenter, who specially selected me to do the reading in church at the school's end of term Christmas Carol Service. It was only one verse from the Book of Isaiah, but I practised it like mad with my mum beforehand. Yep, I definitely liked being in the pulpit with the microphone. My voice sounded very loud and I felt special and Very Powerful. I was higher than everyone else and so they were forced to look up to me. The subtle difference between intoxicating pulpit power and the thrill of spiritual transcendence was hard to discern in those days and I am not sure it got any easier in later life. In fact, I have often confused Divine Power with that glorious trinity of sugar, caffeine and adrenaline.

Teaching

I started school two years earlier than my twin sisters so, at age six, after I had a little bit of knowledge under my belt, I made them sit on chairs in front of me and act as my pupils while I taught them basic letters and numbers. They applied themselves diligently under my tutelage and you will not be surprised to learn that they both excelled academically in later life.

Learning
School was a form of salvation for me. I loved teachers, knowledge and learning. I loved languages, history and sports. I also loved getting top marks and being best in the class.

Bookworm with a Heavy Leaning towards the Supernatural
My personal Kingdom of Heaven was in books. As soon as I could read, I was off on my broomstick into the infinite realm of imagination: witches, fairies, goblins, elves, magic spells and perfect romance between the prince and the princess who hardly knew each other but managed to live happily ever after. Any storybook about the world beyond our physical eyesight and the process of transformation was my preferred research material from age five onwards.

Writing
As well as reading, I loved writing. I can still remember kneeling on the carpeted floor in the hallway next to the open door of the kitchen, where my mum was cooking, and spilling my box of plastic letters in front of me. The letter "N" was orange. The letter "A" was yellow. I picked out two of each from the jumble on the floor and I spelled N-A-N-A.
"Look, Mum. That spells Nana!"
Mum beamed with pride and joy. I knew I was in the flow of magic – to hear the sound in my head and be able to match it with the right letters to make a word. If that is not Divine Creation, then what is?
Whenever relatives would send me or my sisters gifts for our birthday or for Christmas, mum would make us write Thank You letters. It was a bit of a chore but I did not mind. Then, the breakthrough came when I went to stay with my Auntie Pam and her family one summer. She had a small manual typewriter

which she let me “play” with, little realising that this innocent act of trying to keep me occupied awakened a thirst in me to create words and send them out into the world which has still not been quenched fifty years later. With one or two fingers, I doggedly wrote letters to everyone I knew. Once I had discovered the typewriter’s keys to the Kingdom of Words, I did not want to play any other games with Auntie Pam’s kids. They were outside splashing around in the paddling pool and having fun while I was inside becoming a serious writer.

Healing

One of my relatives bought me a nurse’s outfit and a stethoscope that I liked to wear while tending to my sick dolls. My family was sternly instructed to “Be quiet!” when my “patients” were sleeping.

At age 9 or 10, I used to sit quietly in the bathroom after my evening bath and reflect. It was during these “meditation” sessions that I was told that for every sickness that we humans experience on earth, God had provided a herb to cure it. I was also told that I would find the cure for cancer in my lifetime and it would have nothing to do with the typical scientific approach to cancer research.

During one of these sessions in the Silence, I remember making a generous offer to God. It was not without conditions though:
“If You want me to be a nurse and go and help people in Africa, I don’t mind, I will do it. But please don’t send me to the African jungle because I am afraid of snakes.” Apparently, She was willing to comply and sent me to the big city of Johannesburg where snakes are rarely spotted.

Hostess / Socialite

My mum loaned me a spare teapot and some cups so that I could play tea parties in the back garden. After the second broken china teapot (honestly, it was my doll’s fault), leaving no more spares in the kitchen cupboard, this game was vetoed.

Arch Saleswoman

The coal bunker behind the garage in the back garden proved to be the perfect place to set up shop. The top of the bunker formed a natural shelf for stacking my goods. Mum collected empty cereal packets for me and my sisters and donated some tins of baked beans and some fruit. A fold-up table acted as my counter separating me from my customers, i.e. my sisters, who had to come and buy from my choice array of delicacies. It never took too long to get sold out, shut up shop and then go home early.

Media and Advertising

My friend, Sandra, who lived down the road, suggested we put on a show and make some money to spend on sweets. I agreed with anything Sandra said. She was nine and Very Grown Up, plus she went to ballet, tap and singing lessons on Saturday mornings. In my eyes, she was a celebrity. Sandra was as confident as I was gawky. I was seven at the time and, as previously mentioned, had no stage presence.

Well, Sandra and I and my sisters starting preparing for our Grand Show about a week beforehand. With our trusty crayons, we made hundreds of hand-printed flyers (well, maybe twenty) advertising our show and stuck them up on trees and fences in the neighbourhood. This was good. We had committed and gone public. Now the pressure was on to rehearse for the crowds....

Entertaining and Stage Craft

After practising hard every day for a week and figuring out all the different acts and their sequence, the day of the Grand Show dawned. It was going to be a matinee performance in my back garden, starting at 3 p.m.

Sandra and I and my sisters were so busy getting ready behind our makeshift stage curtains (two large blankets pegged onto the washing line in the middle of the garden) that we did not organise anyone to sell tickets and collect the money. Actually, we had not made any tickets, only flyers.

The audience was getting restless—the sky was overcast, it was about to rain and we had to start otherwise we would lose them. The audience consisted of my mother and her friend, Jean, from round the corner, Sandra's mother, Pam, and her baby sister, Karen, and our kindly next door neighbour, Mrs. Lawrence. Sandra flounced onto the grassy stage from behind the blanket-curtains to welcome the crowd. She told them that if they liked our show, they could pay at the end. I thought that was a brilliant way to handle the issue of no tickets. The audience laughed though.

Sandra sang and danced. I did my best as her supporting act. Luckily for Sandra, my best was meagre and she got to shine like the celebrity she truly was. Despite being the obvious star of the production and deserving the lion's share of the profits, Sandra fairly shared out the slim pickings that we had hastily gathered up at the end of the show before it rained. The paltry few coins looked a bit lost in the bottom of my mum's empty peg bucket but it was a reward for our labours and the sweets we bought with it tasted extra-delicious.

Cultivation of public image

My mum's sister, Auntie Cynthia, was a very glamorous ballroom dancing champion and nightclub singer. She smoked and drank, wore make-up and heady perfume and had a lot of boyfriends. She was my early role model and heroine. I even walked around with my teeth sticking out like hers because she was slightly goofy but I thought she was beautiful. She used to give my sisters and me the professional ballroom dancing dresses she didn't wear any more. These divine garments were direct from the

Goddess' wardrobe, sparkling with sequins and with serious places for boobs. Could there have been anything more grown up? Well, all that was needed was make-up and some hairspray to arrange our hair into an elegant style. Sandra was invaluable once again, since she had practised applying stage make-up for the shows she was in. Mum helped considerably by donating some of her old cosmetics.

The true inspiration for my public image came from Cleopatra, Queen of Egypt. At the time, mum was working at the local cinema, selling ice-cream during the intermission. The blockbuster, *Cleopatra,* with Elizabeth Taylor and Richard Burton ran for ages. Mum brought home the programme with photos of the stars and the inspired, creative Sandra faithfully copied Elizabeth Taylor's make up on me, applying heavy black eyeliner on my lower lids and then on my upper lids where it swept out to my temples with an upturned flourish! I thought I looked supremely beautiful and grown-up, a cross between a 1960s mod and an Egyptian princess. Mum, however, thought otherwise and wouldn't let me go out the house until I had scrubbed it off.

Adventuress with a Mission

I was fascinated by the story of Florence Nightingale, "The Lady with the Lamp," a young British woman who felt compelled to go to the Crimea and nurse the wounded soldiers in the Crimean War under extremely hazardous and insanitary conditions. I did not want to be a nurse, but danger, excitement and travel were definitely appealing especially if a mission was involved.

Interesting Footnote:

Later, at university, I studied German and Russian and, much later, in 2002, destiny took me on a spiritual mission from South Africa to Cherkasy in the Ukraine. There I joined my ministerial colleague, Rev. Barbara Leger, and a group of Global Heart practitioners and ministers from the United Church of Religious Science in the U.S.A. We had all felt "called" to offer support to Rev. Barbara Leger and the Ukrainian Science of Mind ministry that she had founded and was leading both in Cherkasy AND in the Crimea. Our journey through the Crimea on our tour bus was fun and exciting but it was hardly hazardous, well except for

1. *the thieves who managed to steal my colleague's passport from his hotel room*
2. *the potholes in the roads*
3. *the creaking, overladen tables of food (waistline hazard) and*
4. *the vodka (brain-cell hazard) that the ever-hospitable Ukrainians provided for us everywhere we went.*

My most dangerous solo journey took place when I was five. My mum gave me two pennies and let me get the 406 bus by myself from our local bus-stop to travel one mile up the hill to Ruxley Lane, the nearest large shopping centre. I was terrified of missing my stop, getting lost and never finding my way home again. A mile is a long way when you are five. The reward, once I got to Ruxley Lane, was to go to the handicrafts shop and buy felt and silk threads for my sewing projects. And then I had to walk back home down the hill because mum did not want me crossing the busy main road at Ruxley Lane. Bit of an anti-climax but worth it for the fresh taste of adventure on the outbound journey.

Perhaps an even more potentially dangerous journey occurred when I was six and my dad took me to buy my first two-wheel bike from a family who lived half way up the hill to Ruxley Lane. I was so impatient to ride my bike that even before I knew what I was doing, or where the brakes were, I was heading downhill like Evil Knievel. Fortunately, my dad caught up with me and reined me in before my bike grew wings and carried me to a crash landing on the moon.

Awareness of Subtle Energies

I remember walking home from school on sunny days, looking up in to the sky and seeing sparkly things swirling around. I took these darting "silver fishes," as I called them, completely for granted. Didn't everyone see that stuff? No, they didn't. And they don't. Years later, at age 26, a psychic friend told me I was seeing Prana—pure energy. He taught me to screw up my eyes and shift my focus in order to see those little fishes again.

Wonder at the Natural Universe

Our next-door neighbours were boys about the same age as my sisters and I. (Reader, I am referring to the family who moved in on our left, not the wimpy sons of the Christian neighbours on our right.) We had a very long garden in those days with a big compost heap at the far end. This was out of sight of my mother even while she was standing at the kitchen sink doing the dishes and looking out of the window up the garden. Somehow, knowing that we weren't supposed to be doing this in full view of the grown-ups, we retired to this sacred spot behind the compost heap and there demonstrated to each other how we peed. A fascinating study that we repeated happily on more than one occasion.

Awareness of Racial Differences

When I was 6, mum took me to Broadstairs, a holiday resort on the Kent coast and we stayed in an hotel for a week. Mum had been ill and needed to rest. She wanted to make sure I would not be bored so she took me into the toyshop on the seafront and told me I could pick out a toy or a game. The toyshop was a positive treasure trove but all I wanted was the brown dolly. She was about 8 inches high with red lips and short black hair. She definitely stood out amongst the white dollies. She was exotic and fascinating. I had never played with a brown dolly or even seen one. I had had no close contact with black people either. There weren't any in our neighbourhood in the early sixties and the only time we ever saw Africans or Jamaicans or Indians was when we drove through London.

The issue was: how to dress her? She was sold to me naked and she needed new clothes! Mum produced a large white cotton handkerchief and showed me a way to wrap it around the dolly's body and tie a knot. Creating different looks for her with that one

handkerchief occupied me for hours but one rainy afternoon, mum was taking a nap in our hotel room and I had clean run out of ideas. Quietly, I crept out of the room and knocked on the door of the nice lady down the passage. I think I had seen her once in the dining room. Fortunately, she was in but was a bit surprised to see me at her door. I held out my dolly to her:
"Please can you show me how to make a new dress for my dolly?"
"Of course, dear. Does your mother know you are here?"
"No, she's sleeping."
"Alright, dear. Well let's sit down on these chairs in the passage and she won't have to come far to find you when she wakes up."
I nodded and waited expectantly. The nice lady was very creative and figured out a brand new look for my dolly. Just as she was finishing the fashion magic, mum emerged half-asleep and completely frantic. She had woken up and seen that I was missing. The nice lady was right; it was good that we had not gone too far away. Mum was embarrassed that I had approached a perfect stranger for help although the nice lady seemed quite happy to be of assistance. And I was jubilant that my wish had been fulfilled and my beloved brown dolly was looking splendid in her new African handkerchief-gown.

Compassion for Slaves

Mum and dad bought us a set of encyclopaedias. In one of the volumes was a drawing of the galley on an African slave ship with the slaves sitting in rows, chained to their oars. There was a short description of the conditions that prevailed in the hold—slaves having to sit in their own excrement, often dying of malnutrition or disease before getting to America. I was at once horrified and full of compassion, hypnotically drawn to that page again and again. My seven-year-old sense of injustice that people could be treated so cruelly, just because of the colour of their skin, was already awakening.

Connecting with the Future: Meeting O.C. Smith, Ringo Starr and Anthony Hopkins

I remember hearing the 60s pop singer, O.C. Smith, sing *Little Green Apples* when I was a child of about six. The song came on the radio while I was standing on my own in the kitchen at home. Something compelled me to stand still and just listen. The memory is profound because the radio was on all the time and no other songs had that effect on me. Then, years later, at ministerial school in Los Angeles, we had the privilege of being taught by Rev. O.C. Smith. He shared in class about how he became a minister and started his first ministry, having the advantage of being able to sing and pull in the crowds, thanks to his years of fame in the entertainment business.

I also recall being in the kitchen on my own as a child listening to the Beatles sing *She loves you Yeah, Yeah, Yeah.* It was 1963. I was five-years-old and I loved the Beatles. Years later as a ministerial student in Los Angeles, I had the privilege of meeting Ringo Starr a number of times and being amongst a small group of people who were around him when he shared his story of his life as a drummer with the Beatles.

Another spiritual giant whom I tuned into as a child was Anthony Hopkins, the actor. I remember reading all about him in the *Daily Express* when he first became famous in the U.K. for his role in the movie, *Young Winston* in 1972. And, even though he is a fellow Brit, I met him in Los Angeles—again, years later—and, as I shook hands with him, I had the opportunity to look into his most sparkling blue eyes of infinite depth.

The Pain of the Prodigal Child

Being a child was not easy. I was in pain and did not know how to fix it. All I wanted to do was grow up so I could leave home and be free. I turned 18. I left home. But I wasn't free. I was still a hurt child. I spent many years blaming my parents for my defective sense of self until I found the Science of Mind teachings in South

Africa at age 27 and a light was ignited inside of me. It was then that I heard that a soul is conscious before birth into the physical realm and chooses an incarnation that will afford the most accelerated and profound spiritual growth over a lifetime. You mean to tell me I actually *chose* my parents?

Yes!

I chose parents who loved me deeply but who were trapped in the vicious rhythm of the karmic dance—the classic power struggle between two egos striving to dominate or avoid domination, matched in misery, paired in pain, destructive unto divorce or death—whichever came sooner.

My soul clearly knew what it needed to shake me awake. As a child, I sensed something was deeply wrong, but I could not name it. So I blocked it and sent it hurtling to the bottom of my memory well. I tried not to feel. I tried to mentally understand why there was so much pain in me and in my family. I believed, hoped, that understanding would be enough to render me healed. It wasn't. At age 10, I decided that I did not want what was being offered in my parents' house. I knew instinctively that there had to be another way to live, and I was determined to find it. It was then that I left home in my heart.

Part 2

TEENAGE YEARS
1969-1977

Chapter 2

The Land of the Free

13. My brethren, I do not consider that I have reached the goal; but this one thing I do know, forgetting those things which are behind, I strive for those things which are before me;
14. I press toward the goal to receive the prize of victory of God's highest calling through Jesus Christ.

Philippians 3:13-14

Interpretation

What is the "goal" referred to in Philippians 3:13-14? It can be any goal that we are trying to reach, but I interpret it specifically to mean the goal of "absolute awareness of our godhood as an ongoing experience." It is important to have this goal in front of us and be constantly developing towards it. The vision of our future selves must be clear so that we can increasingly embody the stellar divine beings that we were born to be.

The verse reminds us that it is necessary to take our attention off the past, both defeats and victories, because the past is not the precedent. Focusing attention on our defeats brings more defeats into our current experience. In every new moment there is a possibility to cut ties with the past, to think, speak and act in a new way—a way that is more aligned with who we choose to be, rather than who we were conditioned to be.

What is God's highest calling through Jesus Christ? A "calling" has often been interpreted to mean religious work of some sort in the role of e.g. a priest, a minister, a monk or a nun. A broader definition of "calling," which does not require a religious commitment, would be a brave or selfless form of service to humanity such as nursing or community development.

But let us expand the definition of "calling" even further. For example, astronauts generally feel a sense of calling, as do artists and musicians, teachers and scientists. In fact, anyone who loves the work they do and turns it into an art form, has been "called." When you do something because you love it so much that you cannot *not do it*, and earning money is not the motivation, you have been "called." And when you express your passion in a way that blesses the world, it means your Christ-Self is activated and you are an instrument for the Universal Power to flow through you; you are tapped into Infinite Love, Joy and Creativity. You are being your best Self and your most authentic Self. This is the prize—fulfilling the purpose for which you were sent to earth, being available to the Spirit to be used as an instrument of Grace in the world. There is no higher calling.

My Story

My godmother, Auntie Margaret, married an American (see the wedding ceremony in Chapter 1) and went to live with him in the U.S.A. when I was still quite small. They settled in Golden, a little mining town in the foothills of the Rockies, just outside Denver. Golden was founded on 16th June, 1859, at the time of the Gold Rush. (Special note: 16th June is my birthday.)

Despite having four children of her own, Auntie Margaret was a fabulous godmother, always remembering to send presents at Christmas and on my birthday, and taking an interest in what I was doing in and out of school. We used to correspond regularly and she invited me to come and visit her in Golden as soon as I was old enough to travel alone. At the time, I was about 12 and I set my goal to fly out to Denver right after my 16th birthday in the summer of 1974.

From the moment I made this decision, my life revolved around this goal. The goal was bigger than simply flying across the world to America—it was about growing up, claiming my freedom, breaking out of the confines of my small self, my family and my familiar world. Yes, America was going to be my Salvation.

On Saturdays I stacked shelves in the local supermarket. In the evenings I babysat. My mother gave me a small allowance for clothes. Everything I earned or received went into my Building Society savings account. Watching my savings grow inspired me to keep saving. My school friends spent their pocket money on the cool clothes that got them attention from the boys at the local college. I didn't care. My eye was on the prize; I had to get to America.

There was no internet in those days so I would go to travel agents and pick up brochures about flights to America and Greyhound Bus routes. To keep myself motivated, I would spread a map of the U.S.A. over the dining-room table and examine the routes from East to West. So many songs I had heard were about towns and cities in the U.S.A. and I tried to pinpoint them all, thereby putting the stakes in the ground of my dream.

By about January of 1974, I had put aside enough for the airfare from London to Denver and was starting to save some spending money. Then, in the May of 1974, a few weeks before I was due to leave, my godmother announced that her mother in England had fallen ill and that she was going to have to fly back to the U.K. for the summer to care for her. I was crushed. My long-awaited prison break had been cancelled.
My godmother assured me that my trip had merely been postponed until a time when she could be available to host me but it was an undeniably devastating blow after saving so religiously for three whole years. What would I do to fill the void? Fortuitously, my German pen-pal stepped in and invited me to come and stay with her family that summer. I accepted. I flew alone which was a big leap in independence and I also became fluent in German which served me well in my development as a linguist. But Germany wasn't America.

Interesting Footnote:
Spirit certainly connected me with my German pen-pal, Agnes. Agnes' friend, Martina, was given my name and address by their English teacher but randomly passed my details to Agnes. Agnes and I enjoyed a brilliant rapport through our letters and, even more so, in person. I went to visit her again two years later during my gap year but then we lost touch. I kept her phone number though and a few years later, when I was travelling through southern Germany, I tried to call her. Her mother answered. Agnes was not at home. She was away at theological seminary training to be a minister....

I did not give up on my dream of freedom that America symbolized for me. I just had to wait another three years. So often in hindsight, it is easier to see how Spirit has a way of orchestrating our dreams much more skilfully than we could ever have managed with our limited human vision and resources.

In 1976, I turned 18 and was finishing school in the U.K. Despite the discouragement from parents and teachers who wanted me to play it safe, I was determined to have a gap year before starting University in October, 1977. But what would I do in that year to earn and travel? Serendipitously, through a chance conversation with a friend at school, I found out about Camp America. It was the perfect solution! So I applied to teach tennis and table tennis at Summer Camp in the U.S.A. from June to August, 1977, and got accepted.
As Camp Counsellors, our return flights from London to New York would be paid for. The contract included two months' work in a summer camp with weekly pocket money, followed by three weeks of free time in the U.S.A. A few days after my 19th birthday, in June 1977, I was finally on a plane to New York!

Camp Red Wing, on the shores of Lake Schroon, was my base for the next two months. It was located in upstate New York, in the Adirondack Mountains and fairly remote. This made it difficult for campers or Camp Counsellors to escape but that did not stop them trying. The nearest "town," Adirondack, was about a mile away from the camp. It boasted a post office and a general store. And that was all.

The peace and conviviality of the first two days of orientation with the other camp counsellors broke into loud chaos when the girls arrived—Jewish American Princesses from New York, mostly from divorced parents. The word "brat" was a favourite among the camp counsellors in our daily complaint orgies. I did not have a clue how to deal with my American charges. Not only were they very spoilt and disobedient, the older ones were into drugs and heavy petting with the boys from the camp across the lake. I was out of my depth.

The camp experience was gruelling. Luckily, the camp chefs were excellent and I was able to handle the emotional demands of my job by regular over-eating. There I discovered the delights of pancakes and maple syrup, plus Gram Crackers roasted over an open fire with chocolate and marshmallows. In addition to the major attraction of food, another sensual delight was skinny-dipping in the lake after dark!

One day, about half way through the contract, the girls were off on an excursion. I took the opportunity to have a meltdown and Sally's mum happened to witness my anguish. Of the five 7-year old campers in my bunk, Sally was my favourite. She was normal and unaffected and she obeyed me. That was novel. Both her parents were working in the camp—it was the only way they could afford to give their daughter the experience of a summer camp that typically only privileged girls could enjoy.
Compassionately, Sally's mum said to me:
"You have to understand, Stephanie, that the spirit of the American nation is confidence, not obedience. We have an 'I can do anything' approach to life."
Aaah, so that is why they weren't listening to me and I felt totally out of control! This insight helped, but I was still out of control.

My fellow counsellors at the camp were glad to learn that I was going "out West" at the end of the summer contract. Many of them said:
"It's a pity you won't be going as far as California. You would love the West Coast."
Their prophecy was accurate, but this was not my time. It would be another twelve years before I landed in California.

When camp was over and I had dried my last tears, after waving goodbye to the "brats" whom I could not control but had somehow grown to love, another camp counsellor drove me up to Montreal where I visited a friend. She helped me buy my bus ticket and at Montreal Bus Station, I finally boarded the Greyhound bound for Denver.

The journey across America that I had been so excited about for so many years took a grubby, uncomfortable 48 hours. The time was no problem but it was oh so boring! Mile upon mile of prairies, cornfields, punctuated by short stops in grimy downtown bus-stations, populated by the disenfranchised, or freeway rest stops where the waitresses had 1950s hairdos and the truckers smelled of nicotine and diesel. The romance of the road had just broken my heart.

It was early one morning in August, 1977, when that grimy Greyhound bus pulled into Denver Bus Station to find my godmother waiting for me. After six years of dreaming and planning, I had finally arrived! My godmother drove me the 40 minutes out to her home in Golden, Colorado. Together with her husband and four children, she spent the next two weeks being a generous host and showing me many fascinating places in the magnificent Rockies. She also introduced me to her best friend, Carol, whom I immediately liked. Carol was joyful and positive and a member of a local Religious Science church where she was planning to train as a Religious Science Practitioner. That meant nothing to me at the time and only proved to be significant later.

When I flew back to England, I was a little disappointed because I had expected a lot from America: total transformation and spiritual awakening actually, although I could never have languaged that at the time. Subconsciously, I was seeking the spirit of the Founding Fathers, the Transcendentalists, those who had birthed the American Constitution based on their spiritual values of religious freedom and equality. I wanted to embody that spirit, to experience my spiritual freedom and had no concept of the inner work that would be involved in order to accomplish that. A summer spent on American soil, drinking sodas and Coors beer, stuffing in pancakes, Gram crackers, ice-cream, chocolate chip cookies, hotdogs and hamburgers and putting on about fourteen extra pounds, was not the kind of "embodying" that would lift me up spiritually but it was my best (and only) strategy at the time.

Nevertheless, the seed had been planted—the seed of expansion and possibility. England felt very small and cramped and huddled together when I landed at London Heathrow at the end of that summer.

Interesting Footnotes:

- *In September of 1989, twelve years after my first trip to America, I followed my "highest calling" and flew to Los Angeles, California, on the West Coast of America, to start my training as a Religious Science Practitioner and Minister.*

- *In 1990, I travelled from Los Angeles to Binghamton on the East Coast of the U.S.A. to spend Christmas with my godmother who had since moved there. She informed me that her old friend, Carol, in Golden, had become a Religious Science Practitioner (licensed spiritual counsellor).*

- *In 1993, I also became a Religious Science Practitioner in the United Church of Religious Science at the Agape International Spiritual Center in Los Angeles and eventually graduated as a minister there in June of 1998.*

- *In September 2006, the United Church of Religious Science, including all its affiliate churches in the world, renamed itself "United Centers for Spiritual Living." In 2008, the UCSL organisation moved its home office from Los Angeles to—you guessed it—Golden, Colorado!*

Part 3

UNIVERSITY
1977-1981

Chapter 3

Love One Another

A new commandment I give you, that you love one another; just as I have loved you, that you also love one another.

John 12:34

Interpretation

If you and I really understood how to love ourselves, each other and our planet, none of the *Ten Commandments* of the *Old Testament* would ever have been necessary. What is more, Jesus would have been a man without a mission! Apparently, then as now, we need some guidance on learning how to love.

Jesus brought forth a new commandment that was different in tone from the "Thou shalt nots" characteristic of the Moses' Commandments. You see, as soon as you tell someone *not* to do something, he or she will probably do it as long as any remaining streaks of a rebellious two-year-old remain inside their psyche. Plus, the subconscious mind does not even hear the word "not," so this kind of negative instruction can be very counterproductive. For example: Don't think of a pink elephant....

Now stop thinking about the pink elephant.

You get the point.

Jesus in his wisdom suggested a positive action we could take towards the common weal:

"Love one another, just as I have loved you," he urged.

His love was unconditional. When people behaved ignorantly around him, he was able to have compassion for them. He could see beyond the smallness of the human condition straight to the sacred heart of all beings.

It is simple, but not easy, to follow this commandment because "love" has become a polluted word and, in our western culture, heavily spiked with meanings that have more to do with getting personal romantic and sexual appetites satisfied than they do with compassion, generosity, understanding, acceptance or loyalty. I heard a good definition recently: "to love is to extend care towards." To truly care for another means releasing the focus from self and, in the act of opening and giving, we become a hollow reed for Divine Power to flow through us.

When we are living in tune with the Law of Love, life works. We enjoy a healthy, prosperous and harmonious existence. It serves us to love one another although, if we ever tried to love for any kind of personal gain, or to get love returned to us, our attempts would certainly backfire. Love has to be an authentic expression of the heart. There has to be a cultivated, conscious choice to offer love regardless of whether those around us are behaving lovably or abominably, and regardless of whether the circumstances are charming or challenging.

My Story

How can anyone tell a love story without using poetry or song? When I was 19, I fell into poetry. His poetry. His song killed me ever so softly. He was a poet and a singer, a revolutionary and a disciple. His name was Tim and he changed my life.

As far as I know, Tim is still alive on earth, and yet I feel him sitting next to me as I write this, as if he were already in spirit. I see him now, as he was then, with his light-blue, V-necked sweater and blue jeans with a key-ring attached to the belt, dark chest hairs poking out from the V-neck and the silver crucifix he always wore hanging from its black leather thong around his neck. He had long, dark, wavy hair, a beard and moustache, a cheeky smile and dark green languid Irish eyes—which were sometimes dancing with humour or fired up with passion but, more often, melancholic. Like Jesus.

We met on September 30, 1977. It was the first day of our first year at Bradford University in West Yorkshire, England. It also happened to be Tim's 19th birthday. Tim's degree course was in Peace Studies. Mine was in Modern Languages. If it were not for the fact that we had both been allocated bedrooms on the top floor of the University Hall of Residence, we might never have met. The sensual hand of fate must have brought us together—he from the Catholic, working-class town of Strabane in Northern

Ireland and me from Protestant, middle-class, Surrey in the South of England.

At that time *The Troubles* were raging in Northern Ireland. The British had occupied Ireland centuries beforehand and the Irish Catholics were rising up against British imperialism and fighting for Home Rule. The I.R.A. (Irish Republican Army) was making an angry political statement by planting bombs in letters addressed to British politicians. Bomb scares were frequent. Daily commuters to London, my father included, ran the risk of being blown up on the trains. Paranoia reigned throughout England.

Against this backdrop of war between the Irish and the English, with all my ignorant, stereotyped ideas about the Irish being either terrorists or thick or both, and with the massive superiority complex of a middle-class southerner, deigning to study at a northern, redbrick, working class university, I embarked upon my degree course at Bradford and encountered my "enemy," Tim. Unbeknown to me, I was about to start my real education about life and death, love and longing, power and prejudice, war and peace, God and sex, and Bradford's speciality: Pakistani curries. I was hungry for it all.

My classic feminine dream in coming to university was to be in a relationship. His classic masculine dream was freedom—freedom for the Irish people from the British crown, the ending of hundreds of years of foreign occupation. As soon as Tim explained the causes behind *The Troubles*, it was obvious to me that the British should withdraw from Northern Ireland.
I supported his dream.
He fulfilled mine.
Tim hadn't expected to find his Juliet in the enemy camp. I would never have thought to look for my Romeo amongst the working class Catholics and I.R.A. sympathisers of Northern Ireland.
Destiny has its own notions.

Tim came from a devout Catholic family. He would not dare to miss Mass on Sunday but more out of fear of the earthly wrath of his mother than of any celestial wrath that God might choose to visit upon him! When Tim's mother sent her son off to university in England, her fear was fully justified that he would go the way of many an innocent Irish lad and kiss his virginity goodbye. She prayed for his immortal soul, pleading fervently with her god of supreme morality that Tim would not be led into temptation by a wicked British girl and that if he was, indeed, teased to the brink of the wicked girl's knicker-elastic, he would have the moral fortitude to say "No." Lamentably, these prayers were merely vain repetitions. *(But when ye pray, use not vain repetitions, as the heathen do: for they think that they shall be heard for their much speaking. Ref.: Matthew 6:7.)*

Would Tim have felt such an urgent need to attend Mass if his soul had not been so joyously compromised by our Sunday morning (and afternoon) indulgence in the "sins of the flesh"? Was he merely showing his face in the chapel to relieve his guilt? Or was it so that he could reassure his mother that he was not a lapsed Catholic? By now he had shown so much more than just his face to his English girlfriend and his morals had lapsed all the way down to his ankles along with his underwear. Could he ever be forgiven by his peers, his community, his family and God for the very venal sin of secretly sleeping with the enemy....?
You see, in the delectable war of the opposites, Tim's English Eve was an irresistible treble agent from the other side. She was:

1) a Brit
2) a Protestant
3) a Woman.

Number 3 posed an even greater threat to his soul than number 1 and number 2 added together! Yet, despite the obvious immediate and eternal danger that Tim was in, his heart and his hormones were sweetly victorious over his head.
Fortunately for Tim, the Catholic Chaplaincy at Bradford University was quite liberal and made allowances for the drinking

and mating habits of the intellectual elite of Great Britain by offering a students' Mass at 5:30 p.m. on a Sunday evening, as well as the regular Sunday morning service. On Sunday mornings, Tim was too busy loving his enemy *(Love your enemies. Ref.: Matthew 5:44)* to go to Mass. And so when the Catholic Chaplain, Father John, saw us rush into the chapel at 5:29 p.m. for the late Sunday Mass, alive and glowing with the aura of sex all around us, he was no doubt very aware that we were not exactly emanating a pure Christian kind of joy, the type that radiates from mystics after lengthy communing on the knees. No, the bright shroud of light we co-habited and co-emanated in the chapel was the kind that radiates from lovers after lengthy horizontal communing without the need for Bibles, bended knees or beads to attain to the higher levels of spiritual bliss and the deeper levels of sensual pleasure....

Have you noticed that the traditional scriptures of the world are sadly lacking in their references to sacred sexual love? It is a widely held belief that the naughty bits of the Bible got "chopped off" at the Council of Nicaea under Emperor Constantine in 325. Perhaps there are sexual references in the Dead Sea Scrolls, which were discovered between 1946 and 1956 in Qumran, Israel, and are still under careful wraps in the Vatican? We may never know. Anyway, despite the fact that Jesus the Christ does not directly share any teachings on sexual love in our current version of the Bible, I choose to believe that, to lovers, he would have said:

"Love one another, worship the divine consciousness of your beloved, honour the sacred essence of each other, surrender your petty ego-self in the purifying fires of love, seek to give and share and delight and comfort, make love to God in the flesh with your whole heart and mind, body and soul. And wake up into Heaven."

Chapter 4

To Russia with Love

2. For there is nothing that is covered that will not be uncovered; and hidden that will not be known.
3. For whatever you have said in darkness will be heard in the light; and what you have whispered in the ears in the inner chambers will be preached on the housetops.

Luke 12:2-3

Interpretation

These Bible verses warn us that it is impossible to keep secrets. This is because there is only One Mind and what is known at One point in Mind is known at all points in Mind simultaneously. The Universe functions according to a pattern of wholeness and interconnectedness. We cannot operate independently for any sustained length of time. We are all interdependent. As holy beings, we were not born to lie and hide so keeping secrets goes against our Essential Divine Nature. We were born to be transparent and to shine our Light.

Furthermore, we are energetic beings, and what we radiate in terms of our genuine underlying thoughts, beliefs and judgements is what others pick up and respond to, regardless of what we may be saying or doing to try and cover up or convey something different.

There is, however, a difference between what is secret and what is sacred. *Sacred* information is not shared because it is held in trust in a confidential relationship. For example, a therapist may not share personal information about their clients that was gained in the context of their professional relationship.

Secret information is not shared because of an egoistic need to hide; the owner of the secret does not want to experience the negative consequences of the truth being revealed. For example, an embezzler does not let on that s/he is stealing company funds but rather carefully covers his/her tracks. This to avoid being discovered, shamed and punished.

My Story

My main motivation in signing up for the degree course at Bradford University was the tantalising hook of four months in Leningrad. At that time, university Russian courses in Britain only offered a month at a summer camp in Moscow. Four whole months behind the Iron Curtain, in the beautiful city of Leningrad, sounded far more exciting and dangerous.

When I registered for the course, I was unaware that there were only 10 places on the Exchange Programme every year, and that the unlucky students would have to stay at a Russian monastery on the outskirts of Paris in France. It never occurred to me that I would not go to Leningrad and that was a good thing, because my clear "in10tion" was rewarded and, when the time came to put the plans in place for our internship year, my name was called out as one of the 10.

Why did I study Russian?
Much as I love languages, I never meant to study Russian but Destiny was once again on the case and one innocent remark by a school friend changed the entire course of my life....
All the fifth formers at Rosebery - we were aged about 15 or 16 at the time - were sitting in one large classroom for an information session on the upcoming school trips being offered in the Lower Sixth form the following year. The most popular option was always the Mediterranean cruise. The boys from the local college went cruising on the same ship so there were plentiful opportunities for tanning and snogging. Oh yes, there were also some educational opportunities at the various Mediterranean ports but they were, of course, a minor attraction. Thinking like a sheep and wanting to stick with the herd, I was assuming I would go on the cruise. Russia did not interest me; cold, drab, no tanning and no snogging. But then my rebellious friend Gillian whispered to me,
"My parents cannot afford to send me on either trip but, if I had the money, I would definitely go to Russia. You never know if the Iron Curtain will one day close for good and you will never have an opportunity to go there again."
"Dang! She is right!" I thought.
In that instant, I changed course, little knowing how momentous that choice to take the "road less travelled" would prove to be. The land of secrets and spies and Siberian prison camps would be my destination.

When my Lower Sixth year began and my "A" level timetable of lessons had been finalised, I joined the two 4th form students in the "O" level Russian class whenever I could. My intention initially was merely to learn the alphabet so that I could read the shop- and metro-signs on my upcoming trip. But Russian got under my skin and, when I ventured into Leningrad and Moscow on our school trip a few months later, I became completely hooked.

Among all the fascinating weirdness that was so different from the West, I felt completely at home in the Soviet Union. My two grey-hair-netted teachers, the group leaders, were amazed at how happily I adapted to the various challenges of Russian life: stinky rusty orange water, which we all bathed in but which I also drank without any side effects, strange foods like black bread with unsalted butter, tea without milk, buckwheat porridge, and greasy beetroot soup (Borscht) which I gobbled up with gusto. Then there was the maze of the Moscow metro, which I negotiated on my own, and the Russian students who joined our coach to practise English, with whom I alone formed pen-pal relationships. One of them, Sveta, continued to send me hardback English translations of Russian classics long after I had returned to the U.K. This feeling of comfort and familiarity had nothing to do with the misery and poverty of the Communist system. No, it was my first taste in this incarnation of the mystical enigmatic impenetrable Great Russian Soul *velikaya russkaya dusha* (pronounced: velli-kie-ya roos-kie-ya doo-sha) and a sense of having been there before, which got stronger each time I returned to Russia.

I came back to the U.K. quite changed and committed to studying for my Russian "O" level alongside my three "A" levels.
Study-aholic.
The next time I went back to Russia was at age 21 as part of the Bradford University exchange programme. The group of 10 students arrived in early October 1979. Temperatures were

already plummeting. Our home for the next four months would be the *Institut imeni Gerzena*, a teachers' training college, housed in an old Russian aristocratic home on the banks of the Neva River. It was close to Leningrad's main street, Nevsky Prospect, and a couple of blocks away from the Winter Palace, famously known as the Hermitage. Our bedroom windows in the Hostel for Foreign Teachers and Visitors looked out over the grand colonnade of St Isaac's Cathedral. The location could not have been more beautiful or more central!

We were warmly welcomed by various officials from the Institute and were introduced to our new "official friends." Each of the 10 Bradford students was partnered with at least two Russians. These were carefully selected English language students who could be trusted to spend time with the foreigners and to practise English, without being contaminated by our "sleazy" western capitalist culture. Needless to say, they were innocent, well-behaved and quite boring. They accompanied us on all our official excursions, arranged by the Institute. They were also supposed to spend every afternoon with us after our morning Russian lessons but we soon learnt how to make excuses and avoid them.

The Bradford groups that had gone to Leningrad in previous years had passed on a list of names and phone numbers of local Russians who were brave enough to have contact with foreigners. Their illegal association with us set them up for close scrutiny by the KGB and to being interrogated and jailed. Most of these Russian contacts were dissidents who were considerably more interesting than our official friends.

The day after our arrival, a group of us went to the Evropeiski Hotel on Nevsky Prospect and got "chatting" in broken Russian to a lonely old Russian man, Sasha, who invited us to come back to his flat for dinner. We had heard about Russian hospitality so we did not think it was a trap. There was safety in numbers so we said, “Yes” and then travelled almost an hour on the Metro with him to the outskirts of the city.

Once we arrived at Sasha’s tiny flat, I assumed we would all sit in the living room while he organised some food for us in the kitchen but I was wrong. Once we had disrobed, Sasha looked directly at me and said somewhat dismissively, as though talking to an underling,

“Just go into the kitchen and make us something to eat. There are eggs in the larder.”

He asked the two boys in the group to sit down and discuss socialism with him. He was obsessed with Jack London, the American author who was a passionate advocate of unionisation, socialism and the rights of workers. I had never heard of him.

Naturally, I was affronted by this blatant sexism. Women were supposed to have greater equality under Communism, weren’t they? That was obviously a theory and not a practice. But you know what? I did what he asked because I liked the weirdness of it,

“Here I am cooking dinner for this Russian stranger and my English friends in a communist flat in Leningrad and I have only been here for one day!”

Everyone liked my food; students always like free food, and Sasha invited us to visit him again. I thanked him but the thrill of more domestic labour did not entice me.

After a couple of weeks, I got into my stride with my new dissident friends. Every night was a party and I got a reputation for being a fun-loving, happy person who drank a lot. The Russians loved me. I fitted right in. Well, the alcoholics and the dissidents loved me. I cannot say the same thing for my Russian language teachers at the Institute.

We had Russian lessons on weekdays, from 9:00 a.m.-12:30 p.m. with a thirty minute coffee break from 10:30-11:00 a.m. Most nights I came home drunk on the last metro and was too tired, too sick (greasy Russian food and too much wine and vodka hardly ever stayed down) and too hung over to get to school for

the 9:00 a.m. start. I compromised by stumbling into the college canteen in time for the coffee break, where I would be served a tall glass of dishwatery coffee, boiled up with lots of milk and sugar. This was my hangover remedy. From there, I graced the class with my presence from 11 a.m.-12:30 p.m. I was probably one of the weakest students in the class. The teacher could not speak English so she explained everything in Russian, which I could not understand. Perhaps I could have asked for help but I was too arrogant and besides, I had discovered a secret weapon, which was the key to speaking fluent Russian....
Vodka.

Vodka loosened up my tongue, my confidence and the Russian rules of grammar. Vodka flowed freely and abundantly and made me sound like an ace linguist. At the end of an evening of partying, when we had drunk the place dry, someone would run down to the street, hail a taxi and buy a bottle of vodka from the taxi-driver's illegal stash at extortionate prices. Vodka allowed me to connect, heart to (sometimes not completely sober) heart, with the Russian people. Among those connections were two very special people: Mila and Alyosha.

Mila was a producer of children's TV programmes. She was married to an opera singer, Alex. Mila was half Jewish and she and Alex had applied to leave Russia under the pretext of wanting to settle in Israel. Unfortunately, they missed the small window of opportunity for hopeful emigrants and their application was refused. This meant that they became "Refusniks" – a slang word used amongst the dissident and disenchanted communities in the Soviet Union for those who had applied to leave and been turned down. Unofficially, Mila and Alex became enemies of the state and they were quietly removed from their employment in the arts and left without work.
Mila was, and is, highly sensitive to energy. She has a natural ability to deeply tune into people and help them deal with their

life issues. Her personal exploration of areas of knowledge that were threatening to the control of the Communist State, such as religion, spiritual psychology, psycho-analysis and western philosophy required her to read books that were banned. She made herself vulnerable to arrest by meeting with trusted friends to discuss these ideas and pursuing contact with foreigners who had easy access to the information she was interested in. Mila's profound wisdom, combined with her warm hospitality and genuine interest and care for human beings meant that there was a constant stream of people to her door, all wanting her to advise them about their human troubles.

One night after I had known Mila for a while and she felt safe enough to open up to me about her gift, she gave me a soul reading. I was astounded at how well she could interpret my past and give me deeper understanding about my present life. She won my trust and I accepted that her perspective on what the future held for me must also be true. This was my first proper experience of the invisible realm beyond what I thought I knew and it changed me forever. Here was my evidence that knowledge and wisdom existed on the unseen levels and that some gifted or sensitive people could translate that to humans on earth with accuracy, honesty and a genuine desire to give assistance and support.

Alyosha was in his mid-twenties, tall and lanky and a bit like John Lennon with his long, dirty-blonde hair and his round rimmed glasses. He was an intellectual, a member of the "Intelligentsia" and was constantly having to outwit the KGB, who kept a close watch on him. He was regularly called in for questioning regarding his anti-Communist activities but always managed to talk himself out of imprisonment. He knew that if he was sent to jail, he would die, either from the inhuman conditions or just plain old torture.

Alyosha and I had a sweet spiritual connection, based largely on partying. He wanted to be my lover but his teeth were so black and furry from the lack of toothpaste that I could not bring myself to kiss him. Alyosha had heard of Bhagwan Shree Rajneesh, the Indian New Age guru also known as Osho, and he asked me to bring him books about him, should I ever return to Russia. It was a big ask, Bibles and New Age spiritual books were banned at the time and both of us would have been arrested if we were caught. Along with Osho's books, Alyosha coveted my favourite item of clothing, a dark blue sweatshirt with the word "BULLSHIT" written in white on the left breast, where the designer's name would normally have been displayed.

Interesting Footnote:

On a future trip to Russia, after much inner struggle and torment, I relinquished the sweatshirt. Alyosha was ecstatic. I also smuggled in the desired spiritual books, having read chunks of them first and, thanks to Alyosha, given myself an introduction to Eastern spiritual philosophy. You can just imagine how extremely nervous I was when a Russian customs official pulled me over at Leningrad airport on entering Russia the following year and asked me to open my suitcase. The books were at the bottom of my case and were wrapped in clothes. I would have been detained, questioned and refused entry if those books had been discovered by someone who knew what they were about. Thanks to the ignorance of that particular customs official, his inability to read English and the Cosmopolitan magazine that I had casually picked up at Heathrow airport, I was spared. The customs official took his time leafing through Cosmopolitan and dwelling lasciviously on the pages with adverts for ladies' underwear. He clearly enjoyed the forbidden fruit of western "porn" and thought he might have to confiscate the magazine. He kept looking at me and then looking down at the magazine. Although it took him a while, he must have realised that I did not fit the profile of an international porn smuggler and reluctantly gave it back without bothering to check the rest of the contents of my case.

Phew!

As foreigners in Leningrad, we stuck out like the proverbial sore thumbs. Our coats and shoes were western and our faces were obviously not Slavic. We were stared at wherever we went, which we got used to but we were very naive and did not realise what an easy target for the KGB we were until the day when we went on a trip to Vyborg.

Vyborg is a fortress town on the Gulf of Finland, about an hour away from the city of Leningrad. Around six of us from the Bradford group boarded the train to Vyborg one icy Sunday morning in January because we had been invited to the home of one of our official friends. His name was Seriozha and he had told his family about the students from England. In classic Russian style, his mother had invited us to a sumptuous lunch, keen to have contact with Russian-speaking foreigners and to learn more about the world outside Russia.

Once on the train, we chatted and laughed in English. We were a very lively group compared to our fellow Russian passengers, who were dour and serious and hardly spoke. When we got off the train in Vyborg, Seriozha was waiting on the platform to meet us. Only one student in our group happened to turn around to notice a Russian man following closely behind us and speaking into a microphone in the lapel of his winter coat....

Seriozha's Mum was as wide as she was tall. She had a plain round face with classic red Russian cheeks and a beaming smile complete with some gold teeth, where the originals had been pulled out. She had lovingly prepared a feast of note for her honoured foreign visitors and urged us all to tuck in. We enthusiastically partook of the home-cooked meal, which was a million times better than the greasy cabbage soup and meat pies served at the college canteen during the week.
Once lunch was over, Seriozha suggested that we might like to see the local museum, which was located in the Vyborg fortress. I would have been happy to stay with Seriozha's Mum drinking

tea and eating chocolates but we knew by now that Russians are enormously proud of their cities and their museums and it would have been offensive to refuse.

As we stood in the fortress, looking at the exhibits of Soviet military glory, three middle-aged men in plainclothes quietly came up behind us and said in whispered Russian that they needed to ask us some questions. Our group leader, Nick, bravely stepped forward and asked who they were. They whipped out their KGB ID cards and made it clear that they would not be entertaining any more questions from us; they were the ones who wanted information. Furthermore, they told us that we would have to go with them to answer their questions. The Museum was clearly no place for this kind of international quiz/interrogation.

Seriozha witnessed our arrest. Brave boy, he did not run and hide but admitted he had invited us to his home and then to the museum. One of the KGB agents stayed behind to talk to him. The other two bundled us into the back of an army van, just like criminals, and drove us to the local police station.

Once at the police station, we were told that we would have to wait for the Chief of Police to come from Leningrad and interrogate us. As it was a Sunday, there was no-one with a high enough rank on duty in Vyborg to handle this unexpected very high-profile international case. We were shown into a meeting hall, which doubled up as a theatre. It had a stage at one end with long red velvet curtains and a lectern. The chairs were arranged in rows. Around the walls were the familiar posters with Soviet propaganda, showing artists' renditions of athletic-looking, dedicated, productive, young men and women modelling the success of the Communist revolution in the factories and on the farms. The reality that we Brits had observed, was very different.

A young Russian soldier, wearing his army uniform consisting of a grey hat with ear flaps, a long grey woollen coat and heavy black boots, was resting on his rifle at the back of the hall. He was given charge over us although, he could not have been much older than 18. On his upper lip were the fuzzy beginnings of a moustache, a faint sign of manhood on his sallow, spotty face with the empty light-blue eyes. Clearly, he was part of the Communist machine. We guessed that he was probably not fluent in English so we used the waiting period to agree on the story we would tell the Chief of Police when he arrived. Nick had understood that we were being arrested for travelling outside the city limits of Leningrad and had, therefore, violated our visa regulations. So our common story was that we did not know about the regulations and we were very sorry for our mistake.

The Chief of Police arrived two hours later; a middle-aged woman, contrary to our sexist assumptions. She was also very round and "busting" out of her police uniform but, in contrast to Seriozha's kind and jolly, mother, this Chief of Police was very stern, bordering on angry, bordering on Very Scary. She had a collection of black and gold teeth but that was inconsequential, because she never smiled. One by one, she called us into her dismal tiny office stacked high with criminal files, and interrogated us in Russian.
"Why did you break law?"
"Sorry, we did not know we were breaking the law."
"Yes, you broke law." "What was purpose of visit to Vyborg?"
"We came to visit Seriozha's family and to see the city of Vyborg."
"Who is Seriozha?"
"A friend from the *Institut imeni Gerzena."*
"What is Seriozha's last name?"
"I don't know."
"What is boy's address?"
"I don't know."
By this time, the Chief of Police was exasperated.

"You must sign here!"
She thrust a piece of paper in front of me and waited until I had signed the pre-printed statement confirming that I had broken the law.
"You must pay fine. 67 Roubles. You must pay now!"
She waited until I had taken the money out of my purse and put it on the desk. This was a king's ransom! Almost half our monthly student income on the Exchange Programme which, by the way, was equivalent to an engineer's salary. But a fine was infinitely better than detention in Siberia.

The interrogation was fairly quick for each one of us and, once we had all had our turn, we were released from custody and taken back to the train station, where we were accompanied on our return trip to Leningrad. No chance to say "Goodbye" to Seriozha or to thank his Mum.

The officials at the *Institut imeni Gerzena* learnt of our misdemeanour through the KGB and they were incensed. In fact, the whole Exchange Programme with Bradford University, which had taken long years of diplomatic genius to set up, was in jeopardy. We were severely rapped over the knuckles the next day and shamed by the Russian authorities into proper social behaviour. But after that there were, fortunately, no further consequences and the Exchange Programme continued the next year as per normal.

In early 1980, as our four-month stay drew to an end, the Russian army marched into Afghanistan. There was some real fear that the borders of Russia might be closed and we would not be allowed to leave. However, that did not happen and we boarded the plane back to the U.K. in early February as planned. By this time, nearly all ten of us had become amateur international criminals. Hidden in our suitcases were illegal letters we had smuggled out for our dissident friends, desperate to get help and support from their contacts in the West. Miraculously, not one of us was apprehended.

Interesting Footnote:

In April 2014, I was in Hungary with my friend Beatrix, an English teacher from Budapest. She had invited me to come to facilitate a sacred ceremony for her 50th birthday. Following the ceremony, we left for a visit to her parents in the south of Hungary. We travelled back to Budapest the next day, by way of Lake Balaton. Beatrix and her family had lived at the Lake for a few years and had remained friends with their old neighbours who had invited us to stop by for a visit.

Delighted as I was to see Lake Balaton for the first time, I was in a lot of discomfort and could not really enjoy it. My back was aching, my spine felt misaligned and I knew that if I could just hang upside down, gravity would pull my vertebrae back into place. But how was that going to happen there?

While we drank tea on the patio overlooking the Lake, the neighbour told us excitedly that he had just opened a new office with the most modern equipment in the local town. It was called "Bat Island." He invited Beatrix, her husband, Justin, and me to come and have a look at it. I was honestly not thrilled at the prospect of dragging myself around looking at bats in cages but I went along for the ride. Little did I know that "Bat Island" was the cute name that the neighbour had given to his chiropractic practice, where he had installed special machines on which his patients could hang upside down like bats to correct their spinal misalignment! In answer to my silent prayer, he asked me if I wanted to try out the equipment....

As if that was not miracle enough, once our tour was over and with spines realigned, we all got back into the neighbour's car. Beatrix and I sat in the back with Irena, the neighbour's wife, who also happened to be an English teacher. Beatrix shared with Irena that she and I had met in Slovenia at an English Teachers' Conference. We had recently discovered that we both spoke

Russian and had both studied at the Institut imeni Gerzena in Leningrad and stayed in the very same hostel for foreign visitors. Irena was amazed.

"I studied there too!" she said.

Really, what were the chances of that?

I studied in Leningrad from 1979-1980, Beatrix attended two different Russian courses in 1982 and 1984 and Irena had trained there as a Russian teacher in 1990. Irena shared that when she had come back from Russia to Hungary, she did not admit to speaking Russian for fear of looking suspicious. She had quickly turned her focus to speaking and teaching English. Russian was most unpopular in Eastern Europe after the fall of Communism and English became the first foreign language to be taught in schools.

Part 4

AMSTERDAM
1981-1985

Chapter 5

Desperately Seeking Self

Ask, and it shall be given to you;
seek and ye shall find;
knock and it shall be opened to you.

Matthew 7:7

Interpretation

With our outer-focused and other-focused Western minds, we might immediately interpret this saying of Jesus to be about asking and seeking and knocking in the outer world in order to get the things we want. That certainly is a valid interpretation, but when we consider that the metaphysical route is usually an inward journey and involves a transformation of consciousness, then this biblical instruction is not just about obtaining something of human value.

Jesus is offering us a technique for spiritual growth rather than simply a method of acquiring. We are advised to ask the indwelling Spirit for what we need. We are urged to seek to know the Whole Presence living Its Life as us, to be a sleuth for Truth, to discern Beauty, to follow our Inner Guidance.

When you knock on the door of your heart, be persistent. Don't leave until there is an answer. Demand to be taught, shown and assisted in your understanding of what is true and who you need to become in order to live your life with power and purpose. The doors of your consciousness will be opened to the Infinite Possibility of your Being and all will be revealed from within, in the perfect way and at the perfect time.

My Story

It was 1981 and the final term of university was drawing to a close. I still had no idea how I was going to solve that niggly little issue of my future career as a graduate nor what I was going to do with the rest of my life. On Wednesday afternoons, while my fellow students had been attending careers lectures in Middle Management, I had been doing the important work of meeting with my feminist group and demonstrating against pornography.

My feminist anger and political views had been awakened in January, 1978, early on in my university degree course, when I read Germaine Greer's seminal work, *The Female Eunuch,* from cover to cover and absorbed it like medicine for my wounded female psyche. Germaine changed my perception of reality at the core of my feminine being, and this changed my life.

In addition, I was being politically awakened by the education I was receiving from Tim regarding the imperialist nature of the British government and its global exploitation under the guise of colonization—specifically in relationship to *The Troubles* in Northern Ireland.

Feminism and her bed-fellow, Socialism, were obviously going to be my vehicle for my budding saviour complex. Naturally, I became a Socialist-Feminist. I planned to rescue downtrodden women, third world colonies and underdogs in general. Passionately, I dreamed of bringing down the patriarchal British Empire and changing the world with my newfound political and social ideals. Finally, I had a label and an identity to be reckoned with – or so I thought. I did not know then that to simply rebel *against* the status quo is a position of powerlessness. Victims are never victors.

After we received our degree results, my boyfriend, Tim, went home to do a well-paid summer job in Northern Ireland. He felt duty-bound to support his widowed mother and younger siblings. Together, he and I planned to save some money over the summer and meet up in September to go travelling. That did not transpire. (More details about our relationship are coming in a future book.)

So what next? Stay in Bradford? Go on the dole and try to pretend I was still an irresponsible student like some of my older university friends had done? No, there had to be more to life than this!

I must have asked inwardly for some guidance. Possibly an anxious muttering of: "What the hell am I going to do now?" without really expecting anyone or anything to respond. But

then, one night, shortly before the last day of term, I had a dream....
In the dream, I was told to go to Amsterdam. Finally, a clear and concrete plan was in place! Obediently, and also because I did not have any better ideas, I quickly packed up my stuff in Bradford, got on the overnight boat from Harwich to the Hoek of Holland and emerged from Amsterdam's Centraal Station three days later.

There I was, bleary-eyed in the early morning sun, surrounded by the guttural screeching of the Dutch seagulls. On my back was my clean, bright, royal-blue, hardly-used backpack, to which was tied my vivid orange, hardly-used sleeping bag. I had very short, spiky, wine-red hair, and I was wearing a maroon Chinese jacket, long dangly earrings and no make-up—looking for all the world like a switched-on Socialist-Feminist from a middle-class background, experienced at the bohemian lifestyle and a force to be reckoned with in the intellectual circles of world changers.

Not.

It was only going to be a two-month stay that summer, however, I fell in love with Amsterdam. I worshipped the fringe element: the hippie communities in the squats, the air of experimentation with consciousness, both the dark and the light, the spiritual journey with mind-expanding drugs and waist-expanding booze. But there was more that delighted me: an extremely sophisticated and liberal social system, the stunning beauty of the old merchants' houses along the canals, the bicycle brigades, the proximity to other European cultures and languages, the art museums, the freedom. Yes, freedom! This was *exactly* what I had been missing during all those years at school and university! I was fed up with academia. Now it was time to discover what was real so I became a passionate spiritual seeker. Simultaneously, my human survival instinct turned me into a desperate job seeker.

After two weeks of knocking on the doors of prospective employers, and being promptly rejected, I finally landed a plum part-time job as a toilet cleaner in an office building. My two-hour shift was from 6-8 p.m. every evening so it left me time in the day to continue seeking work. The toilets taught me to be humble and grateful but, after three days, driven by a need to pay rent, which the toilets were simply not satisfying, I surrendered to job-hunting at McDonalds. It was then that the Goddess of Fortune and Fast Food smiled upon me.

Let me give you a little background on my glittering career with McDonalds. During my gap year, in 1977, before taking off for Camp America, I had worked for McDonalds on Reguliersbreestraat in Amsterdam. It was just for a month while I was travelling through Europe but oh, how I loved it for this job made me cool and grown-up.

One of my co-workers, Faye, was a real hippy from Australia. She lived in a squat with her Dutch boyfriend and a moving collection of other hippies and travellers. They had taken possession of a one-bedroom flat in an old building where there was no bathroom or shower. This meant that the solitary cold water tap in the kitchen had to be shared between five people. Faye's friends were vegetarian and spiritual; they smoked dope, slept on mattresses on the floor, had different sexual partners and wore socks which did not match. Every night was a party. Every morning was a blank.

You can only imagine how sorely I was tempted to give up my place at University so that I could attempt to become a full-time hippy in Amsterdam but the job at McDonalds made me seriously reconsider. You see, despite Amsterdam's seductive lure of seediness and the joint-promise of true spiritual freedom, I got clear that I did not want to do a minimum wage job for the rest of my life. I decided that I would go to University and get my degree in Modern Languages and then I would be a highly paid

world-changer by working as an interpreter for the United Nations.
Big Ego led to Big Fall....

Four years after I left the McDonalds on Reguliersbreestraat in Amsterdam and, having graduated with an honours degree in German and Russian from Bradford, I found myself dossing on my friend's couch in the Bijlmermeer on the outskirts of Amsterdam and working as a part-time toilet cleaner. Said friend, Dorothy, was also a co-worker from the former McDonald's job with whom I had stayed in touch over the years. She was definitely not a hippy which meant she had a proper job and a proper flat and slept on a proper bed with only one steady boyfriend and her socks matched.
Dorothy pointed out rather harshly, along with some tactless hints about me "paying my way" that a few more McDonalds branches had recently opened up in the city and, if I was lucky, I might get a full-time job in one of them which would give me a decent wage. Furthermore, she had the audacity to suggest that if I was serious about job-seeking, I should get up early every morning, dress smartly and be pounding the pavement and knocking on the doors of prospective employers rather than slobbing about till 5 p.m. then throwing on a pair of jeans to go and clean toilets.

I felt sick.

The next morning after this little pep talk, during that humid July of 1981, I ventured into the new McDonalds branch on Nieuwezijdsvoorburgwal. (This is quite difficult to pronounce if you are not Dutch.) And right there, behind the counter, was my answer to prayer in the short, brown, round, form of the Duty Manager. I recognized him! Really, what were the chances?

The Duty Manager's name was Hassan and he was an Egyptian. We had worked together at the Reguliersbreestraat branch four years earlier when I aspired to being a hippy. At that time, Hassan was the restaurant cleaner, an immigrant into Holland, hoping to make a better life for himself and his family. On the night before I left the job in 1977, I passed him as he was mopping the floor and I happened to strike up a conversation with him about his home in Egypt and his dreams for his children in Europe. He was both touched and surprised that one of the European staff would bother to talk to him. Mostly he was ignored or looked down upon.

While I had been studying at University in England, Hassan had worked his way up to Duty Manager at McDonalds. Miraculously, he also recognised me when I walked into the new branch four years later. Like me, he was also desperate; he urgently needed temporary summer staff to serve the hordes of foreign tourists. Without further ado, *he* asked *me*, "Do you want your old job back?"

Beggars can't be choosers. Seekers can be choosers but I felt like a beggar. Gratefully, I chose to accept the job even though it was the much-spurned late shift from 4 p.m. - 12 midnight and involved eight fatty-sweaty hours per day standing at the till, asking the summer tourists profound questions, such as: "Would you like ketchup OR mayonnaise with your fries?" and invariably getting the answer
"Yes."
Aaagh! But, hey, it was better than cleaning toilets by a long-shot (or even by a long drop?).

Nine months later, as soon as I escaped out of the McDonald's frying pan, I was into the fire of Canon, Amsterdam—a Japanese company where my militant feminist ideology and uniform attire were not graciously received:

- ♀ short spiky hair;
- ♀ no make-up;
- ♀ no bra;

- ♀ baggy harem pants;
- ♀ extra large, hand-knitted, shapeless sweaters;
- ♀ big clompy boots;
- ♀ Palestine Liberation Organisation (PLO) chequered shawl;
- ♀ long dangly earrings and
- ♀ a dismissive scowl towards all humans with a penis.

But, Alleluya, it was a day job and allowed me to go to classes in the evenings. I attended as many courses as I could, desperately seeking spiritual awareness and knowledge. These included:

- Dutch;
- Japanese;
- Tai Chi;
- Karate;
- Self-Defence;
- Yoga;
- Macrobiotic Cooking;
- Zen Meditation;
- Transcendental Meditation;
- Massage;
- Astrology;
- Psychic Development;
- Healing the Aura and Chakras;
- Crystal Healing;
- Keep fit and
- Hairdressing (because, as you might remember, I wanted to be a hairdresser when I was a child).

In addition to classes, I read like a fiend—mainly feminist literature but also self-improvement and spiritual books. With my Canadian friend, Joanne, I started a feminist literature group. And through it all, so that I could relax from this relentless pursuit of esoteric knowledge, I drank beer and smoked dope—as you do, when you aspire to belong to the elite class of dropouts living in Amsterdam.

Of course, at that time, I had no idea what was happening behind the curtains on the stage of my destiny. Why was I living in a Dutch culture and learning Dutch?
In South Africa there are two major groups of white settlers who put down their African roots in the 17th century: the British and the Dutch. The Dutch people are known as the "Afrikaners" and still speak a derivative of Dutch known as Afrikaans.
Isn't it amazing that a whacking nineteen years before I started my ministry, at a time when I had not even heard of the Science of Mind, let alone thought about becoming a minister, Spirit had gone ahead to prepare the way? *(I will go before you, and make the crooked places straight; Ref.: Isaiah 45:2.)* So, when I eventually started my ministry in South Africa, my knowledge of Dutch allowed me to understand a substantial amount of spoken and written Afrikaans as well as appreciate the Afrikaner mentality. This cultural training enabled me to integrate more successfully which, in turn, eased the way for me to spread the Science of Mind teachings.
Of course, this special attention to my divinely tailored curriculum was lost on me, caught up as I was in the not-so-merry-go-round of my centre stage drama. The Amsterdam years were a time of huge discovery and huge disappointment. I loved the learning. I loved opening the door to spiritual wisdom, but I didn't love the fact that for all my reading, learning, drinking and doping, I was still chock full of self-hatred and loneliness. On Tuesday nights, after my psychic healing class, I positively flew home on my stolen bike, feeling completely joyful and at one with the universe, but the next day it was always business as usual....

Depression.
Something was missing. I did not know what it was. There were frequent thoughts of suicide. Why did I feel so empty? I was

disappointed that the mental expansion did not change the old underlying sense of defectiveness and pointlessness that I felt in my darker moments. There was something wrong with me, I was sure, and I did not know how to fix it. Avidly, I kept seeking, but mostly outside myself. There had to be a teacher or a book or a class somewhere that would fix me forever.
Didn't there?

One cold, dark, wet, winter's day, my plaintive prayers were answered in the form of a book called *Creative Visualization* by the American, New Age author, Shakti Gawain. My teacher from the U.S.A., Gayle Raborn, who taught the Psychic Healing workshop I attended on Tuesdays, had recommended this book to her students. Those were the dinosaur days, pre-internet and pre-Amazon.com. The book had to be specially ordered from the U.S.A. It took forever and was very expensive. Forking out cash in advance and delayed gratification were abhorrent to me. Needless to say, I did not order it even though I was sure that spiritual books were right up there, next to God, in their capacity to save the Afflicted and the Lost. I fit nicely into both categories and devoured self-help literature without ever putting any of the suggestions into practise. Sometimes I did not even take the book off my shelf at home let alone crack it open because merely having it in my possession was the key to transformation.

On this particular miserable, rainy afternoon, I was on my way home from the dentist. Wait, did I say "dentist"? I meant "demon-ist." He had just pulled out my four wisdom teeth without any anaesthetic or sympathy! My gums were bleeding from all four gaping holes and the cotton wool pads, a thoughtful parting gift from the demon-ist's nurse, had maxed out on absorption. I needed a powerful distraction while I recovered from this bloody torture and I was hoping to buy something light to read before slinking back off to my flat to literally lick my wounds.

The feminist bookstore, Xantippe, my usual place of pilgrimage, was too far to walk in the rain. And so, on an emergency basis, I dashed into The Gay Bookstore & News Agency because it was the nearest bookstore to my flat in Leidseplein and right opposite my tram stop. There, on the shelves, amongst all the gay literature and soft-porn photography, and only visible to a true seeker, was one lonely copy of *Creative Visualization!* I snapped it up, carried it home jubilantly as if it were sacred prey, and then devoured it from start to finish.

No sooner had my wisdom teeth been yanked out, than this spiritual wisdom came rushing in. The universe abhors a vacuum. This book was written for me. I had asked, I had sought, I had knocked and suddenly the door within had opened. The enormous power that was being made available to me through Shakti Gawain's elucidation of visualisation and affirmations left me reeling. With a sense of both delight and horror, I recognised then that I could actually create my own reality—I no longer had to be a victim of the rabid forces beyond my control, mainly consisting of:

1. My parents;
2. My employers;
3. Men, and
4. Money.

This was exactly what I wanted—power! I was drunk on the anticipation of my soaring new life as "Queen of Everything." The last page was entitled: "Your life is your work of art."
"No," I contradicted Ms. Gawain, suddenly sober, "my life is a prayer."

With that, I shut the book and did not dare look at it again for another year.

Part 5

SOUTH AFRICA:
The Apartheid Years
1985-1989

Chapter 6

Keeping the Vision

Where there is no vision, the people perish,
but he who keepeth the law,
happy is he.

Proverbs 29:18,
King James Bible

When the wicked men multiply, the people are ruined;
but he who keeps the law, blessed is he.

Proverbs 29:18,
Holy Bible
from the Ancient Eastern Aramaic Text,
translated by George Lamsa

Interpretation

What is a vision?

- An image, a feeling, a sense of what is possible despite a complete lack of evidence or agreement in present conditions;
- The impossible dream;
- A brighter future;
- A possible reality larger than one individual can achieve in a lifetime;
- A powerful objective that we are forever striving towards but never fully accomplish or manifest;
- A piece of Heaven being revealed on Earth in magnificent ways that blesses the Whole.

If you and I do not have the awareness of an expanded possibility for our lives i.e. something that is beautiful, true and healing for ourselves and all others, we are contracting and perishing. There is no static state in the Spirit. Either we are moving heavenward or hellward. Either we are expanding our lives or contracting our existence. Heaven and hell are both here and now. Heaven is an expansion of consciousness to include more of the qualities of the Divine. Hell is a contraction in consciousness and a deeper sense of separation from the Divine and all that is Good.

The good news is that it is natural for us to eternally evolve into greater and grander versions of Who We really Are. If we stay true to the future vision of Who we want to be and what we want to accomplish, the Universe supports us with a massive YES and goes about the business of delivering on our vision according to our clearly formulated desires.

My Story

When I landed in South Africa on December 16, 1985, to visit my mother for a short two-month holiday, I had no intention of staying. I had no vision for my life either, apart from generally

changing the world to more closely match my personal specifications. The rather grandiose idea of going to work for Mother Theresa in India had occurred to me and I was happy to talk about my "plans," but I think that was only to comfort myself and to impress others with my selfless heroism. I actually never did anything about it.
No, in the sorry absence of a real vision, my best "plan" after my two-month holiday would have been to return to my debauched life in Amsterdam. In the few months before my first trip to South Africa, I had been selling diamonds by day and living in a squat with a gangster/drug dealer by night. I liked my double life. It was exciting if not terrifying. Adrenaline is a drug all of its own. But I digress....

My mother had emigrated to South Africa in 1984 after she was finally divorced from my father in the U.K. She loved the sunshine and the lifestyle and had found a job and made plenty of friends. One of my two sisters, Hannah, had already gone to visit her, fallen in love with a South African Jew and decided to immigrate so that she could be with her new boyfriend. That worked out quite nicely; she converted to Judaism and they got married a few years later. Mum had invited my other sister, Debbie, and me to visit her, little knowing how much that first trip would change my entire life. Debbie had to return to college in the U.K. after her three-week holiday in South Africa but I had booked a longer stay because I did not have

- a steady job in Europe (my contract with the diamond company had finished) or
- a place to live (my boyfriend had vandalised the squat and we had broken up) or
- a plan (see above.)

When I first arrived in Johannesburg, I was full of political left-wing righteousness about Apartheid and judged my mother harshly for her acceptance of the system and her enjoyment of her white privileges. You see, while I lived in Amsterdam, I had been an attractive (not), beer-drinking, dope-smoking armchair socialist, marching in my head against the racist policies of the South African government. I certainly had no wish to participate in that corrupt culture and add my white presence to the imbalance in the system.

So why did I even go, you might be asking yourself? Well, the only way I could morally justify a trip to South Africa was to reassure myself that it would be a one-off duty visit to my mother, during which time I would have the uncommon opportunity to see firsthand if what I heard and read in the media about Apartheid was true. This foray into the front lines of the war against colonialism would certainly deem me a socialist hero upon my return to Europe as well as a profound authority on the sensitive subject of South Africa.

Spirit had other plans.

On the day I stepped off the plane on to South African soil, I felt as if I had been transported to another planet, another dimension of time and space. I noticed a few things right away which were in stark contrast to Europe:

1. The light was blindingly bright.
2. The heat was intense and burned through my winter clothes.
3. The flowers were like a tropical explosion and the colours were extraordinarily vivid.
4. The earth was a dark orangey-red because of the iron-ore content.
5. Only white people drove cars.
6. Africans walked barefoot along the roadside.
7. All the houses had very high walls and some had electric fences on top of the high walls. Many had guard dogs barking in the front yard.
8. The bars were closed because it was a Sunday and there was no alcohol to be bought anywhere. This is how my Aunt

could justify the two-litre box of wine that she brought with her to meet us at the airport and celebrate our arrival....

Yes. Definite culture shock.

With its mine dumps and mine shafts, single-story buildings, and acres of rough, undeveloped land, Johannesburg reminded me of an old mining town in the Wild West of America, thrown up in a hurry during the time of the Gold Rush. And, indeed, as I learned later, it was just that. The African name for Johannesburg is "Egoli" or "City of Gold." It was originally founded in 1886 as a result of the South African Gold Rush. Until that time, it was simply unsuspecting desert sitting on a gold mine.

On my first night, typical of the weather patterns on the Highveld (Afrikaans for high plateau) where Johannesburg is located, there was a thunderous rainstorm complete with biblical lightning flashing across the sky. Due to atmospheric pressure on the outside and the pain-body pressure on the inside, now that I was once again in the tense orbit of my biological family, I suffered a migraine. With elephants stampeding inside my skull, I got out of bed and padded into my mother's living room where I sat cross-legged in the dark, trying to meditate to ease the pain.

Suddenly, through the din and banging in my head, I heard a still small Voice say:
"You have been prepared. I have brought you here. Now it is time to get on with the work."
"WHAT? What work? Who, me?" I asked, startled and curious.
I had no idea what this message meant. Unfortunately, the Voice did not specify further. I continued to sit in the dark, waiting for more information. Nothing. Only Silence. Not a deep mystical Silence though. This was an irritating silence when I could really have done with a bit more input from Upstairs.

You will be relieved to know that, upon arrogant reflection, everything became clear: I knew, with absolute significance, that I had been divinely appointed to single-handedly fix Apartheid—rather like a modern-day Joan of Cl'arke but, sadly, with three key elements missing:

1. Humility,
2. My maidenhood,
3. A warhorse, aka car, to move me around the urban battlefields,

   3a. A driver's licence.

Mustering up the troops was harder than I had envisaged. In fact, not one troop was ever mustered. There was no proper battle plan either. Eventually I realised my sphere of power, as God's righteous warrioress, was limited to advising my mother's friends that they should no longer employ black maids or gardeners because the exploitation of cheap black labour meant they were reinforcing a corrupt political and social system. Yes, you can imagine how that went down!

My mother's friends patiently advised me that I did not understand the situation in South Africa. I eyed them suspiciously. It sounded like justification for abuse to me. Strangely, my mother's friends stopped inviting me over. Now I had no friends and my mother was embarrassed about her belligerent and socially inept daughter. The battle was not going well.

Discouraging though it was, this experience turned out to be one of my important lessons in "Learning to be a Liberator."

1. Don't confront people with their ignorant attitudes or appalling behaviour at the first meeting or even the second.
2. Wait till you build trust by being consistently present and compassionate, over time, and by being the example of someone living inside the vision of a better world not just a big talker.

3. Get permission before you share with others exactly how they are screwing up in your esteemed opinion.
4. Permission may never come.

What I came to understand was that the white European colonialists had fostered a culture of dependence amongst the black indigenous peoples in South Africa, and so, if white people did not hire black people to work, the black people would be faced with poverty and hunger. For many blacks without employment, the choice would have been to starve or steal.

Hope for changing the world, or at least the immediate Apartheid problem, showed up in the form of Rev. Gladys Harrison at the *Centre for Abundant Living* in Westdene, Johannesburg (later renamed to the *1st Church of United Religious Science* in South Africa).

"Coincidentally," I found out about Rev. Gladys and her spiritual centre when I happened to pick up the *Link-up Directory* in the local chemist. *Link-up* was a list of all the alternative organizations and practitioners in the Johannesburg area. (By the way, Reader, I don't believe in coincidence any more—hence the inverted commas; I am convinced that everything is orchestrated.)

The name *Abundant Living* piqued my interest. Was it indicating a spiritual way to get rich quick? My holiday money was running out and I could certainly have done with some extra cash. This old familiar feeling of financial neediness turned out to be my very human hook into the Science of Mind teaching.
Poor in Spirit and purse, I dialled the number. Rev. Gladys answered.

Until that conversation, I had had an outworn concept of ministers as serious, sombre (mostly male) people, but this female Rev. Gladys was happy to be alive and kept laughing as she told me her miserable story of being born with a partial stomach, undergoing endless operations and, finally, turning to the Science of Mind technique of affirmative prayer when the doctors had given her just a few months to live. She had defied the medical establishment. Not only had she survived and thrived, but she was now running her church full time at the age of 60!

OK, I have to admit that I respected her. Generously, I would allow her to be one of my foot soldiers in the good fight against Apartheid. To my dismay, Rev. Gladys had better things to do. She had a clear vision of establishing her Science of Mind ministry in South Africa and she was constantly about her Mother-Father God's business. *(And he said unto them, How is it that ye sought me? wist ye not that I must be about my Father's business? Ref.: Luke 2:49, King James version.)* Rev. Gladys was working on her own consciousness and helping people to heal theirs, and she was not about to blow her energy resisting the evil of Apartheid. Hmmm.... no support for my cause there, then.

After that major set-back, I heard about the *Sowetan*. It was a radical black newspaper with its offices in the Soweto Township. Soweto was and is a huge sprawling settlement of mostly urban black people, living on the breadline on the borders of Johannesburg.

"If I worked for the *Sowetan*," I reasoned, "I would be in on the front line and I could write the articles that would crush Apartheid with the Power of the Pen!" (Actually, I had no training in journalism but this was an insignificant fact and, therefore, easy to overlook.)

I decided to tell Rev. Gladys about my plans. I felt sure she would support my revolutionary stance and my brilliant strategy.

The opportunity to have a tête a tête with Rev. Gladys presented itself during my next trip to the *Abundant Living Centre* where I had begun volunteering. Just to reassure you that I had not become holy and selfless, my reason for volunteering was so that I could sneakily spend time being unofficially mentored by Rev. Gladys. Being of service to the vision of the church wasn't that compelling to me at the time whereas getting a spiritual fix was.

When I shared with Rev. Gladys my grand vision to be a journalist for the *Sowetan*, she told me with her endearing bluntness that I would not be much good to anyone if I were in jail or dead, and this was going to be my likely fate if I tried to work in the township. I was crestfallen. What about my dreams to fight for the underdog, save the world, be a hero whilst all the time remaining pleasantly comfortable? (To be ashamedly honest, Reader, I didn't actually want to *die* fighting for my principles.)

Wisely discerning that I was a classic "rebel without a clue," Rev. Gladys suggested the following strategy in an attempt to channel my loose-cannon passion for fixing the outer world (so that I could avoid peeking at the domestic crisis in my own head):

1. Get a clear vision of what you want to see happening in South Africa, write it down and describe it in details.
2. Ask yourself what role you could play in fulfilling that vision and write it down.
3. Ask yourself what you can usefully do in the next 24 hours towards fulfilling that vision and then get on and do it.

Amazingly, I did what she suggested.
In part, at least.

1. My vision was to have black people and white people sharing power in a democratic government and speaking the language of international politics – English.
2. My role could be teaching black people English.
3. I didn't know what to do in the next 24 hours, so I just thought about it—for approximately two and a half years.

The catalyst that moved me into action on my vision was an overseas trip to Holland for a holiday, one year later, in 1987 where I watched the newly released movie, *Cry Freedom,* in a public cinema in Amsterdam. The movie had, not surprisingly, been banned in South Africa due to its subversive nature. It depicts the life of Steve Biko, a brave, outspoken, Black Rights activist in the late 1960s and early 1970s of Apartheid South Africa, and his growing friendship with the white South African journalist, Donald Woods.

In the movie, we see how Woods was put under house arrest and how he and his family had to escape from South Africa, under cover, because of his increasing involvement with Biko's cause. Biko was captured by the white Afrikaner police and beaten to death in prison. While in exile in London, Woods wrote a book, entitled simply *Biko*, about the life of Steve Biko and the South African "cry for freedom." Right after I saw the movie, I went out and bought the book.

As I travelled around Amsterdam to visit my friends, I felt afraid of reading this dangerous book openly on the tram. Furtively, I would slide it out of my handbag, being careful not to expose the title on the cover, half-expecting to be arrested by the South African secret police who might be travelling on that very same tram.... Clearly, after less than two years of living under South African Apartheid, I had become paranoid; terrified of the potentially fatal consequences of exposing myself as an enemy of the system.

The *Cry Freedom* movie stirred me deeply in my sleeping soul. It shamed me into realising how numb I had become to the iniquities of daily life in South Africa. It stimulated my fighting spirit, and spurred me on in the battle for equality and justice.

Interesting footnote:

It occurs to me as particularly ironic that I had this transformational experience in Holland, the very country from which the Dutch sailors first sailed to South Africa en route to India, the land of tea and spices. The Dutch employees of the Dutch East India Company who later settled in the Cape of Good

Hope became known as Afrikaners. They were mostly farmers (known as boers) and slave owners. It was the national Afrikaner political party that coined the term "Apartheid" and legalised the separation of blacks and whites when the Afrikaners came to power in 1948.

Apparently, my fighting spirit went underground and another year passed after my return to South Africa from Holland. It was only in 1988, when I finally told Rev. Gladys about my desire to teach English to black people. The timing must have been right because she had just hired a black gardener, named Peter Kekana, who was very bright and educated and had just started a school for black domestic workers. In fact, Peter was so committed to education as a path to freedom, that he had worked all day as a gardener and studied all night by candlelight in order to pass his exams. His goal was to help his students get through the lower level school exams in English, Afrikaans and Maths and then, ultimately, take them through Matric, their South African school-leaving certificate. A good grade in Matric would allow them to apply for university and, even if they did not choose that academic route, they would still have many more opportunities for better paid employment. They would no longer be sentenced to cleaning or gardening for their white boss for the rest of their lives.

Rev. Gladys had allowed Peter to use the church premises on Saturdays for his school. In the days of Apartheid, it was illegal for blacks to meet in public places and they could be arrested for doing so. The white government would have assumed that they were agitating and so kept them divided in order to rule. The only legal place to meet was in a church. Naturally, the churches in the black neighbourhoods became the base for revolutionary activity. While the Sunday services were taking place in the churches upstairs, the anti-Apartheid activists were meeting downstairs in the basements.

Rev. Gladys introduced me to Peter. When I offered him my services as an English teacher, he nearly cried. For him, I was an answer to prayer, a sign that Spirit was fulfilling his vision.
"Could you teach literature as well as language?" he asked, not wanting to push his luck, but pushing his luck all the same.
"Errr...What kind of literature?" I asked, hesitating.
"*Macbeth*," Peter answered.

Two of Peter's students were studying Shakespeare's *Macbeth* for Matric. "Coincidentally," Macbeth was the only Shakespeare play I had studied for my English literature exams, then known as "O" levels, at grammar school in the U.K. It must have been fifteen years ago though, because I was only 15 at the time, and I was not sure I knew the play well enough to teach it, but I said "Yes" to Peter's request and then prayed a lot.

At that time, I had had very little experience teaching English and then only to individuals or very small groups. While I was in my first year at Bradford University, I volunteered to teach English to some young Pakistani immigrant women. The important language revolved around health care, nappies and bottled milk. In my final year at Bradford I had done a short TEFL course (Teaching English as a Foreign Language) because I knew that I wanted to travel the world and, for that, teaching English was a perfect vehicle.

English language lessons at Peter's volunteer school began on a Saturday morning. I was so nervous before my first class; worried that I would not be able to teach English effectively and even more worried that they would not accept me as a white teacher. My fears were unfounded. Showing up for them meant the world. Peter introduced me and my twenty-five black students welcomed me with open arms and an eager enthusiasm to participate in my lessons.

Alpheus and Joseph, my two literature students (both in their early twenties) who worked as gardeners by day and who studied at night, met with me a couple of times each week and we worked our way through *MacBeth*. Naively, I assumed they would struggle to relate to the capers of the nobility of mediaeval Scotland. Wrong! Born and bred in the townships, steeped in a brew of religion, superstition, tribal politics and crime, they knew more than I about murder and bloodshed, treachery and betrayal, witches and magic, ancestral spirits and their wandering ghosts.

On the last night of the course, we did a radical and illegal thing: I invited my students out for pizza to celebrate and they accepted, but without being able to hide their nervousness and reluctance. You see, in the South Africa of that time, white people and black people were not allowed to mix socially as equals. Black people could live in the homes of white people – usually in a converted garage or in a small shack on the property – and they could wait on white people at social events but friendships and sexual relationships were punishable offences. The offenders could get a prison sentence if they were caught by the white Afrikaner police or discovered by the government spies and informers.
Reader, I did not tell you earlier that, as well as meeting my beloved Tim on my first day at Bradford University, I also met a fellow student called Noelle who quickly became my best female friend. Noelle, who also came from London, was on the same course as Tim: Peace Studies. Interestingly, her parents were South African Jews who were forced to leave their home in South Africa and escape to the U.K. in order to avoid a prison sentence for the above-mentioned offence of mixing with blacks and speaking out against the Apartheid system. When I met Noelle in 1977, my mother was still married to my father in the U.K. and no-one knew, except God, that mum would visit South Africa in 1981, my last year at University, and decide to permanently emigrate in 1984. No-one knew that I would come out to visit her

in 1985 and start fighting against the Apartheid system just like Noelle's parents. Hmmm, you gotta admit that Spirit was up to Something.

But let's get back to the story. In the South Africa of 1989, the white maitre D' at the pizza restaurant did not want to let Alpheus and Joseph inside. He did not want to risk being reported and losing his job. Nor did he want to risk all his restaurant guests walking out in righteous indignation. Realising that all three of us were about to enter the white stronghold of the restaurant, he hurried out onto the pavement to apprehend us. There he strongly suggested to me that my black "servants" should wait outside or in my car while I ate alone. I explained that they were my students, not my servants, and that we were planning to eat together. Head drooping in shame, he led us inside. Nervously and reluctantly, he provided a table for us in a corner of the restaurant far from the other diners. All eyes of the white diners and the black waiters were upon us as I strode defiantly to our table and Alpheus and Joseph shuffled behind me, unsure about how to behave as guests in a white restaurant.

It was a first for Alpheus and Joseph not to be in a position of servitude. We were stared at throughout the meal despite the maitre D's attempt to make us inconspicuous. I could read their prejudice all over their frowning faces:

- How dare I sit at a table with black people?
- How dare I talk to them as friends and equals?
- How dare we share one very large pizza off the same plate?

The restaurant breathed a sigh of relief when we left and the archaic order was restored with only a slight blip on the screen of racial awareness.

There were other illegal gatherings with my black students. Peter Kekana secretly arranged a farewell celebration for me in July, 1989, before I left for America to study for the ministry. On the

appointed Saturday afternoon, I arrived at the meeting place in the park close to Rev. Glady's church to find my black students waiting for me. They were wearing their Sunday church choir robes and, despite their meagre income, had brought bags of food for a picnic. With Peter directing them, they broke into song. The African gift for singing in harmony is profound and has always made me homesick whenever I have heard it in later years outside South Africa. Then Peter gave a speech about how much they appreciated their only white teacher and how much my English lessons had inspired and motivated them to persist with their education. When it was my turn to speak, I struggled to articulate through my tears. I shared how terrified I was on my first morning of lessons. They laughed. They had never guessed. I also shared how it had been my vision all along to teach English to black people to assist them to be able to share power in government. This raised a cheer from the students. Peter broke in and said:
"Stephanie, we understand that you have a calling to be a minister and you have to go to America to study. But, honestly, we wish you would stay here with us and become the new President of South Africa!" The students cheered again. "Stephanie for President!" was the chant. I was overwhelmed and could no longer talk. The ceremony ended with prayers, hugs and tears and the breaking of bread. Luckily, we were not seen. Peter had deliberately chosen a place well hidden behind the trees.

The second illegal gathering was a farewell party I hosted in my home, also in July, 1989. I invited Peter Kekana and four other black teachers from the volunteer school. They did not have transport so I went to pick them up outside the church an hour before the party started. In the car, one of the teachers, Stephen, surprised me by confessing that since he had met me, he had had to accept that not every white man was his enemy. It was one of the highest compliments I had ever been paid. This elevated sense of mutual respect and connectedness, so rare in the days of Apartheid, came plummeting down to earth in the instant that the first white guest, Sheila, came through the door and handed one of my black colleagues her coat. Quickly, I explained that my black colleagues were my guests not the hired help. Sheila was embarrassed but she apologised to my black friends which was a rare and beautiful thing. Later, she admitted to me privately that she had not been expecting such a posh party with black "waiters" and had simply done what she had been conditioned to do all her life.

From a racial integration perspective, the party was not the greatest success. Only Peter Kekana was comfortable interacting with both blacks and whites. But a statement was being made and we were not arrested for it.

Despite all the inhuman laws and restrictions on black people, a free South Africa with racial equality and justice was emerging. All around the world, South African exiles, writers, artists and musicians had been singing the freedom song in harmony with Nelson Mandela and the other political prisoners on Robben Island. The soul of liberation cannot be imprisoned forever. A democratic South Africa was a vision whose time had come.

Interesting Footnotes:

On 4th July, 1989, Nelson Mandela had his first secret meeting with the President of South Africa at that time, P.W. Botha. Mandela was serving his 26th year in prison.

In August, 1989, P.W. Botha abruptly resigned and F.W. de Klerk was appointed as Acting President. He continued the secret talks with Mandela regarding his release from prison and an eventual democratic political system based on "one person one vote."

On 2nd February, 1990, President de Klerk announced the unconditional release of Nelson Mandela. This was less than a year after the, hitherto, completely obscure "Restaurant Revolution of 1989" with my students, Alpheus and Joseph, the illegal gathering in the park and the illegal party in my home.

In April, 1994, four years after Madiba's release from prison, the "unpredictable impossible" happened: Nelson Mandela became the first black president in South Africa!

South Africa now has a democratic constitution where black people and white people share power in the government and where the predominant language of government is English, in amongst the eleven official languages of the Rainbow Nation.

Chapter 7

Love Your Neighbour (but only if he is single)

Thou shalt not commit adultery.

Exodus 20:14

For the wages of sin is death; but the gift of God
is eternal life
through our Lord Jesus Christ.

Romans 6:23

Interpretation

Moses brought the Ten Commandments to the Israelites while they were in the desert on their 40-year journey to the Promised Land. The Commandments were basic lessons in love, guidelines for a community to live together in peace. If the Israelites were going to reach the Promised Land alive and in one piece, Moses had to put a stop to extra-marital affairs and the fighting it caused. Wisely, he did not try to use his personal authority to control the behaviour of his people. The Commandments came from the Highest Authority – God.

There is a Law of Love that governs the Universe. If you and I think, speak and act in integrity with this Law of Love, we live a blessed life. The capacity to speak our Word and create our reality, to stand for something until it becomes true in our experience, is a God-given gift, an essential aspect of our creator-nature. The marriage vow to "love, honour and cherish till death us do part" is a classic example of giving our Word.

If you and I treat our Word loosely, as though it does not mean anything, whether it relates to a public vow taken at the altar or any other promise we have made, we will have to experience the consequences of undermining our Self and breaking the trust of others around us. If we, deliberately or unthinkingly, hurt betray or sabotage other people, the painful effects of our thoughts, words and deeds will come back to bite us. The effects of adultery might look like guilt, shame, possible exposure and humiliation, hurt caused to family members, breaking of trust, divorce and even death.

Adultery

There are different types of adultery and we are free to commit all of them except that, as noted above, we have to take responsibility for our actions and be willing to accept the consequences.

With regard to dealing with adultery as a result of dissatisfaction in committed relationships, I learned a lot from two spiritual teachers Neale Donald Walsch, author of the *Conversations with God* series, and Marshall Rosenberg, a worldwide teacher of *Nonviolent Communication*.

Neale advised that the married person having an adulterous affair always has the opportunity to tell his or her marriage partner the truth that s/he is having sex with someone else. This gives the marriage partner the freedom to leave the relationship, start their own extra-marital affair or decide to stay in the relationship and be monogamous with full knowledge of what is going on outside the marriage.

Marshall advised that the honest and most loving way to leave a relationship is to admit to ourselves that we could not figure out a way to get our needs met with our partner. This saves us from demonizing our partner and making him or her wrong if we are not consistently happy, fulfilled, nurtured, inspired, seen, heard, respected, cherished and orgasmed multiple times.

Sin

The word "sin" has commonly come to mean "a spiritual crime that will taint your soul forever and fast-track you to Hell while you quake in your boots." From the metaphysical perspective, however, sin means

- a sense of separation from God or your Good
- missing the mark
- living inside the identity of your little human ego self
- making mistakes as a result of ignorance of the Universal Law.

No one is essentially sinful. We are all ignorant of the rebound effects of our actions until the light goes on inside and we become conscious of how we are the perpetrators of what is happening in our worlds, not the victims.

If you and I live our life feeling separate from the Source of Life, Love, Well-Being and Good within us and we try to get that good from people, places and things outside ourselves, then we are cut off from the abundant blessings of a life lived in tune with the laws of the Universe. We will suffer and feel empty in our soul. This is a form of death while still living in the body.
So "the wages of sin is death" can be translated to mean: "the consequences of ignorant human behaviour reduce aliveness and well-being."

With regard to adultery as a sin, it is given to us to choose how we use our bodies and express our sexuality. May we, henceforth, be responsible and honest and share our holy body temples as instruments of love, generating ongoing aliveness within ourselves and our sexual partners, and blessing all beings with this conscious flow of love.

Interesting Footnote:
In 1631, two London printers accidentally left the word "not" out of the seventh commandment in the King James version of the Bible. The verse then read, "Thou shalt commit adultery." This legendary book is now known as the "Wicked Bible" or the "Sinners' Bible" or the "Adulterous Bible."

My Story
Even though I had only gone to South Africa for a two-month holiday to visit my mum, righteously convinced that I would never stay in such a politically and socially corrupt country, I not only stayed, but I officially emigrated!

Initially, my low self-esteem was as deep as a diamond mine and, much as I wanted a real, available boyfriend to be all of the following:

- Lover;
- Worshipper;

- ♂ Therapist;
- ♂ Healer;
- ♂ Masseur;
- ♂ Knight;
- ♂ Champion;
- ♂ Protector;
- ♂ Sugar Daddy;
- ♂ Provider;
- ♂ Treasurer;
- ♂ Chef;
- ♂ Chauffeur;
- ♂ Cheerleader;
- ♂ Entertainer;
- ♂ Adult Parent

  and
- ♂ God

I was not averse to affairs with married men!

Neil's lively wit and winsome charm won me over. Discernment failed me in those days. We met in the bar of a restaurant in Rosebank Mall while he was having some beers with a friend and I was looking for work as a waitress. He pretended to be the manager and interviewed me. I could see I was impressing him and thought I had landed the job. When would I start work? It was only then that he admitted he had been lying to me and bought me a glass of wine to make it up to me. Aw, how can you not fall in love with a man like that?

I gave up trying to get work as a waitress or barmaid since I was pathetically incompetent at both forms of service. Instead, I started a fledgling aromatherapy-massage business from my mother's flat.

Neil and I began dating. He did not divulge to me that he was married, but it became obvious quite quickly as he was usually only available to meet on weekday afternoons, very rarely in the

evenings and never at weekends. When confronted, he confessed. I should not have been surprised as our whole relationship began with a lie and he well knew that all it took to open my heart in forgiveness was a glass of wine. Well, maybe two glasses of wine for very big lies.
Initially, I was indignant about the deliberate deception, but chose to carry on blithely with our post-meridian trysts. The forbidden fruit was made so much the sweeter by the garnish of the adrenaline rush that very nearly—with the help of abundant alcohol—digested that acidic forkful of guilt.

On one of a those sultry, yet sordid, afternoons of lunch followed by a carnal dessert, I raced back to my mum's flat for an early evening aromatherapy client. She did not show up. I checked my answering machine. She had cancelled, but so had two more clients who were due to come the next day. Suddenly I had no income. Eeek!

In a panic, I phoned my spiritual teacher, Rev. Gladys, and asked her to pray for me for a prosperous business. Rev. Gladys asked a few well-aimed questions and I ended up confessing about my married boyfriend. She bluntly confronted me with the spiritual truth that I was committing adultery and that I was stealing.
Ouch!
"If anyone here is guilty, it is Neil, not me!" I blurted out defensively. "After all, Neil is the married one and he chose to break his vows to his wife!" Wasn't I simply his willing colluderess?
Rev. Gladys refused to dabble in shifting blame or degrees of guilt. She maintained that I was the one who had called her for prayer, therefore, it was my consciousness that needed to be healed of its false beliefs, not Neil's.

Ouch, again!

Rev. Gladys went on to say that if I chose to steal from another, I would be stolen from. I assumed she meant that one day, in the distant future, I might be in a monogamous, committed relationship with a boyfriend or husband who would cheat on me. I quickly decided that I would take my chances and deal with that when it happened. In the meantime, I would continue to indulge my hormones with Neil.

Then Rev. Gladys "blessed" me with the punch line:

"The Law is working all the time and you do not have any control over when or how the consequences will show up in your life."

Finally, it clicked: I had stolen from Neil's wife and suddenly my rent money was being "stolen" from me because my clients were cancelling. AHA! There was a direct connection. We have only one life, not many separate lives.

The lesson I learned is that I cannot expect to have my good at someone else's expense. There is only One Life and I am part of That. I cannot hurt another without hurting myself as well, even though I might seem to be a separate entity from my brothers and sisters on the planet. The Spiritual Law that governs the universe is impersonal and ever-operative, and much as I want to think that I am special and above the Law, I am not.

It took me a long time to learn the lesson: you and I are free to do whatever we want in this life as long as we are willing to bear the consequences of our thoughts, words and actions. There is no freedom without responsibility.

Interesting Footnote:

Rev. Gladys prayed for me and my business prospered. I stopped seeing Neil and prayed for an available boyfriend. The answer manifested in the form of the man who lived in the flat next door—a confirmed bachelor! My sex life was guilt-free and Jesus' commandment to "Love your neighbour as yourself" (Ref.: Matthew 22:39) had erotically taken on a new depth of meaning.

Chapter 8

Know the Truth

And you will know the truth,
and that very truth will make you free.

John 8:32

Interpretation

Anything that you and I know the Truth about will set us free to live a more expanded, grace-filled life. Knowing the Truth means we have freedom and choices. Conversely, if you and I are living in ignorance or falsehood, our experience will be one of contraction and blockage. It will seem as if people, places and things have power over us and we may have the temporary experience of being a victim, either waiting for, or trying to force, change on the outer levels of our experience.

Knowing the Truth is applicable to every area of our experience. For example:

- When you were 5 years old, knowing the truth about how to tie your shoelaces, set you free from dependency on others to do the job for you.
- Once you knew the truth about numbers and mathematics, you were free to count then add, subtract, multiply and divide.
- Once you knew the truth behind letters and how they were put together to form words and sentences, you were free to read anything.

The Truth may be uncomfortable in some cases but once confronted, freedom is the result. For example:

- An individual might get a diagnosis of a life-threatening medical problem from the doctor. It is better to know than not to know because then the individual is free to make decisions regarding their future course of action.
- A person might come out of denial about an addiction s/he is trapped in. The very act of acknowledging that s/he has an addiction which s/he is powerless over, is already a huge step towards freedom.
- An individual might have a fantasy about becoming a great musician but then acknowledge the truth that they have not taken any action to turn that fantasy into a reality. This sets the individual free to devote their time

and attention elsewhere rather than wasting it on a fantasy.

- A person might be in deep debt and a lot of fear about confronting the exact amount that s/he owes along with the accruing interest. Once facts are faced, the individual is free to take corrective action or seek help with repayments.

On our journey of unfolding, as more and more Truth is revealed through our conscious seeking, we become liberated from the false concepts of our human experience, our superstitions and our inherited beliefs. We are all fundamentally spiritual beings having human experiences and creating reality through our predominant thoughts, words and actions.

Do you know the truth about yourself—both your spiritual nature and the darker, denser side of your human personality? Do you understand the Spiritual Laws of the Universe and how to work with them through prayer and affirmations? Knowing your power as a conscious divine being and knowing that your Word is Law in the universe, you are free to express and create at will and to design the life you want to lead. Knowing the Truth about "Who" we are and what we are here for—not just as a nice mental concept, but as a living reality— changes everything in our lives instantly and we begin to walk this earth as the bright gods that we really are.

My Story

It was the beginning of February, 1986, and my two-month holiday in South Africa was drawing to a close. In fact, I was already booked to fly back to Europe in mid-February. However, I felt strongly that I should take the one-year Science of Mind I course being offered by Rev. Gladys at the Abundant Living Centre in Johannesburg. It was starting in the first week of February and would end in November 1986.

In a wild act of faith, and as my declaration to the Universe that I intended to stay in South Africa, at least for that year, I ripped up the return portion of my roundtrip ticket back to the U.K. and registered for the course! At the time, I did not know how I would get a visa to stay in South Africa, or how I would support myself, let alone pay the course fees. (The Irish writer, Flannery O'Connor, said: "You shall know the truth and the truth shall make you odd.")

Serendipitously, on the very first night of class, I met a fellow student, Anuschka, who gave me a job in her company. This helped me get my temporary work permit as well as provide a small income. Anuschka and I remain close friends and spiritual journeywomen to this day.

The other significant person I met on the course was Greg. He always showed up at class in his business suit, having raced over from his office or from his latest wheeling-dealing escapade with a client-victim. The business suit fooled me. I thought he was a professional man, grown-up and prosperous. Jesus told us not to judge by appearances. He knew it would get us into trouble. *(Judge not according to the appearance, but judge righteous judgment. Ref.: John 7:24.)*

Greg and I started dating on 1st October, just before the final end-of-course exams in November. There was an instant familiarity, as if we had known each other in a past life. (Reader, I have since learned that that familiar feeling I had at the beginning of a new romance was because my partner embodied the painful conditioning that was passed on to me by my human family of origin. He felt so familiar because I recognised this place of suffering. It was just like home! But oh, how easy it is to be fooled in the beginning when the fantasy is alive and well. Have you ever heard yourself hope: "Surely this one is the 'The One' and I will never be hurt again"? Oh dear....)

Our early romantic dates generally adhered to an original and exciting format:

1. Going to a restaurant for dinner,
2. Imbibing copious amounts of fine South African wine, and
3. Going dancing—i.e., back to Greg's place to do the horizontal mambo before crashing.

The morning after a typical date also had its own predictable routine:

1. Getting into Greg's car so that Greg could take me home before driving to his office
2. Getting out of Greg's car because it would not start
3. Resentfully pushing Greg in his big silver Volvo down the hill until the engine started.

Greg always used to park his car on the street outside his house under a Jacaranda tree. During the night, a shower of purple blossoms would fall on the car and in the morning, the car would look as if it had been romantically adorned with confetti. Unromantically, however, Greg never had money for car repairs (or rent or debt repayments). That should have been my clue, right there. Love may indeed be blind. But romantic fantasy is both blind and total-lobotomously stupid.

One night, two weeks into our Grand Romance, Greg and I went on an evening date in the typical way only there was something critical missing from the predictable formula. We started drinking and simply forgot

1. Dinner!

Ooops! After abundant liquid refreshments and no solid food to line our stomachs, we were both the worse for wear by closing time. Greg was well over the limit, but his drunken cockiness was convincing him that he was Nikki Lauda's mentor. We stumbled out to the car, Greg perfectly willing to drive us home despite his stupor. Fortunately, the God that protects drunks and babies intervened; the Volvo would not start. For once, I was grateful that Greg's car was so dysfunctional.

Greg called an emergency tow truck and then we waited inside the parked car for nearly an hour. To pass the time meaningfully, Greg told me drunkenly, over and over again, how much he loved me. Then, with great difficulty—as in the case of someone suffering from a stroke, who is also constipated—he slurred out a proposal of marriage. I, who had been rendered legless, swept off my feet by rose-coloured alcohol, accepted without a second thought. My befuddled brain was incapable of stringing two thoughts together—especially not two thoughts in a row, one after the other and in sequence.

Our passionate, grape-sodden, pre-nuptial kiss was rudely interrupted when we suddenly saw, in the dark gloom of the empty parking lot, a bright light beam in the distance. A true knight in shining armour - alias our tow truck driver in his gleaming yellow tow truck - moved on to the scene. He rescued us before we could slobberingly seal our pre-nuptial agreement in the backseat of the Volvo. This was a clear case of "coitus interruptus" but, unusually, by a third party! Thankfully, he got us home safely.

The next morning, hung-over but riding high on romantic fantasy, I was afraid that Greg might have been too drunk to remember his proposal. As I felt him stir and then fart (two essential signs of life), I cautiously asked him:
"Greg, do you remember what you asked me last night?"
"Yes," he answered. "I asked you to marry me."
I think I was relieved.
Then in the next breath, he mumbled,
"Doll, won't you make me some steak and eggs for breakfast?"
Look, he did not make that request in italics but that is how I heard it.

WHAT!? How dare he? Outraged and incensed, I was well aware that this was not a polite request. This was a patriarchal, husband-like, assumption that I was going to cook him breakfast!

Three key questions disturbed my hungover brain cells:

1. How had I suddenly become Greg's chattel, his domestic servant and his breakfast chef?
2. Where was the romance now that he had proposed?
3. Where were my feminist ideals?

For all my exam-taking skills, I could not answer question 1 and 2 but the answer to question 3 was easy:

Down the toilet.

Getting married and having a man commit to me was much more important than my principles. In those days of magnificent theory, unsolicited preaching and zero practise, I wasn't willing to do the work of loving and committing to myself.

As soon as we could, my betrothed and I got an appointment with Rev. Gladys and announced that we wanted to get married. "OK...." said Rev. Gladys, forcing a smile while mastering a desire to puke.

At the time, she was not authorized to legally marry us, however, she informed us that Dr. June Jones, a Divine Science minister and licensed Marriage Officer, would be coming to Johannesburg from Port Elizabeth on 29th November to marry another couple and she might be able to do a second wedding for us on the same day. Greg and I were eager to take advantage of this opportunity. Reader, here is a timeline:

1st October, 1986 - our first date

16th October, 1986 - the drunken proposal in the Volvo

29th November, 1986 - the wedding date.

Some possible obstacles:

1. Greg could not afford a ring (or car repairs or rent);
2. We had no money between us for a deposit on a flat;

3. It was going to be Greg's 4th marriage at the age of 32 and because of this, our respective parents were not willing to fund a major society wedding or even a simple registry office affair;
4. We both had unfinished business with previous partners which we weren't planning to heal, or even address, before our magical wedding day;
5. Adultery was a recent experience we both had in common;
6. We were both about to fail our Science of Mind I exams because we had not been disciplined or mature enough to do our homework;
7. Our addiction to the romantic fantasy and our regular fuelling of that addiction with alcohol and copious copulation meant that we were blissfully unaware of any of the above-mentioned obstacles.

Rev. Gladys did not think we would be quite ready.

Diplomatically, Rev. Gladys strongly recommended that we not rush into such a deep commitment but, if we were insistent upon tying the official knot of wedlock on November 29th, then we should have at least three counselling sessions with her before then.
Rev. Gladys confessed that she had no power to judge the agreement that two souls make before they enter this incarnation and, therefore, she did not know what we were striving to learn, individually or together, through a marriage. However, based on her knowledge of us over the previous nine months in the Science of Mind class, she could tell we had a lot of growing up to do, and she was not willing to co-sign something that she did not, in her heart, believe was a true marriage.
That was integrity for you. It should have earned our respect for Rev. Gladys and maybe some deep consideration of our hasty plans to wed. However, Greg and I were offended and thought she must be jealous of our happiness because she was not the

best looker and had a couple of very unhappy marriages behind her.

Rev. Gladys then closed the session by praying for guidance and clarity for us regarding our plans to wed. Despite her concerns, we believed God was magic and, before we said Goodbye, we made an appointment for our first proper counselling session.

Stubbornly clinging to our romantic fantasy, we left Rev. Gladys' office. We were a little despondent but comforted by the old adage that "the path of true love never runs smooth." Unbeknown to us, Rev. Gladys' prayers started working right away. We had an almighty fight in the car and stopped speaking to each other, just like all "mature" couples. Conflict resolution skills were not in our toolkits.

Reader, if you have ever had any experience with Spiritual Mind Treatment, which is the name for the Science of Mind technique of affirmative prayer, you might also have noticed that everything unlike the thing you prayed for comes up first to be addressed and cleared away. In our case, anything unlike love—fear, projection, pain, judgement, etc.—was leaking through on to the stage of our drama. As was to be expected, we didn't want to see it.

A few hours later, when speech tentatively resumed, we decided to call the whole thing off. At least we had come to an agreement about something. Then we kissed and made up and as the fuzzy, warm, kiss-chemicals kicked in, we changed our minds. The wedding was on again! We decided to go ahead with the counselling (only in the hopes of changing the other to match our fantasies but we did not admit that to each other, of course).

The Happy-Ever-After notion did not release us from its straitjacket. Doggedly we drank, argued and then used sex to make up for our fights. These were particularly fierce after each of our three counselling sessions but they also occurred in between sessions as well. Meanwhile, the Universe made it abundantly clear that ours was a marriage made in hell and carefully sabotaged our plans to tie the official knot of entanglement on 29th November.

The sabotage took the following forms:

- No wedding minister
- No wedding ring (or engagement ring)
- No venue
- No catering
- No wedding dress for the bride
- No 3-piece suit for the groom
- No formal invitations
- No wedding guests
- No place to live
- No family support
- No maturity
- No commitment
- No clue

Even though our resistance to Truth was mighty, we stopped pushing for the 29th November date and agreed to postpone our wedding plans until the following year. I then began the process of applying for permanent immigration into South Africa with the intention of eventually marrying Greg and settling down, not guessing that I would be making our bed in hell. *(If I ascend up into heaven, thou art there: if I make my bed in hell, behold, thou art there. Ref.: Psalms 139:8.)*

To start off with, we would move in to our own little place together and, since by this time we had both failed our end-of-course Science of Mind 1 exams with distinction, we would romantically repeat the year-long course together starting in January, 1987. Yes, we would be the ultimate happy couple, spiritually enlightened and contented, an example to all. What is more, we would be the envy of all those who were still searching for their divine soul-mate but who had not yet been blessed with our good fortune.

In December, 1986, I flew back to the U.K. to pack up my things and ship them over to South Africa. Greg was supposed to come with me, but none of his shady business deals had come through and he had such a bad credit history that he could not get a loan to pay for the flight. He surrendered and "let" me go alone. Much later he admitted that he was terrified that once I was away from him, I would meet someone far more worthy and never come back. As you will see, Reader, his fears were realised, but not in the way that either of us imagined.

Soon after I landed in London, I visited my friend Louise. Had I heard of a book called *Women Who Love Too Much,* by Robin Norwood? I hadn't. She wanted it for Christmas. Next, I saw my sister, Debbie, who asked the same question. Yes, I told her, Louise had mentioned it. Debbie wanted it for Christmas too. I could take a hint. I bought the book for Louise and for my sister, and I snuck a look at it on the train. Oh my God! It was written for me! I then bought a copy for myself for Christmas and could not put it down. Thank you, Robin Norwood, for telling me the truth that set me free.

Reader, if you have not come across this book, it is for and about women from dysfunctional families who attach themselves to loser guys, usually violent, addictive, impoverished young boys in adult male bodies. The women who "love too much" try to love these men better at the expense of their own life, always hoping that the man will eventually change, grow up, wake up, and return all the love and commitment that their "loving" devoted female partners have showered upon them.

Ooops! I fit the profile perfectly. So did my mother. So did just about every woman I knew.

While Robin Norwood was carefully dismantling my romantic fantasies, I was busy gathering together my things that had been left at my dad's house in the U.K. and trying to decide what I would ship to South Africa. One night I came across a raffia box that I recognized from my childhood. It had been used for storing my plastic beads and other childish knickknacks. I opened the box and began sorting through its contents. Suddenly a whacking great silver ankh (the Ancient Egyptian Key of Life) appeared in the middle of the plastic toys! What a find! Or was it a gift from the Other Side? It stimulated some penetrating questions:

- ♀ How did it get there?
- ♀ Who gave it to me?
- ♀ What was it doing in my box of childhood trinkets and toys?

All of these questions remain unanswered to this very day.

The ankh had become a very important symbol for me since the time I read the book *Initiation* by Elisabeth Haich, two years earlier, at age 26. The meaning of the Ankh was explained in this book: it is a symbol of Divine Power and Eternal Life, associated with the Pharaohs of Ancient Egypt. I felt an instant resonance and decided I had to get one and I had managed to procure a series of three small silver ankh necklaces before this "Mamma of All Ankhs" showed up in my raffia box. What I had begun to observe is that whenever I was off my spiritual path, I would lose my current ankh. As soon as I was back on the path, another ankh would show up in my world.

This big ankh on its silver chain was about four inches long and rested perfectly on my heart chakra. It was a symbol that I was definitely on the right spiritual path—the path of recovery from co-dependency and various other addictions—although it was going to take me another three years before I had the courage to join a support group for the adult children of alcoholics and start to examine my faulty wiring.

Sad Footnote:

I wore the ankh every day for the next 17 years until it fell off while I was sleeping on a plane to Amsterdam, en route to speak at a Science of Mind conference in Mexico City. I was devastated; it was my most precious possession.

Having discovered the truth about my relationship problems, and now sporting the sacred symbol of an Ancient Egyptian Priestess on my heart, I could not go back to Greg with my former unconscious relationship fantasy intact. I did want to go back to South Africa though, and continue with my spiritual studies, so I decided to give it one last try with Greg. I even moved in with him as we had planned. While I was in the U.K., he had carefully sought out a lovely little place for us to begin our co-habitation: a room in his parents' house! The relationship was never the same though. I had changed too much while I was away in the U.K. The co-dependent insanity lasted a few more months before Greg's behaviour became violent and destructive. In a drunken rage, he hit me and I left him. Yes, I was bruised, but more importantly, I knew the truth and I was free.

Interesting Footnote:

A few months before I went overseas, I had started going to a Yoga class twice per week. The class was taught by a beautiful woman called Jackie and it was held in the Scout Hut between Selby Street and Bolton Road in Parkwood. It was about 30 minutes walk from Illovo where I both lived and worked. Twice a week, on Tuesday and Thursday afternoon, I would speed walk from Illovo over to the Scout Hut for the 5 p.m. yoga class. On one such occasion, I was running and puffing down Selby Street and I thought to myself:

"If I lived on this street, it would be so much easier to get to Yoga."

Well, while I was overseas in the U.K., Greg's parents bought a house on this very street! Not only that but it was right next door to the Scout Hut! And this was the very house I moved into with Greg in January 1987 when I returned from the UK. So all I had to

do was hop over the low dividing wall and I was ready to stretch and pose.
P.S. I still arrived late.

Chapter 9

California Dreamin'

7. And the Lord said to me, Do not say, I am a child; for you shall go to all that I shall send you, and whatever I command you, you shall speak.
8. Be not afraid of their presence; for I am with you to deliver you, says the Lord.

Jeremiah 1:7-8

Interpretation
The ancient teachers and prophets used the image of a rewarding or punishing parental figure to try to convey the idea of the invisible working of the Universal Law of Cause and Effect. These advanced beings had to explain this abstract concept of the invisible Law in a simplistic way to the uneducated masses so they came up with an image that the majority could relate to: each human being was the child of a loving, raging father.
The ancients had no problem believing in the concept of a punishing and rewarding God. When things went wrong in their worlds, such as failing crops, childlessness or sick cattle, they believed that the Lord God was punishing them for their sins. Conversely, when things went well in their human worlds, it was, they believed, the direct result of finding favour with God. In their minds, God was a larger-than-life-but-invisible human autocrat and definitely located outside themselves.

More than 2000 years later, that image of a personal, parental, father figure – the old man with the long grey beard who regularly rages but is still believed to be essentially benign and loving – dominates in our collective awareness of God. It will continue to dominate until it is questioned by a critical mass of courageous individuals, examined and cast out. Then a new image can take its place in mainstream thought.

Whenever you see the word "Lord" in a Bible text, try translating it to the word "Law" instead. Another way to translate it is "Lord of my own being" which means "my Divine Self." It is the Inner Power that guides and protects each of us – if we allow It. This Inner Voice prompts us, puts holy ideas in our heads, truthful words in our mouths, and compels us to express them so that all around us might be healed of the false sense of self (little human ego). Maybe you have felt that inner pressure and the accompanying human resistance, the fear of the fall-out if you actually told the truth and became vulnerably exposed in your authenticity? Maybe you have experienced the torment of trying to suppress the inner promptings and the negative consequences of actively going against the Voice of your intuition? (Intuition means "Inner Teacher.")

Take heart! When you and I are covered in prayer, when our attention is on the Spirit, no one can touch us. Outer authorities or even imagined enemies have no power to hurt us. They are simply not vibrating at our frequency. It seems as if we are invisible to them and we move freely to where we need to be, to say and do whatever is required so that we can be of maximum service to God and our fellow human beings.

My Story

One night in 1987, during a church board meeting, Rev. Gladys asked the board members where we saw the church and ourselves in five years time. That simple question changed the whole course of my life. It gave birth to a vision within me. What I saw was a multi-racial ministry in South Africa where black people and white people could worship together under the same roof. I even saw myself as the minister. At that time Apartheid had a stranglehold in South Africa and there was no obvious indication that the Old Guard of white Afrikaners in the government would ever relinquish their power. A multi-racial ministry was a dangerous and impossible dream in those days. So, I simply pulled the duvet over my vision's head and left it at home to sleep.

A year later, in 1988, my aromatherapy and reflexology business seemed to be failing and I could not make ends meet. Clearly, I had to get a j.o.b. I started writing out some serious affirmations about "perfect work," "perfect position" and "abundant prosperity." Within a mere 20 minutes of writing out these affirmations, I got a call from an employment agency and was offered the position of receptionist/secretary at a small business that had just opened in Rosebank. The business owners liked me so much that they decided to take me on permanently. They paid me a massive salary, much more than my mother was earning as a top executive secretary, and gave me regular increases in accordance with my affirmations for prosperity.

Much as I enjoyed working at this small company with the big salary, I was not fulfilled; being a secretary was simply a means to an end. My real life was lived after dark. Not in any bars or nightclubs, as you might think. (Were you really thinking that?) Nor was I a lady of the night....
Oh, just a minute, I have to segue here for a "bit on the side" of my main narrative.
There was a slight temptation to pursue that line of night-work when I was serving hamburgers at McDonalds in Amsterdam on Nieuwezijdsvoorburgwaal. McDonalds was next door to a strip club and I figured that the strippers were earning a lot more than I was for the similar job of catering to men's appetites. However, I had to face facts: with my aggressive feminist image of very short hair, no make-up, no bra and bovver boots, I was fairly sure I would not make it past the interview so I did not apply.

Surprising as it may sound, my real life was lived at church! Yes, I cringe when I write that. It seems so, well, holy.... even, dare I say it, Christian!
Most nights of the week, Rev. Gladys held an event, a class, a meeting or a volunteer project of some sort. With my old stereotyped ideas of church-going folk, based on my experience of our neighbours when I was a child, I never believed that church could be fun but it was. There was so much joy in fellowshipping with one another, learning more about the Truth of our divinity, calling each other out when we heard negative statements with a comic condescending, "Would you like to rephrase that?" and telling stories of the miracles we had witnessed every day by changing our mental beliefs. Our time together was pervaded by laughter. I wanted more of this. Plus it was clear to me that I was

not meant to be a secretary all my life but I did not know what else to do to earn a living.
I was frustrated.
And I was constipated.
Since the physical state is often the mirror of an inner mental/emotional state, I knew that this energy blockage in my body was the outward sign of an inner contraction; life energy was not flowing through me. In other words, I was not expressing my real purpose on earth.

Desperate for change, I asked Colleen, one of my Science of Mind classmates at church, to pray for me to know my purpose.
"Yes, with pleasure," said Colleen and she got busy knowing the Truth for and about me and my Divine Purpose during her regular morning prayer practise.
Within a few days, the following answer to my prayer request kept repeating itself to me:
"Go to California and do the ministerial training."
With joyful relief, I noted that the message was simply:
"Do the ministerial training."
And not:
"Become a minister,"
which would have been terrible and triggered me into deep resistance.

With my accustomed short-sightedness, I assumed I was merely meant to go through the spiritual learning process. Eternal student that I am, I embraced the message wholeheartedly out of a deep need to fix myself and an equally deep belief that this training would be "The One" that would knock my poor self-esteem on its head or cleanly gouge it out of me forever (just like all the other trainings were also "The One"—until they were not. Sob.)
Continuing on a faulty track of ignorant assumptions, I foresaw that as soon as I completed my training, Spirit would reveal the fabulous, cushy, special job that would be waiting for me, a job

that would not be nearly as scary, grown-up or responsible as becoming an actual minister in a country where it was illegal for black people and white people to mix together socially. No, I was obviously just meant to do the training for my own edification and personal growth.

This was not the first time that Spirit had dropped hints about me becoming a minister. The first quiet "call" to ministry had actually whispered itself to me two years previously but I had ignored it. It came in 1986, during my initial two-month "holiday" in South Africa. My mother had invited me to come to one of her toastmistresses' events at the Wanderers Club in Illovo. I "happened" to sit next to a Dutch lady from Amsterdam called Nellie, who was a spiritual teacher. Yoga was her main passion, but she had a wide esoteric knowledge on all aspects of divination including astrology, numerology and healing. We had an instant rapport, speaking Dutch and English interchangeably, and she spontaneously invited me to visit her at her home in Margate on the South Coast. I could not drive at the time and did not know how I would get to the South Coast but I was eager to go. Magically, a ride manifested through another toastmistress friend of my mother's, Anna the exorcist, who was planning to drive down to the coast on holiday and could drop me off at Nellie's in Margate. Perfect.
So, two weeks later and after the long eight-hour car journey from Johannesburg, I showed up at Nellie's front door.

Nellie had a library that would make any aspirant drool. I read and drooled deliriously. One particular treasure chest of esoteric wisdom that leapt off the shelf at me was a book by Dr. Catherine Ponder, a famous American Unity minister and author. In the introduction, she wrote a short paragraph about how she was sitting in her study one Saturday night working on her sermon for church the next day. As I read those lines, I thought to myself:
"I want that life."

I could imagine myself being in that study writing those sermons. Quickly, I dismissed it. Instead of reflecting on that idea or, God forbid, praying about it, I chose to sit at Nellie's feet on the beach by the Indian Ocean, where she instructed me in the esoteric mystery teachings while I, with eyes closed, feigning meditation, secretly worked on my suntan.

Interesting Footnote:
I actually met Dr. Catherine Ponder 10 years later at a Science of Mind conference in Anaheim, California, where she was the keynote speaker. She was already elderly and frail looking but immaculately turned out and when she spoke, you listened. When I got to the front of the book-signing queue, I was able to tell her that her book had inspired me to train as a minister and brought me from South Africa to the U.S.A. She was delighted, of course. And, clearly, it was not the first time that she had heard such a testimonial about her life-changing work.

Early one Margate morning, while still with Nellie and jogging on the soft white sand (no pun intended but can you imagine that black people weren't allowed to go to the "white" beaches during the days of Apartheid?), enjoying the sights of the palm trees waving in the breeze under a blue cloudless sky, the sparkling azure of the Indian Ocean and the intense African sunlight, I suddenly knew I had landed in paradise on earth. I felt completely alive and free. My heart cracked open. Despite its abhorrent politics, I was falling in love with the land, the beauty, the people and the pulse of South Africa.

Before I leave the subject of Nellie, I have to tell you a couple of side stories about how she helped me on my journey.
Right before I left Holland to come to South Africa in December, 1985, I happened to be reading a book by the actress, Shirley MacLaine, called *Out on a Limb*. In the book, Shirley describes a part of her spiritual journey of awakening in which she goes to Lima in Peru to connect with aliens. At that time, the aliens made

themselves visible to spiritually developed visitors but the scientists, who came with all their sophisticated equipment, did not enjoy a single sighting. There and then, I set the intention to see an alien. I assumed I would have to go to Peru but the intention manifested far more conveniently through Nellie who told me soon after I arrived in Margate:
"I want to introduce you to my friend, Nine Merrington. She is a wonderful healer. She comes from the planet, Saturn. And so does her husband Charles."

Well, I was not sure what to expect but Nine looked amazingly normal except for her eyes. They were large and blue and penetrating. Like laser beams. I loved Nine from the beginning. She is a medium and a healer with a huge heart and endless patience for the limitations of humanity. When she speaks to me, I still do not understand her, but to be in her energy field and to feel her brilliant blue eyes boring through the density of my conditioned mind, is enough.

Nine had become well-known in the local area when she wrote her first book: *On the Death of my Son*. It was the story of a young man called Mike who had died suddenly in a car accident. Mike's spirit was able to communicate across the Veil to Nine and then through Nine to his father who was still on earth. Thus, Mike was able to give his father the reassurance that he was still alive but in another dimension. Nine's next book on the same theme is called: *I Died Young: Mike Speaks from the Afterlife.*
As a catalyst for transformation and a pure channel for communication from the spirit world, Nine has helped and healed thousands of people from all walks of life and in many different countries. I feel very privileged to have met her and to have been the recipient of her love and wisdom in this lifetime.
Nellie also gave me a lot of support to get my aromatherapy and psychic healing business off the ground. She knew a lot of people in the alternative circles of Johannesburg and she gave me the phone number of Arthur Chambers, a holistic massage therapist

who had rooms in the Illovo Centre, a mere three minutes walk from the flat where I was staying with my mum.
When I met Arthur, we had an immediate rapport. He was an elderly, thin, wizened, Merlin type of being from Yorkshire where I had attended University. Trusting Nellie's recommendation, he let me use his second massage room in which he kept his stock of Aromatherapy oils.

One day, soon after I started seeing clients at Arthur's rooms, he asked me if I knew how to use a pendulum. I did. My astrology teacher in Amsterdam had taught me. So he said:
"Just go to the cupboard and swing your pendulum over the oils so that we can see which oils want to work with you."
I did as instructed and a number of oils leapt out at me right away - energetically speaking, of course. Arthur then gifted me those oils as well as an endless supply of Sweet Almond Oil to use as a base. He never asked for money for the oils or the room rental. I think he was an angel.

And now back to the story.
The second inner nudge towards ministry came a few months after the first nudge at Nellie's. It was soon after I had started studying Science of Mind with Rev. Gladys. During our class one night, Rev. Gladys shared some of the experiences she had had at the United Church of Religious Science Ministerial School in San Jose, California. As I listened, I felt a quickening in my heart as though a cage door had been opened and a trapped bird had taken flight. Inspired and excited, I stayed behind after class and asked how I could apply. Rev. Gladys gave me all the information. However, instead of filling out the application form and pursuing the dream, I got drunk one night with my new boyfriend, Greg. (See previous chapter.) He had proposed. I had accepted. So, naturally, "Ministerial School Application" did not get ticked off on my "To Do" list that week and not for the next two years either.

This time, however, after Colleen prayed for me and I had heard the clear message about doing the ministerial training, I saw the opening and I stepped into it even though my "Yes" went hand in hand with some human trepidation; no-one likes to leave their comfort zone, even if it is a fleas' nest of discomfort, and no-one likes to step away from the herd and be vulnerably alone. Somehow, I knew it was a "now or never" decision, but nevertheless I faltered. While there was still time, I looked for the loophole in my destiny: how could I do the ministerial training in America, yet stay in my comfort zone in South Africa? It was a stupid question. There was no answer. Not even a stupid one.

The decision was made for me irrevocably while I was house-sitting for a friend over Christmas and New Year, 1988. In the middle of the night on December 30, I got up to go to the loo but, unfortunately, forgot about the two steps down into the guest toilet. In the darkness, while I fumbled around for the light switch, I stepped confidently into thin air, fell crashing against the toilet bowl, cracked my ribs and was then incapacitated and in great pain for the next few days.

Stuck in bed, alone on New Year's Eve, I wondered what I could do to amuse myself while staying still and out of pain. (It still takes a lot for me to get still, but Spirit had to use *really* drastic measures in those days!)
Hah, I had it!
I would write my New Year's Resolutions, just for entertainment, not because I had any intention of keeping them. After all, why would anyone want to submit to the disciplines of:

1. Losing weight?
2. Cutting down on one's alcohol consumption?
3. Keeping one's knickers on?

Much to my surprise, as I put pen to paper, clarity broke through like a thunderbolt: I only had one important goal and that was to start the ministerial training at Santa Anita in Los Angeles, California, in September, 1989.

How did I know about the Santa Anita Ministerial School? It had crossed my path quite recently through a friend at Rev. Gladys' church, actually Dr. June Jones' daughter, Diane. It was an independent metaphysical school with a three-year ministerial programme. In order to apply, all I needed was two years of experience in any metaphysical teaching. I qualified! The entry requirements were a lot less stringent than for a United Church of Religious Science Ministerial School, and so it meant I could begin my ministerial training almost immediately instead of waiting another two years or more until I was a fully licensed Religious Science practitioner under Rev. Gladys. Typical spirited horse that I was, bolting at the starting gate, eager for spiritual food and no discipline, I strained to rush out on to this new race track/spiral of evolution.

Interesting Footnote:
Talking of bolting horses, Santa Anita is far more famous for its horse race track than it is for its Ministerial School. One Sunday morning in 1990, a few months into my ministerial training, I was on my way to the Santa Anita church with some wayward minister friends who were visiting from out of town. They wanted to go to the racetrack instead, so we skipped church and joined the throngs of gamblers at the track. Guided by my intuition, and with help from my pendulum, I bet on the horse that won the next race and earned myself a few dollars. And the horse's name....? "Heaven Scent."

After I had written the goal down to move to California and enrol at the Santa Anita Ministerial School, and also made the commitment in my heart, I learned that Dr. Margaret Stevens, the Senior Minister of the Santa Anita Church, would soon be coming to Johannesburg with a posse of other New Thought Ministers to speak at the three-day INTA (International New Thought Alliance) conference. How is that for synchronicity? I wrote to tell her of my intention and to ask if we could meet. She replied affirmatively.

It was a huge South African thrill to be at the INTA conference in the very plush Sandton Sun hotel and to be taught and inspired by the American leaders of the New Thought movement. But, so scared was I of speaking to Dr. Margaret and following my destiny into the Unknown, that I avoided her throughout the conference until the very last day. When I finally approached her at the eleventh hour, she admitted to being both surprised and concerned that I had not introduced myself to her earlier. Nevertheless, she hastily arranged a time and place to interview me the next day just a few short hours before she was due to leave Johannesburg and fly back to the U.S.A.

There we were sitting opposite each other in her friend's flat in Illovo. It was the moment I had been waiting for exactly as much as I had been dreading it. Dr. Margaret was dignified and beautiful. She sat serenely, like a noble queen on the light green velour sofa, radiating kindness and gentleness, while I squirmed and tried to disappear into the back of my armchair.
"And so why do you want to be a minister, Stephanie?" she queried. The dam broke. I simply blubbered incoherently for the next 20 minutes. Miraculously, through the snotty, inarticulate mass that I was, her spirit understood my hopes, my fears, my pain, my doubts, my longing, my passion, my vision, my heart and my sad lack of Kleenex. My stellar interview techniques notwithstanding, Dr. Margaret ended our meeting by awarding me a place at her school at Santa Anita in Los Angeles, California, starting in September, 1989.

Most people were supportive when they heard about my plans to study in America. Here are some of their responses:

1. **Jackie, my yoga teacher**

Jackie was delighted to hear that I would be following my dream and going to the U.S.A. to study for the ministry. She told me that, "coincidentally," another one of her students had recently left for America to train to be a United Church of Religious Science minister. His name was Edward Viljoen. Did I know him? No, I didn't.

Interesting Footnote:
Many roadblocks were encountered by South African students who tried unsuccessfully to get American residence permits so that they could study for the ministry. The most they could manage were short part-time courses. Three months max. So it was amazing that in 1989, two South African students ventured forth to California to become metaphysical ministers: Edward Viljoen and I. Just imagine that the two of us could have been doing our asanas on neighbouring yoga mats and had no clue about our shared path!

I contacted Edward when I got to LA and we spoke on the phone. And then "coincidentally" a mutual friend of ours, Karin, came out from Johannesburg to visit Edward. She was the link that brought Edward and me together for the first time. Our paths have crossed many times since. Rev. Edward chose to stay in America when he finished his training and he has gone on to become one of the leading lights in the Religious Science movement as well as directing the thriving Santa Rosa Center for Spiritual Living in Northern California.

2. Rev. Johanna Meiring, a local minister

Rev. Johanna Meiring was a lovely Afrikaans lady and a Religious Science International Minister. I met Rev. Johanna briefly when I first lived in Johannesburg in 1986 but we did not have much contact because her church was largely Afrikaans-speaking. When I was about to leave South Africa, I made an appointment to speak to her and told her about my mission to go the U.S.A. to train as a minister so that I could eventually return to South Africa and start a multi-racial church. She was delighted. I did not even ask her for money but she reached into her handbag right away and wrote me a cheque for R100 to support me on my mission. This was such a generous gesture to one who was not even a member of her congregation.

3. My boss

My boss and his wife, who co-owned the company in Rosebank, were very sorry to see me go but they appreciated that I was following my passion. My boss gave me regular raises after I announced my news in order to support me financially in my mission. Really, what boss does that?!

4. Avril, my landlady

In November, 1988, I moved into the house of my friend from my first Science of Mind class, Avril. At that time, neither of us knew that we would both be in Los Angeles the following year but shortly after my move, Avril decided to leave for America in April, 1989. Avril is a classical guitarist and was planning an international guitar concert tour which would end in Los Angeles where she intended to spend time with her American boyfriend. By January 1989, it was clear that I would be leaving for America the following August. Avril was delighted that I was following my dream and that we would be in the same U.S. city at the same time.

Interesting Footnote:

After I moved to America and started renting my own cottage in Los Angeles in January, 1990, Avril parted ways with her American boyfriend and came to live with me before returning home to South Africa. It has been a strange reciprocal landlady-tenant relationship with Avril, always underlying a special friendship throughout the years.

Many people did not approve of, or understand, my choice to become a woman of the cloth. Here are some of the more negative responses:

1. **Disapproval from Mum**

When I told my mum, she was concerned for my happiness and well-being.
"Does this mean you will have to be poor and celibate, darling?" she inquired tentatively.
Mum did not want me to be an impoverished, dried up spinster. She would have preferred me to be wealthy and happily married. This was her dream for *her* life.

Interesting Footnote:
Before I left for America in August 1989, I visited my mum, and asked her to write down her vision of her perfect husband. Previously, I had given her the little book "Your Word is your Wand" by the metaphysician, Florence Scovell Shinn, and she had had great success working with affirmations. Mum duly made a list of qualities and attributes she desired in a life-partner. Five months later she met the man of her dreams, her South African Prince Charming, who also happened to be an extremely wealthy property developer. One year after their first date they were married and recently celebrated their Silver Wedding Anniversary after 25 gloriously happy years together.

2. **Horror from a client**

When I told a client my news, while he was waiting in reception to see my boss, he looked me up and down, slowly and lasciviously, and then said:
"Well, that's a waste of a damned good body!"
He, like a lot of men, wanted to have sex with me urgently before I became a woman of the cloth and off-limits.

3. Downright scorn from Rev. Gladys

When I broke the news to Rev. Gladys, I thought she would be thrilled but instead she was angry. She did not approve of Dr. Margaret Stevens' training school, which was an independent metaphysical ministerial school. Angrily, Rev. Gladys declared that I was selling myself short and that I should wait another two years until I had finished with my practitioner studies in South Africa. She advised that once I had my Religious Science Practitioner qualification, I would be eligible to study for the ministry at a *quality* ministerial school in America i.e. a Religious Science school. Rev. Gladys' ambition for me was to qualify as a Religious Science minister so that I could eventually take over her Religious Science church in South Africa.

After I got that adverse reaction, I cleverly intuited that my idea to ask Rev. Gladys for help in raising funds through the Johannesburg church to support me on my quest would probably not fly.... I held my tongue even though I was desperate and did not know of any other likely avenues for funding. Sadly, Rev. Gladys and I parted from each other in a very strained way.

Crying, I slunk off home. Rev. Gladys was my first formal spiritual teacher. She had changed my life. I looked up to her, admired her. Her ability to convey Truth had set me free. I trusted her judgement. Her disapproving reaction had really thrown me. Was she right? Was I about to make the biggest mistake of my life with this premature ejaculation into the Santa Anita Ministerial School?

A song started playing on the car radio just as I pulled up outside my flat and was about to switch off the engine. Transfixed, I sat and listened. It was the Mamas and the Papas singing *California Dreamin'*. This is what I heard:

> *I'd be safe and warm if I was in L.A*

California Dreamin' on such a winter's day.
Stopped into a church I passed along the way
Well, I got down on my knees and I began to pray.
You know the preacher likes the cold, he knows I'm gonna stay
California Dreamin' on such a winter's day....

Was that a message from God, or what?!

In August 1989, I packed up and left South Africa bound for Los Angeles, California, and began my studies at the Santa Anita Ministerial School in September, 1989.

Sadly, I never saw Rev. Gladys again.

Part 6

AMERICA
1989-1999

Chapter 10

The Battle is not Yours

By faith the walls of Jericho fell down
after they had been encompassed seven days.

Hebrews 11:30

Interpretation
Jericho was the first city that was taken and destroyed by the Israelites after they entered the Promised Land.

The "walls" in this Bible verse have a number of interpretations. For example:
1. The ego defences that keep Love out and stop us from releasing Love from within.
2. The people places or things that seem to be blocking our good.
3. A lack or restriction of any kind in the area of relationships, health, work or material supply.

Seven is the number of completion. So a metaphysical interpretation of the verse would be something like:
"If an ego defence/an unhealed part of ourselves is lovingly encompassed in prayer for seven days until the inner work is complete, the seeming barrier to our good will crumble and melt away as if it never was."

The wall or barrier was always a false perception of self or the world, but needed to be annihilated in the laser beam of a loving, compassionate gaze.

My Story
On 9th September, 1989, I landed in Los Angeles and on 12th September, I started Ministerial School at Santa Anita.
A number of "walls" or challenges had already been overcome before I even arrived.

Job and U.S. Visa
I had entered the U.S.A. with a one-year tourist visa and the promise of a job from a Santa Anita congregant. This would help me get the much-coveted Green Card (i.e. legal residence status in the U.S.A.) while I completed my three years of ministerial training.

Accommodation

One of the final year students at school, Mary Reninger, was a good friend of Dr. Margaret Stevens and, when she heard that I was coming from South Africa to study at Santa Anita and needed a place to stay, immediately offered her spare room. She lived in Covina, about a 20-minute drive from Santa Anita.

Transportation

Along with accommodation at Mary's, came the offer of transport to Ministerial School classes on Tuesday and Thursday evenings, as well as to the Sunday morning church services.

Some "walls" or challenges took a little longer to overcome:

Driving

I was terrified of driving on the right hand side of the road for the first time and on the massive 5-lane highways, the likes of which I had never seen in my life. I was also scared of getting hopelessly lost. (Mobile phones and satellite navigation systems had not been invented then.) Once I got orientated and understood North, South, East and West and the way that the streets were laid out in a logical grid system, it was easy to find my way but, initially, many Americans must have wondered how I was ever going to lead my sheep if I could not manage a simple compass!

Language

Divided as the Americans and the Brits are by a common language, I still naively expected that communicating would be the least of my problems in America. Wrong! Everyone around me had American accents which I could understand, even though I cringed at the "bad" grammar, but they did not understand me. Not that they would always let on. One elderly congregant had the honesty to say to me after a deep conversation on Sunday after church:

"Oh honey, I didn't understand a word you were saying but I just LOVE listening to your accent!"
I had to learn to speak slowly and turn up the volume. Mexican-American waiters in restaurants still looked mystified when I ordered "water" and did not know what to bring me. As soon as relinquished my British manners and learned to scream "WAAA-TERRRR," everyone was happy.

Starting Ministerial School
How can I describe the first night of school? Sometimes, when you dream about something for a long time and then it actually happens, it has a feeling of unreality about it. I was in a new dimension and I felt as if a Higher Hand had simply plucked me out of South Africa and set me down in my seat at that long rectangular table in the upper room that was the Santa Anita Ministerial School. This was it! I had arrived. I knew I was in the right place, I definitely belonged and yet I was a total outsider.

The student body was much smaller than I expected. There were only nine students: three in the final year, four in the second year and one more besides me in the first year. One man and eight women—a fairly typical ratio amongst New Thought ministerial leaders. We were all white. That is not so typical in New Thought but the Santa Anita community happened to be a fairly white-bred population at that time.

The Dean of the Santa Anita School, Rev. Russell Williams, welcomed us and asked us to introduce ourselves to each other by speaking about our first sense of being called into ministry as well as our vision. As my fellow students shared their very unconventional plans for their ministries, I began to feel more and more liberated. Only a small percentage of them actually planned on being pulpit ministers in a New Thought church. Until this point, I had not realised there were any other options. I had been told by Spirit to do the ministerial training and I was obeying orders but, honestly, I could not see myself operating in a traditional church set-up. I doubt if you could either for all the reasons which have been covered in the preceding chapters.

One of my new classmates, Pam, actually did want to be a pulpit minister and relayed the story of how, as a young girl, she used to arrange all her dolls in rows and then preach to them! She was raised going to the local Unity Church, and she had experienced physical healings through prayer, so she was well equipped to carry the message from the pulpit. I could not help but be impressed with her extraordinarily early recognition of her future path.

One student wanted to work with "Youth at Risk." Another wanted to be a hospital chaplain. Another wanted to work in the field of recovery from addiction. Another did not know what she was going to do; she just felt compelled to go through the ministerial training with the faith that she was being led and that her ministry would be shown to her in due time. I knew then that I had found my tribe! I felt validated; I did not have to become a pulpit minister with all the maturity and responsibility and selflessness that that would require. I simply had to go through the training and see where the Spirit took me. That sounded superbly vague and, therefore, entirely comfortable. Phew, off the hook!

When it was my turn to introduce myself and my vision, I remember being overcome with emotion, gripped by a Force much larger than myself. Holding up my pen in front of everyone in a very dramatic way, I declared, through my tears, that I wanted to use the power of the written word to heal Apartheid in South Africa. In that moment, I claimed my seat around that table. The shift had occurred from "inferior little outsider and ministerial imposter" to "I am in my power and I belong here as an equal." We were all taken aback by the energy that moved through me. It galvanised everyone in the room and compelled my new colleagues to listen in absolute silence, spellbound.

UCRS Practitioner I Training

In addition to attending Ministerial School on Tuesday and Thursday evenings, I had contacted the Home Office of the United Church of Religious Science in downtown Los Angeles and asked if there was a church near Covina where I could start my two-year practitioner training. There was not. The nearest location was in downtown Los Angeles at Founders Church, the very first church to be established in the Religious Science movement. Fine, but it was about 30 miles away. How would I get there?

The staff at Founders put me in touch with an African-American named Helen, a fellow Science of Mind student who lived near Covina and she kindly picked me up and drove me to and from my Practitioner I class every Monday night. Not only was Helen black but half the students in the class were too.

Having lived for four years under Apartheid, I was inspired and excited to witness African-Americans carrying themselves with dignity and confidence and an air of prosperity. One of the African-American students who particularly impressed me with his strong conviction of Truth was Michael Hayes. You will read about him in another chapter. These African-American practitioner students at Founders had no fear of speaking up in class – they even argued with the white teachers! And those white teachers were no lightweights. They were Rev. George Bendall and Dr.William Hornaday. Both were close friends and associates of Ernest Holmes and had become two of the great leaders of the Religious Science movement. It was such a privilege to be in their presence. I was in awe of them and would never have dared to argue. I could only listen in amazement as my fellow students courageously stood up and spoke out. It made me aware how far behind South Africa was, a land where the majority of black people had no self-esteem and very little education and still lived in fear of the white authorities.

Employment

The initial euphoria disintegrated when the promised job offer fell through. The congregant at Santa Anita, who had offered to help me with employment, was a scientist in the NASA space programme. He had seen my C.V. and, based on my degree qualification, assumed he could easily get me a job at NASA as a German and Russian translator. (Later when we started dating and then living together, he confessed that he had fallen in love with my C.V. and was keen to have such an intelligent, spiritually-focused, young woman as his girlfriend!) He told me to contact his secretary to organise the paperwork. Said secretary was an Australian immigrant and painfully familiar with all the legal restrictions around foreigners working in the U.S.A., and particularly for the U.S. Government Space Programme where security was perhaps the highest in the land. There was no way.

I prayed.
My ministerial class at Santa Anita prayed.
My practitioner class at Founders prayed.
I called the World Ministry of Prayer at United Church of Religious Science Home Office. The Religious Science practitioners prayed.
Everyone assured me that God had not brought me this far to abandon me. My Practitioner teacher at Founders put me in touch with a Science of Mind student who was an immigration consultant. This man, Darren, told me I needed to find an employer who would offer me a job that no one else in the U.S.A. could do, and then he could apply for a visa for me without me having to interrupt my training by leaving the U.S.A. There was hope. But who would employ me?
More prayers.
In October, after I had been in school for a month, one of my classmates at Santa Anita, Lori, invited me over to her home in Long Beach for the weekend. While we were together, she told me that she had been trying to set up an interview for a new job as a Personal Assistant. She did not really want this full-time job

because she was already overloaded doing freelance work and Ministerial School part-time but she needed the extra money. Lori was frustrated that every time an appointment was set for an interview, either the employer cancelled or Lori couldn't make it.

"Who is the prospective employer?" I asked.

"Marilyn Ferguson," Lori replied.

Quite calmly, a voice came out of my mouth saying,

"The reason it has not worked out for you is because it's my job."

Reader, let me tell you how I knew that...

Earlier that year, in June 1989, when I was still living in Avril's house in Johannesburg and getting ready to move to America, there was a book by my bed called, *The Aquarian Conspiracy,* by Marilyn Ferguson. A bestseller in the 1980s, it highlighted the New Age movements that were developing in all sectors of society. What fascinated me was the last page. It was a subscription form to the *Brain Mind Bulletin,* which Marilyn published every two months; a synthesis of Science and Religion. This intelligent little magazine contained articles about the leading edge discoveries in the scientific world which proved the validity of what mystics had been saying throughout the ages. I decided to take out a subscription as soon as I got to America.

There were many things to contend with in my first few weeks in America and I did not take out a subscription to the Brain Mind Bulletin straight away, as planned, but suddenly, there I was with Lori, being told about a job opening in Marilyn's company. Perfect synchronicity.

Lori was taken aback by my remark, but then considered that maybe she was, indeed, being blocked from the interview because the job was not right for her. She then kindly set up the interview for me and even drove me the two hours out to Lake Arrowhead to meet Marilyn at her mountain retreat.

Our "interview" consisted of a walk through the woods and a chat about everything except the job. Marilyn said to me,

"I have the feeling that I know you. Have we met before?"
"Yes, it was probably in Atlantis," I answered, matter-of-factly. Honestly, Reader, I was not trying to be spiritual or facetious but that response seemed to clinch the deal. An applicant's C.V. had very little to do with Marilyn's decision-making process when hiring new staff. No, in her typical unorthodox style, Marilyn proceeded to have my astrological chart drawn up and interpreted, and also have a sample of my handwriting analysed by her graphologist friend. Then we went over the results together to confirm my suitability for the position, after which she offered me the job. And so it was that in December, 1989, I became Marilyn Ferguson's Personal Assistant and the Office Manager of the *Brain Mind Bulletin*. The subscription was no longer necessary. And Darren and I could proceed with my visa application.

Working for Marilyn catapulted me into a world that I could only dream of in South Africa. Here I was suddenly surrounded by the movers and the shakers in the New Age movement: authors, publishers, artists, psychotherapists, spiritual leaders and visionary business owners. Dr. Louise Hay was one of that illustrious crowd and she wore all those hats. She had been my hero in South Africa. Her best-selling book, *You Can Heal Your Life,* had come out in 1986 and I had gobbled it up. Louise had a way of writing that made the Science of Mind sound human and digestible unlike Ernest Holmes' very intellectual *Science of Mind* textbook. She herself was a living witness of the efficacy of the teaching as she had healed herself of cancer by releasing her old beliefs, forgiving people who had hurt her and adopting a new positive attitude to living with the help of prayer and affirmations. Louise had been a Religious Science pulpit minister for a while and then moved on to helping the gay community during the AIDS epidemic and after that started her own publishing company called *Hay House*.

On my first day in the office, Marilyn asked me to make a call:

"Just get Louise Hay on the phone. She wants to publish my new book and I have to talk to her about it."
So I found the number for Hay House, the receptionist put me through and I, yes I, ACTUALLY SPOKE to Louise Hay! A few years later at a Religious Science convention, I met her in person and had the opportunity to tell her how much she had changed my life and inspired me on my path towards becoming a minister.

The Fall of the Berlin Wall
Marilyn Ferguson (deceased 2008) was an ultra-deluxe experimenter with consciousness. Every week she would send out a request to all her friends and associates to pray for a particular cause in the world. The week of my interview was in late October, 1989, at a time when there was intense political activity in the Eastern European Bloc. Marilyn asked me to join in with her prayer circle to bring down the Berlin Wall in East Germany.

This prayer request took me back sixteen years to 1973 when I was 15 and still at school in the U.K. We learned about the Berlin Wall in a history lesson. It was built in 1961 when I was only three. Having already learned about the history of World War I and II, I saw the potential of World War III breaking out in this very city where families and friends had been divided between East and West, between Communism and Democracy. I wanted to bring the Wall down to avert the war. By the time I was 15, I could already speak German quite well and I was learning Russian at that time. Ambitiously, I imagined I would be an interpreter for the United Nations and help the two powers communicate through their differences. They would forget their near-fatal squabble; they would kiss and make up and play nicely with each other. Alas, such noble flights of fantasy.... But, in defence of the fantasy, it was at least powerful enough to drive me to university and a degree course in translating and interpreting.

From 1977-81 I studied German and Russian at Bradford University in England. One morning, during an interpreting class, I was sitting in a booth with my headphones on, interpreting a recording of a speech by a German politician into English when I suddenly had an epiphany:
"This is unadulterated B.S.!"
Was I really training to translate B.S. from one language to another? Surely that would be colluding with the conflict rather than cleaning it up? Deeply discouraged, I walked out of the class, ideals and ambitions decimated for the next ten years - until Marilyn Ferguson's prayer request.

So I joined Marilyn's circle in the prayer-work. And now, get this, Reader: the following week after Marilyn's prayer request had gone out, the Berlin Wall came down!

Hmmm, prayer works.

I did not need German or Russian. I did not need to become an interpreter. I did not need to move to Berlin. All *we* needed to do was to surround the Wall with love, along with many others of like mind and heart, and have faith in Divine Demolition, breaking up the situations and circumstances that no longer served the Highest Good of the Whole.

The Fall of Apartheid

There is another story I want to tell you about a wall tumbling down. In this case, I mean the invisible wall of legally sanctioned separation between black people and white people in South Africa: Apartheid.

In November 1989, while the Berlin Wall was coming down and Eastern Europeans were flooding to the West, Nelson Mandela, the anti-Apartheid activist, who had led the armed wing of the

ANC (African National Congress), was serving the 27th year of his life sentence as a political prisoner. The wave of freedom was clearly passing over the world though and, even though the South African public did not know it, Mandela's release was secretly being negotiated by a select committee of the Afrikaner government.

Marilyn Ferguson gave me the honour of choosing a South African theme for the next focus of the prayer circle. Much inspired and encouraged by what had happened with the Berlin Wall, we joined in consciousness to pray for liberation from the Apartheid Regime in South Africa. I asked the circle members to visualise a maternity ward in a South African hospital with a white mother and baby next to a black mother and baby in alternate beds, thus signifying the birth of a new integrated generation.

Three months later, on 11th February, 1990, prayer was answered when Mandela was set free and the official dismantling of Apartheid began.

Interesting Footnote:
My vision is manifesting and continues to unfold. Now white mothers and black mothers are having their babies in the same hospitals. Not only that, more and more children are being born to mixed-race couples to create the Rainbow Nation called South Africa.

Nelson Mandela comes to Los Angeles

Soon after his release from jail, Mandela went on an eight-city tour of the U.S.A. Amid a mass of publicity, he actively garnered support from the Americans for the end of white minority rule in South Africa. On the morning of June 30, Marilyn generously suggested that all the Brain-Mind Bulletin staff drive down to the City of Los Angeles to see him. Mandela was going to be helicoptered directly to the City Hall steps in order to address the waiting crowds.

By the time we arrived, there was no way we could get anywhere close to City Hall, but Marilyn's husband had a cunning plan. He had identified an apartment building that overlooked the City Hall steps and he led us up the fire escape to the balcony area where we stood squashed in with others who also had no business being there except for this uncommon opportunity to witness and honour the living legend of Mandela.

On the balcony, there were a number of African-American families with their young children who clearly did not understand whom they were waiting to see or why. One little four-year-old black girl heard me talking in my funny accent and looked inquiringly up at her daddy for an explanation of my alien presence. Daddy took the cue.

"Where are you from?" he asked.

"I come from South Africa," I said proudly. And to the little girl, I said,

"That is the same place where Mandela comes from."

Now the little girl looked even more confused. She thought "African" meant "black." And in South Africa "black" meant "prisoner." That much she knew. So how come my skin was white and I was roaming freely?

With adorable innocence, she looked up at me with her big brown eyes, wide open, and asked:

"Did they let you out of jail too?"

Well, yes, "they" did. "They" brought me to California, the land of spiritual freedom.

God bless that little black girl from the City of Angels. She helped me realise that we are all "doing time" until the walls around our heart are caused to crumble, our small identity as humans falls away and our true identity as free spirits is unleashed.

Employment with InSynergy

Before we completely leave this chapter and the theme of breaking down walls in the world and in all areas of my new life in America, I must just tell you about my next employer after Marilyn. His name was Doug Kruschke and he ran a management consultancy business in Santa Monica with his wife, Diana.

After one year as her P.A., it was clear that Marilyn and I had come to a parting of the ways. As I was walking up the stairs to her office to hand in my notice, she was walking down the stairs to talk to me about terminating my contract. We parted on good terms, both intuitively knowing that my time there was over. I agreed to work off a month's notice after which I would leap into the void of unemployment.

I was still in a difficult situation legally so it would not be easy to find an employer who would hire an alien even though my visa application was being processed at the time. But I needed an income to cover living expenses and school fees. Amazingly, I did not panic. By this stage in my spiritual journey, I had become very clear that I needed to apprentice myself to a visionary, to learn from someone who knew how to cast a vision and implement it. Developing that ability was so important to me that earning an income was actually a secondary consideration.

My intention must have been strong because on Tuesday night at Ministerial School, a couple of days before I left Marilyn's office, I was divinely nudged from within to approach our teacher, Rev. Linda McNamar, at the end of the class and ask her if she could help me find a position.

Let me tell you a little more about Rev. Linda because she played a key role in my journey. She was a minister from the Huntingdon Beach Religious Science Church under Dr. Peggy Bassett, then one of the largest, most rocking churches in the entire Religious Science movement. Rev. Gladys, my first Science of Mind teacher in Johannesburg, had met Dr. Peggy and often used to sing her praises because of her phenomenal success as a spiritual leader who knew how to manage the business of a mega-church.

Rev. Linda was and is a brilliant educator in the Science of Mind. In fact, in 1986, Rev. Gladys had invited her to come to South Africa to visit the Science of Mind communities and offer a series of lectures and workshops. At that time, I was still a newbie at the Religious Science church in Johannesburg, full of self-hatred, believing that I had nothing to offer and "hiding my light under a bushel" in the form of spotty skin, a beer belly and baggy clothes. *(Is a lamp brought and put under a basket or under a bed? Is it not put on a lamp stand? Ref.: Mark 4:21.)* Amazingly, I was approached by the church committee members who were preparing for Rev. Linda McNamar's visit and asked if I would join them. Who, me?! But what use would I be? Well, they saw something in me that I could not see in myself. It was my first volunteer assignment in the church community and the beginnings of some self-esteem.

Rev. Linda's trip to South Africa was cancelled for a number of reasons but fast forward almost five years and there I was in Ministerial School at Santa Anita being taught by Rev. Linda herself!

Rev. Linda was delighted when I asked for help with my job search because she had been approached by Doug Kruschke a few days prior. Doug had asked her if she knew anyone suitable to be his new administrative assistant as his previous one had just left.... Synchronicity is a wonderful thing.

Doug was no ordinary management consultant. He led Win-Win Conflict Resolution workshops within the Church of Religious Science and he was the personal management consultant to Dr. Peggy Bassett. In early 1991, Dr. Peggy had asked him to lead a weekend workshop on *Synergy* for the ministers in the Religious Science movement. Rev. Linda was one of the participants.

Linda duly connected Doug and me. That Friday I had an interview with Doug and his wife Diana and the following

Monday, I started working for InSynergy. I was unemployed for precisely one week.

My prayers were answered in that Doug was a visionary who helped his clients get in touch with their vision for their professional and their personal lives and then showed them how to implement it in a win-win way. Spirit over-delivered, though, with this Divine Appointment as Doug's assistant, and gave me so much more than I had asked for.
Once per month, Doug facilitated a Ministers' Synergy Team meeting in which the Religious Science ministers from Southern California would come together for the day and discuss the challenging issues in their ministry in a safe and supportive environment. I was permitted to sit in on these meetings and, not only meet the heavyweight ministers in the movement, but get an uncommon insight into the private concerns that they would not be at liberty to share outside this sacred context created by Doug.

Not only was Doug a wonderful teacher, but his wife Diana brought her special magic to my development as a minister too. She taught me how to design and facilitate a sacred ceremony using the knowledge and skills she had developed by apprenticing herself to Native American Indian teachers. My limited knowledge of ceremony was based entirely on the empty rituals I had witnessed in traditional religious organisations. Thanks to Diana, the extraordinary power of ritual and ceremony was conveyed to me. When facilitated properly, it is alive and spontaneous and magical; it sets the tone for transformation, connection, healing, upliftment and community building. It lives in a dimension outside time and space and is a portal into the Infinite. Leading ceremonies, both traditional and unusual, has become one of my greatest passions in life.
Note: Reader, further information about ceremonies can be found at the back of this book.

So, one by one, the “walls” and challenges of my new life in America were overcome. However, the biggest wall, which I was in denial about and which was blocking me from the sunlight of the Spirit, was yet to be confronted. Read on.

Chapter 11

Caught in the Act of Being Human

3. Then the Scribes and the Pharisees brought a woman who was caught in adultery; and they made her to stand in the midst
4. They said to him, Teacher, this woman was caught openly in the act of adultery.
5. Now in the law of Moses it is commanded that women such as these should be stoned: but what do you say?
6. They said this to tempt him, that they might have a cause to accuse him. While Jesus was bent down, he was writing on the ground.
7. When they were through questioning him, he straightened himself up and said to them, He who is among you without sin, let him first throw a stone at her.
8. And again as he bent down, he wrote on the ground.
9. And when they heard it, they left one by one, beginning with the elders; and the woman was left alone in the midst.
10. When Jesus straightened himself up, he said to the woman, Where are they? Did no man condemn you?
11. She said, No man, Lord. Then Jesus said, Neither do I condemn you; go away and from henceforth, do not sin again.

John 8:3-11

Interpretation

From a metaphysical standpoint, every character in a Bible story usually represents an aspect of our consciousness. In this particular story

- Jesus represents our Adult Christ Self, the perfect blend of Love and Wisdom, able to witness and observe with detachment and yet also compassion—not getting involved in the drama nor taking sides.
- The woman caught in adultery is that part of ourselves chasing after our perceived good, regardless of whether such a pursuit hurts others or ourselves.
- The men who want to stone the woman are our inner critics, the beat-up voices inside us.

Jesus shows us how we can best relate to our split-off selves and become integrated or whole. He clearly understands that part of our human journey is to do the things that do not work – the things, which we hope and think will bring us real happiness or peace of mind, but which always fail miserably. We have been given free will and we are compelled to experiment in this way so that we can consciously discover how to live and love.

The woman caught in adultery was simply looking for love. This, in itself, is not a crime. Her strategy, however, of having an adulterous affair, is how she deviated from the law of her society and the Universal Law. Jesus tells her:

"Don't do it again!"

He is warning her that if she insists on doing harmful things she will keep reaping the detrimental consequences of the Law, both societal and universal.

The inner critics believe that they can help us to improve and change by punishing us and making us suffer. That never works. What does work is to take responsibility for the error, make amends and move on in greater awareness and freedom.

My Story

My graduation from Santa Anita Ministerial School was on 14th June, 1992. It was the greatest day of my life and could not be marred by the fact that I had invited both of my parents along with their painful relationship. They had had no contact for eight years since their divorce and my mother's immigration to South Africa.

My father arrived at Los Angeles airport from England in an Oxfam charity-shop suit with trousers that were about two inches too short. His front teeth were missing due to his recent involvement in a pub fight that he obviously did not win. I assumed that the fight was right before his flight and that he had not had time to see a dentist. But no, the fight was a few weeks prior. Alcohol was his priority, not dentistry or clothing.

My mother arrived from Johannesburg looking stunningly beautiful, well-dressed and happy with her wealthy new South African husband on her arm. They stayed at an expensive hotel in Santa Monica while my father dossed down in my tiny spare room.

The red rag and the bull confronted each other in the Santa Anita parking lot right before my graduation ceremony. I played my role of "hurt child" and "peace-maker," suggesting to my parents that they could at least be civil and shake hands. They did that grudgingly. Snorting silently, they refused to speak to each other and sat on opposite sides of the church for the ceremony.
The whole event was an outstanding opportunity for me to witness the pain and insanity of my parents' relationship and it catapulted me right back into the lion's den of my childhood.
However, this was my big day and I was not going to let anybody ruin it, least of all me with my toxic childhood memories.

Once the guests were all seated and I stood in the foyer of the church, waiting to process down the aisle, the ceremony took on a power of its own. My childhood was forgotten as I started walking down the aisle of the Santa Anita church towards the altar and into my future. How inspired I felt when Rev. Dr. Michael Beckwith stood to give the keynote speech. How strongly I felt the surge of power when I knelt down at the altar and Dr. Margaret Stevens blessed me and placed the ministerial stole around my shoulders. And how alive I felt when I stood in the pulpit and gave my graduation speech about my vision for South Africa and all the obstacles that had been overcome to get me to this point of readiness.

You might have heard the name Rev. Dr. Michael Beckwith? He is the founding minister of Agape in Culver City, Los Angeles, a vibrant spiritual community which recently celebrated its 30th anniversary. He became internationally famous in 2006 with the release of the movie *The Secret* about the Law of Attraction. The movie led to interviews on *Oprah* and the *Larry King show*.
How did I meet this enlightened being and why was he speaking at my graduation ceremony?

Well, when they heard about my vision to found a multi-racial ministry in South Africa, my fellow ministerial students at Santa Anita strongly recommended that I go to one of Rev. Dr. Beckwith's Sunday services because they thought he would be a good mentor for me. As an African-American, with a dynamic speaking style and a rapidly growing multi-racial congregation, Rev. Michael was fast becoming a leading light in the Religious Science movement.
So it was that in mid-1991, I entered the doors of Agape for the first time and my soul was rocked to its core. This was what I had been searching for—the palpable presence of Spirit throbbing through the room and blasting through the outworn concepts in my mind and the hurts in my heart. I fell in love with the giant spirit of Rev. Dr. Michael and loved him as I have never loved another before or since. Furthermore, what I saw at Agape was a perfect manifestation of my vision for South Africa. There I

witnessed black people and white people holding hands, singing, praying and serving together in a joyous, vibrant, multi-coloured spiritual community. The precedent had been set. I knew that if this could happen in America with its own turbulent history of racism, then it could happen in South Africa too.

In February, 1992, when my Santa Anita ministerial graduation ceremony was just over three months away, Rev. Russell asked my fellow graduate, Linda, and me to select a keynote speaker for the event. We asked Rev. Michael and, miraculously, he said "Yes" because he could. Nowadays, one has to book him years in advance.

When I spoke about my vision at my graduation ceremony and how profoundly inspired I had been the first time I had witnessed the living manifestation of a multi-racial ministry at Agape, Rev. Michael was listening. After the ceremony he put me in touch with one of his Agape Practitioners who was organising an Agape trip to South Africa a few months later in November of 1992. Rev. Michael would be speaking at the New Thought centres in Johannesburg, Port Elizabeth, Durban and Cape Town and also in the townships.

My inner child had taken a back seat during my graduation ceremony but she could not be totally suppressed. She got a bit restless with all the pomp and seriousness in the church so, as soon as the ceremony was over, and the guests were processing into the Fellowship Hall for tea, the little inner rebel came out to play. My photographer friend, Kelly Taaffe, who was also a ministerial student, encouraged me to pose for some irreverent photos around the back of the church and met with very little resistance from me – as you will see from the cover photo of this book!

My mother and her new husband left in a huff soon after my graduation. My mother was incensed that I had had the audacity to invite my father to my ceremony because his presence had spoilt the whole occasion for her. Meanwhile my father was intent on killing the pain of seeing his ex-wife happily married to a wealthy successful colonial - the man he would never be - and stayed long after the party was over for a few more drinks.

On the day my father left Los Angeles, 28th June, 1992, I did something I thought I would never do since I had judged all Americans so contemptuously for it: I started therapy. You see, despite passing all my ministerial exams and having Rev. in front of my name, and despite being 33, (the same age as Jesus at the peak of his ministry,) I still had an ever-present sense of defectiveness and, in my heart, I knew that I was simply not adult enough to return to South Africa and take up the mantle of ministry. Being in the same room as my parents for a few hours on the day of my graduation had successfully brought all my childhood wounds to the surface and I could no longer ignore them or try to do a spiritual by-pass on the pain. My gem of a therapist, Maxine, was an Inner Child Counsellor as well as a Religious Science Minister. I believe she saved my life.

In July of 1992, I joined the South Africa Vision Team at Agape consisting of four beautiful African-American women who had been praying and planning together for a year to bring about this special trip. We all hoped to raise enough funds to personally accompany Rev. Michael to South Africa.

Now that I had become more involved at Agape over that summer after my Santa Anita graduation, it became an obvious first choice as the centre where I would complete the final year of my Practitioner Training (Prac. II) to become a licensed spiritual counsellor in the United Church of Religious Science. Rev. Gladys wanted me to complete this entire 4-year Practitioner training in South Africa before leaving to start ministerial school in the U.S.A. but, as you have seen, Spirit's curriculum overrode all human plans and preferences.

And so it was that in September, 1992, three months after I had graduated as a minister from Santa Anita and started Inner Child therapy twice per month, I registered for the final year of my Practitioner Training (Prac. II) at the Agape International Center of Truth.

12-Step Meeting

One of our first homework assignments at the beginning of the final year of the Practitioner training was to visit a 12-step recovery meeting such as Alcoholics Anonymous or Overeaters Anonymous. We were to observe how people with addictions approached their spiritual path in case any addicts might seek out our services as counsellors once our professional practices were up and running.

The man I was dating at the time, David, was a long-term Science of Mind student, a friend of Rev. Dr. Michael and a sober member of AA for nearly seventeen years. He took me to my first AA meeting to do my homework assignment. I played the role of the detached observer, feeling sorry for the poor alcoholics and not relating to anyone who shared their story of recovery from the podium.

A few days later, on 8th October, 1992, I went for my weekly therapy session. My therapist, Maxine asked me to share my experience of the 12-step meeting. I told her how I had not identified one bit with anything I had heard. Later I found out that almost every alcoholic reacts with the same denial at their first AA meeting. Sagely and gently she helped me make the admission to myself that I had a problem with alcohol.

What?
You mean, *moi*?

Really, this was the last thing on earth I expected! I was horrified. How could it have come to this? Surely being an alcoholic meant I was the lowest of the low? Ashamed to my core, I did not dare to lift my head among humans any more.

Overwhelmed with the magnitude of this realization, and the fear that I would now have to learn to live without alcohol, I raced directly from Maxine's office to the practitioner class at Agape. Rev. Nirvana Gayle, also an African-American and then an Assistant Minister at Agape, as well as a close childhood friend of Rev. Dr. Michael's, was facilitating. After the opening prayer, he asked us to report on our experience at the 12-step meeting. I stood up first—actually, I was lifted out of my chair—and said:

"My name is Stephanie and I am an alcoholic."

Then, I burst into tears, the shame of my condition filling every cell, crushed by the utter defeat, the hopelessness of being an alcoholic just like my father. Dad was one of the stereotyped alkies - not that he was lying in the gutter with a dirty raincoat and a flask of whiskey under his arm, but almost. I was ashamed of him. Much later I grew to understand that this is where the disease of alcoholism takes its sufferers and that my father was not essentially a bad person, but simply a sick person.

My raw sharing triggered others in the class to be honest about their own addictions. It was an intense evening of healing, involving the divulging of dark personal secrets that many of us had never previously dared to bring to the light of conscious awareness in a public forum.

At the end of the evening, I went up to thank Rev. Nirvana for facilitating the class so sensitively and for making it safe for me to be so vulnerable. It had certainly not been my intention that night to go public with my new awareness of my alcoholism. As usual, Spirit had Its own agenda.

When Rev. Nirvana held out his arms and gave me a long hug, I felt as if the Christ was hugging me and I was a woman who had been caught in the midst of a shameful act. I felt the years of fear and shame wash off me. They literally drained away in the presence of his great love. His compassion purified my soul. I knew I was not tainted. I knew I was pure and the disease did not define me. I knew that nothing I had ever done under the influence of alcohol could condemn me. I felt completely loved and accepted in a way that I had never been able to love and accept myself.

Bless you, Rev. Nirvana. Thank you for being there for me in that very moment and for helping me to gently put down the hateful stones I had been levelling at myself.

Interesting Footnotes:
That night's Practitioner class inspired Rev. Nirvana to begin the visioning process for a new ministry at Agape. It was to be called "Freedom Path" and it was designed to help people deal with their addictions from a spiritual standpoint. I had the privilege of being one of its first leaders.

The beloved Rev. Nirvana Gayle made his transition on 9th August, 2016. He had helped thousands on their path of spiritual growth. He was larger than life so he must be larger than death too.
This poem came through me upon his passing:

A bright light has gone out
And departed the earth,
Whisked up to the stars
For a cosmic re-birth,

While I stay and weep
Missing him so,
But his legacy remains
This I know
Because of who I've become
From loving this soul
My life has been blessed
Through him, I AM whole.

Chapter 12

Prosperity

For to him who has, shall be given and it shall increase to him;
but to him who has not, even that which he has shall be taken away from him.

Matthew 13:12

Interpretation
At first glance, this Bible verse seems to suggest a universal unfairness, i.e. if you have certain things already, you will effortlessly get more of them and if you do not have much of anything, then even that paltry little bit will be removed, seemingly by an external giver and taker.

If we look at it from the metaphysical perspective, though, we must turn away from the outer circumstances in the physical world of our experience and put our attention on the inner realms of consciousness.

The critical factor is not whether you and I "have" or "do not have," but whether you and I have the *consciousness* of "having" or "not having." The actual amount we possess is all relative and not a real consideration. For example, a millionaire might have a fleet of yachts and seek just one more to add to her collection; thus, she might be living with a poverty complex of "not enoughness." A tropical island fisherman might have one boat that allows him to fish, feed his family and still have fish left over to sell. He might be living in a consciousness of wealth and abundant overflow. Consciousness is everything.

Let me give you some more examples to clarify.

Finances
An individual living in a consciousness of "not enough" or "only very little," has beliefs such as

- There is never enough money to pay the bills
- I cannot afford luxuries
- My employer does not pay me what I am worth
- The tax man takes all my profit
- Inflation has eaten up my pension
- I will never be able to pay off my debts

And the human solution to all that is:

"One day, when I win the lottery...." rather than "How can I change my consciousness and heal my relationship with that expression of Divine Substance called money?"

Lottery winners have proven that the external "fix" of a large amount of money does not solve anything. In a state of "not enoughness," individuals experience the misery of watching their financial resources dwindle through taxes, fines, pay-cuts, unexpected losses or expenses or sheer extravagant overspending and wastefulness. They always have less and less of that elusive thing called money.

If you believe that you always have lots of money and all your financial needs are met in beautiful ways that prosper you and the entire universe, you will most likely be rolling in abundant financial resources. You will be filled with joy because you understand the Law. You know that God is your immediate and Eternal Source of Supply, that all your needs are met in time and on time, that nothing can ever be taken from you because you are One with the Inexhaustible Supply of Infinite Wealth and Abundance.

Let us also examine this verse from a different view point, bearing in mind that whatever we put our attention on expands because the Law only knows how to multiply.

Health

An individual who has a consciousness of having a lot of physical health problems, problems that the doctor, medication and surgery cannot seem to heal, will have the experience of the health problems mounting and multiplying until the eventual conclusion of "death." If the individual makes their body, their suffering and their failing health the only subject of their conversation, both internal and external, these health challenges will intensify and dominate the individual's life experience.

If, on the other hand, you give thanks for the health and aliveness that you do have, you value the amazing body temple that you inhabit and you nourish it lovingly with rest, nutrition and exercise, the life-force will multiply within you and then more good health will be given to you.

Relationships

If an individual has a sense of "not enough love" in their relationships, nothing they do to get love will work. No amount of people-pleasing, manipulation, begging, sexual partners or having babies will achieve their desire to feel loved. If an individual experiences relationships as power struggles, where they feel like the victim, not seen, not heard not loved, then their repeated focus on those relationship problems means that they will have to experience more of the same.

However, if you have been doing your spiritual work and come to realise that your previous relationship problems were based on a false sense of self, on a sense of emptiness trying to get filled. If you now have a relationship with your Higher Self and you know you are whole and complete unto yourself, you will notice that the old style of relationship that you used to have just does not feature any more in your life. Even the people who used to trigger you have either de-selected themselves from your life or they cannot hook you in like they used to because of your refusal to indulge in your old beliefs and behaviours. You will notice that you have fewer and fewer unhealthy relationships and more and more supportive and enriching connections with others. Eventually, even the few bad relationships you once had will be taken away.

The Solution

The way out of the "lack of good" trap is to practise a consciousness of gratitude. Be grateful for the little you do have and soon it will grow. Make a case for yourself. Prove to yourself that you have more than enough for your needs *right now*. For example, you cannot wear all the clothes in your wardrobe anyway, and you cannot read all the books on your bookshelf right now, and you probably have more food in the cupboard than you can eat right now. The key is to know that *right now* you are taken care of and you will be supplied in the next moment of now, too.

The way out of the "abundance of problems" trap is to desist from feeding the problems with attention, worry and complaining. Instead, focus on the areas of your life where you can witness success, ease and grace.

As an example, one Sunday I had a headache during the church service in Johannesburg and afterwards when I complained to Rev. Gladys, she told me that I should put my focus on a part of my body where there was no pain, like my arm. I didn't like being told that, but I tried it and it worked.

Is your glass of water half-empty or half-full? It is all in how you see it, or rather how you choose to see it.

My Story

I always had money issues, the constant experience of poverty even though you and I are members of the elite eight percent on the planet who have food, shelter, cash, clothes—and enough education to read this book.

Spiritually I was bankrupt and I was painfully aware of the "void" inside that I tried to fill with things and people outside of myself. But, no matter what I achieved or purchased, no matter whom I seduced or manipulated to do my will, it was never enough. I dipped in and out of varying levels of terror with regard to not having money. On one particular occasion, I remember it was in June, 1994, I was going through my "monthly curse" i.e. rent was due and I did not have enough to pay it. My sense of "not enoughness" was doubled on that occasion because I wanted to go on the annual Agape Practitioner Retreat in Lake Arrowhead. Sadly, it was a luxury I could not afford.

At the time, I had just moved to a new flat in Mar Vista on the West Side of Los Angeles, about a mile from the Pacific Ocean (poor me), and my new chequebook with my new address had arrived in the mail. Casually, I threw out my old chequebook and left it in a bag of rubbish that I tossed in the communal dumpster in the alleyway behind my apartment building. The idea of shredding it never occurred to me. Yep, you can guess what happened.... A homeless person sorted through the trash and picked up my chequebook. She or he then went into the bank and cashed three cheques on different days for an amount of $25 each. $75 in total.

When my next statement arrived in the mail, I saw to my horror, that the balance in my account was $75 less than it should have been. Oh no! There must have been a mistake.

Angry and terrified and girding up my spiritual loins for a righteous battle *(She girdeth her loins with strength, and strengtheneth her arms. Ref.: Proverbs 31:17)* with the bank over their glaring ineptitude, I learned from the bank customer service rep that it was both possible and legal at that time to cash a cheque over the counter for an amount of up to $25 without showing ID or having the signature verified. Eeeek!

The experience was a direct manifestation of the Law at work. My fear of lack was producing even more lack in my life. Money was being taken from me without me even knowing it. I had to correct this so I quickly started working to shift my consciousness to a sense of "havingness." I started by getting really grateful for all the money I had in my bank account and in my purse, disregarding the fact that rent was due and I did not have enough to cover it.

The day after the heartless bank statement had arrived, an Agape friend, Michael Hayes RScP, came over with a gift. (Do you remember that I was impressed with his spiritual stature when I met him in the Practitioner I class at Founders Church in 1989? Since then we had both gravitated towards Agape.) It was a late birthday card with a dollar bill on it as a symbol of prosperity. Michael had already prayed over it and blessed it for me. Well, I thanked him and I then saturated that one dollar with blessings and gratitude. I chose to see abundance in a single dollar and affirmed that I was wealthy and supported.

That afternoon, the mail arrived with a letter from my best friend, Harriet, who had recently moved back to the East Coast. I opened the envelope expecting to read about her new life back East but, to my surprise, a cheque fell out! In her accompanying letter, Harriet shared that I had inspired her on her spiritual journey and, as a result, she had decided to tithe to me in order to support me further in my spiritual work. (Note: Tithing is an ancient custom of giving 10% of one's income to the source of one's spiritual food so that the individual teacher or organisation can focus on carrying their message of inspiration without concern for financial support.)

When I looked at the amount on the cheque, I fell to my knees inside and cried, humbled and awed by God's grace. It was well over $200 – more than enough to make up the rent AND cover the Practitioner Retreat fees in full. What's more, Divine timing was immaculate: the cheque arrived on the day of the deadline for the Retreat registration! Alleluya! Praise God. A lesson I shall never forget.

Chapter 13

Forgiveness

21. My Lord, if my brother is at fault with me,
how many times should I forgive him? Up to seven
times?
22. Jesus said to him, I do not say to you up to
seven times, but up to seventy times seventy-seven.

Matthew 18:21–22

Interpretation

Even though this verse of scripture clearly indicates that we should forgive up to seventy times seventy-seven, the way I have always heard this verse is "seventy times seven." It matters not. The message is to keep forgiving until you and I are finished forgiving and our consciousness has returned to a state of innocence where all we can see is the Divine Presence in our brother or sister and the Divine Presence in ourselves.

Forgiveness does not occur from a high pedestal of spiritual superiority where you and I deign to release the peon below us from our wrathful and justified punishment. It means that you and I take radical responsibility for what occurred, admit that we are the creators of all that shows up in our experience and release the "transgressor" from blame because, after all, you and I summoned that person to read their lines and play their part in the script that we wrote and she or he did a perfect job. Ouch! But true. And there is freedom and power here once the addiction to victimhood is surrendered.

My Story

It was 1994. I was living in Mar Vista, still working for Doug Kruschke and very active at Agape teaching, speaking, counselling and facilitating groups.

My mum and I had not had a great relationship for most of my life. I was living in America while she was living in South Africa. This was good, I thought. We were about ten thousand miles apart. Only I had not acknowledged that she was living rent-free inside my head.

One of my earliest childhood memories is when, at age 2 ½, I was farmed out to an aunt of mine while my mum went to hospital to be observed before the birth of my twin-sisters. It was bad enough being separated from both my mum and my dad during this period, but, being a prisoner in the large, cold house of a large, cold, angry aunt, was traumatic. Once my mum came home from hospital with my twin-sisters, the inevitable occurred—the newborns got all the attention and, as the oldest child, I was relegated to a supporting role. My mum did her best to make sure I was not pushed to one side, but too little too late; the separation had occurred and it never re-joined – well, not during my childhood anyway. Nor during my teens, my twenties or my thirties.

One day in April, 1994, I had a visitation from an angel in the fleshly form of my dear friend, Gwen. The angel commanded me with great urgency and importance:
"You have to forgive your mother. Your resentment is holding you back and you can't be a minister if you don't practise what you preach.'

Gulp! She was right.
Rats!
I was under the misapprehension that the divine privilege of being a minister was to tell *other people* how to clean up *their* act. God forbid that others less qualified (e.g. my close friends), should usurp that Divine Authority and tell me how to clean up my act! The egoic armour of being beyond reproach had taken an almighty bullet!

Gwen shared how she had also had a difficult relationship with her Mum and how she had consciously practised forgiveness as a way to get free. Wow, so mature, so responsible, so spiritual! And Gwen was not even officially studying this spiritual stuff. In fact, she was doing her Masters in Political Science.

Gwen patiently reminded me of the Bible verse about Jesus instructing the disciples to forgive 70 x 7. She informed me that I had two choices: I could write

1) Seven affirmations a day over a period of 70 days saying, "I now forgive my mother"
   or
2) 70 affirmations each day for seven days saying, "I now forgive my mother."

She thought the first option was the better choice because it would not be so intense and my mind set would probably change more permanently if I did the work over a longer period of time.
I agreed. Sullenly. Reluctantly.
And silently, vowed not to do it.

Gwen, bless her, called me the next day to check up.
"Hi, Stephie! Have you done your seven affirmations?" she chirped, irritatingly.
"Er no, I was just about to." (Big fat lie.)
"Do them now, Stephie! Stop resisting. I love you." Click.

Damn! Why did she have to be so relentless? I hate it when angels are pushy. But, you know what? I did them. As I squeezed the blood from my pen, I wrote:
"I forgive you, Mum, for ...."
and then I wrote a list of seven childish, whining complaints.
Actually, I did not forgive her at all. I was going through the motions in order to do this stupid exercise that Gwen had recommended. I had no desire to forgive her. I preferred to be right and unhappy. I preferred to make her the demon and me the saint, her the crab and me the naked toe.

That evening there was a message on my answering machine when I got home. Guess who?
Mum!
We had not spoken or corresponded for about two years. Consider, Reader, that this all happened in the dark ages of the BT era—BT stands for Before Technology (unfortunately for

British Telecom), and the advent of the Internet, email and Skype.

Mum's voice sounded faint, weak, like she was dying:
"Stephanie, I need to talk to you. Can you call me back?"

Panic! Was she about to pop off the planet? Did she want to make her peace with me? Was I supposed to be urgently making my peace with her? You know when a parent uses all three syllables of your name that something is about to erupt. I called her back.

"Hi Mum, are you alright?"
"Yes, I am fine."

Phew, relief.

"I called you because I am planning to come to California in July and I would like to take you on a bus trip up the coast from Los Angeles to Seattle. It will be just over a week. I want the two of us to be together so that we can talk. Would you like to do that? You have to tell me now because the travel agent is holding the tickets and I have to confirm 'yes' or 'no'."

Hmmm, no pressure there then.
"Er, yes."
"Good. That is settled then. I'll see you in a couple of months. Bye."
"Er, bye," I said.

Stunned, I checked the calendar and counted the days. Can you believe that there were exactly ***70 days*** from the date of her call to the date of her arrival in Los Angeles?!

The impending doom of my mother's visit really upped the ante on my daily forgiveness affirmations with the result that I got really, really sick with a horrible flu and an ear infection. From a metaphysical perspective, the blockage in my ear indicated the nature of my resistance and lack of willingness to hear anything that might contradict my old encrusted attitudes, cherished since childhood.

Fortunately, before I got sick, I had shared my story about my mother with a dear friend called Gene Taylor. Gene and his wonderful wife, Barbara, were both Religious Science Practitioners at Agape as well as leaders of the Freedom Path Ministry. Gene was one of the kindest, most compassionate men I have ever met. He counselled me to write a eulogy for my mother, as if she had already died and I were singing her praises at her funeral. He advised that this was a wonderful spiritual exercise to help people in conflict to focus on the essence of love in each other.

With tears, I wrote the eulogy while I languished in my sick bed. I acknowledged mum for the love she had shown us on her terms and in her way. She had, after all, done her job. In very trying circumstances with my alcoholic father, she had made sure I survived till I was 18 and independent. That is the responsibility of a parent. She had delivered. She was not my *fantasy* parent and it was this that I had judged her for so harshly. She was not the fairy godmother type who always said "Yes" to me with a beaming countenance, who was always well coiffed, patient, tireless and magical. She was not my friend Sandra's mother who let Sandra stay up late even on school nights. But she was my mother. She had agreed to let her body be used that I might have an opportunity to incarnate. Further, she had also agreed to take care of me until I was ready to take care of myself. Any way you look at it, those are two very big unselfish and long-term agreements that should not be entered into lightly. And they weren't – at least not by my mother. She

- cleaned;
- planned the meals;

- shopped;
- cooked;
- did the gardening;
- washed the laundry;
- hung the washing out to dry and raced to get it in before the rain;
- ironed all the clothes and sheets;
- managed the family finances;
- saved;
- selected and booked family holidays;
- made sure I went on all the school trips, including the expensive ones to Austria and Russia;
- learned to drive and bought the family's first car;
- drove me and my sisters to school then drove herself to work;
- took time off work if my sisters or I were sick;
- marched down the school if the other kids were giving me or my sisters a hard time;
- helped me with my spellings before a test;
- baked cakes;
- preserved fruit and vegetables;
- knitted sweaters;
- darned and mended
  and
- always made a big deal of birthdays and Christmas.

It sounds like she was a stay-at-home mum but she managed to hold down a full-time job to supplement the family income and protect us from financial ruin in the times when my father drank his salary or emptied the family savings account.

Naturally, mum could never understand what I had to forgive her for, since she had only ever done her best to look after me and make sure I got educated so that I could have a better life than she had had. That was a gift of love, right? She had fulfilled her duty as a mother, right? Errr.... Well, I still reserved the right to dehumanize her to make myself look good. Immature, I know. Cruel even. But that is how it was until I wrote the eulogy for her and began to change my bratty, ungrateful point of view.

Mum flew to California, as planned, and we did our bus tour up the Pacific Coast. It was not an easy journey and I, insisting on resisting, kept the eulogy safely locked up in my suitcase throughout the trip. Finally, on that last day of our time together, before we went down for breakfast in our San Francisco hotel, I told mum I had something I wanted to read to her. We sat opposite each other on our twin beds in the hotel room. She, expectant and anxious. Me scared of the atom-splitting activity in my heart. I pulled the eulogy out of my suitcase and began to read to her. Before long, she was in tears and so was I. We hugged. We celebrated. We feasted on a late breakfast of Belgian waffles with strawberries and cream in the restaurant of our San Francisco hotel. Nothing had ever tasted more delicious.

Returning to Los Angeles, I felt as if a big stone had been plucked out of my heart. Indeed it had. Forgiveness had done its tender quarrying, all the way down to the Mother Lode.

Chapter 14

Divine Appointment

You did not choose me, but I chose you, and I have appointed you, that you also should go and produce fruit and that your fruit might remain.

John 15:16

Interpretation

We have been appointed and anointed to fulfil our Divine Purpose by the Power that made us out of Itself. If we do not surrender to this purpose, life will be difficult because we are going against the flow. Our purpose in being here is to leave the world a better place by contributing our unique being with all of our gifts, talents, abilities and resources. If we work with the intention of expressing more of the Divine Principles into the world such as Love, Beauty, Abundance, Creativity etc., then our work will have lasting value and we will leave a legacy for those who come after us. Once we are in the flow of giving to Life, rather than trying to get something from Life, we are in alignment with the Law of Life and everything we need comes to us easily and effortlessly in order to serve the greater good of the Whole.

My Story

In June 1992, I graduated from Santa Anita as a minister.

In August 1993, I graduated with a Practitioner Licence from Agape.

In January 1994, I started teaching Science of Mind classes at Agape and was co-leading the new Freedom Path Ministry as well. Meanwhile, I was still working for Doug Kruschke and going to Inner Child therapy sessions and 12-step recovery meetings. Life was full and fulfilling. South Africa and my vision seemed very far away until one day in the summer of 1995 when Dr. June Jones burst into my bubble.

Do you remember Dr. June Jones from my story about my relationship with Greg? She was the New Thought minister in Port Elizabeth who was licensed to marry us but who was uncannily unavailable to us on the planned date of our wedding. Dr. June and I had met on a number of occasions while I was still in South Africa and she was thoroughly supportive of my decision to study at Santa Anita as Dr. Margaret Stevens was a very good friend of hers.

On this particular occasion, Dr. June was visiting America expressly to receive the Joseph Murphy award for her outstanding contribution to the New Thought movement. Through a mutual friend, I found out that Dr. June was staying in a hotel around the corner from my flat in Marina del Rey and I made plans to visit her there. I walked into her hotel room looking forward to a casual chat. Instead I got a divine boot up the bum:

"Hi June. Howzit?" I asked, smoothly remembering my South African lingo. Her reply took me completely off guard.

"Stephanie, you had better jolly well hurry up and come back to South Africa. We need you there. Rev. Gladys is ill and is giving up her church. I won't be able to carry on much longer either and all the other metaphysical ministers are dying off. We need young blood like you with all your enthusiasm and energy to bring in young people and families and get New Thought going again in South Africa. When do you plan to come home?"

"Er, dunno. I don't have any plans right now." I answered, sounding like a pothead.

"Well, Gladys needs you to take over her church!"

"I can't do that. I am not qualified to take over a Religious Science church." I righteously defended my position.

"Well, you had better jolly well do whatever it takes to get yourself qualified then!"
With this exhortation from Dr. June, my audience with her was complete. These words were the final words we exchanged before Dr. June left her body some time later.

The power of Dr. June's intention had the effect of propelling me into action and I applied to start at the Religious Science School of Ministry at Agape in October, 1995. Meanwhile, Rev. Linda McNamar, who taught at both the Santa Anita School and the Religious Science school, and who had helped me get my job with Doug Kruschke, also helped me get my transcripts sorted so that the modules I had completed at Santa Anita would count towards my qualification as a Religious Science minister. I had my interview. The panel accepted my application and once again, I was back at school two or three evenings per week with homework, internship hours to complete and exams.

My second ministerial graduation was in June, 1998. By this time, I had completed a further two years of study at the Holmes Institute (the new name for the United Church of Religious Science Ministerial School, based at Agape) and in August, 1998, I was officially granted status as a Fellow of the United Church of Religious Science.
What next?
I had no plans.

Look, I had never forgotten my original vision to start a multi-racial ministry in South Africa but I was still enjoying life in California and certainly did not have any immediate desires to go home. Being a part of the Agape community was a very compelling reason to stay in the U.S.A. I loved all my teaching and counselling work and being surrounded by so many friends and powerful teachers who were consciously on the spiritual path, such as Marianne Williamson, Neale Donald Walsch, Dr. Louise Hay and Deepak Chopra. Last but not least, by this time I was living right by the beach in a luxury apartment in Marina del Rey, California.

Interesting Footnote:
When I first moved to this particular Marina del Rey apartment complex in 1994, I was sharing the space with Wendy, one of my

Agape friends. Truly there are no accidents because the very apartment we moved into was the same one in which Rev. Dr. Michael Beckwith had held his initial prayer and vision meetings when he was preparing to start the Agape ministry.

Sad Footnote:
Wendy Taylor edited my first two books. I was hesitating to ask her to edit this book too and was not sure why. Then I learned that she made her transition unexpectedly on 22 October 2016 after brain surgery. Bless you on your way, dear Wendy. Thank you for your gifts of words and friendship. I will never forget you.

No, there was no way that I was going to prize myself out of my sunny comfort zone, especially not before establishing my Green Card status that would have allowed me to return to the U.S.A. at will.

Well, you know by now what happens when I have a cunning plan for my greatest comfort.... It rarely coincides with God's Universal Purpose for my life. In fact, it backfires. Spectacularly.

In December of 1998, I heard the news that the next Parliament of the World's Religions would be held in Cape Town, South Africa, in December 1999. The Parliament is a gathering of religious leaders, which is held every five years for the purposes of dialogue and global inter-faith peace work. The 1999 Parliament was going to be the first year in which the New Thought movement would be recognized as an official world religion and Rev. Dr. Michael Beckwith had been invited to be our global New Thought representative, as well as to present the former President of South Africa, Nelson Mandela, with the Ghandi-King Peace Prize.
Oh, how I longed to go to the Parliament, to be in Cape Town again and to witness Rev. Michael on stage with Nelson Mandela! It would be a magnificent reconciliation of both my

worlds in South Africa and America, the perfect cornerstone in my vision, the culmination of all my hopes and dreams.
But I discounted the idea.
I was too attached to America and would not risk being refused re-entry after a reckless trip to Cape Town.
Regardless of my little human preferences to stay put in America, Something Huge had already been set in motion but it was outside the range of my awareness. In other words, God was scheming again behind my back.

One of the projects at Agape that drew me was the 1999 *Season for Nonviolence*, created to honour two of the world's great peace activists who were both assassinated: Mahatma Ghandi and Martin Luther King, Jr. The *Season* begins on 30th January on the anniversary of Ghandi's death in 1948, and it ends on 4th April, the anniversary of King's death in 1968. Eisha Mason, RScP (Religious Science Practitioner) initiated and organised the annual three-month *Season* on behalf of Agape to examine and heal the violence within ourselves, within our city and upon our planet.

In January 1999, shortly before the official beginning of the *Season*, we were invited to a weekend workshop at Rev. James Lawson's church, Holman United Methodist Church, in South Central Los Angeles. What a privilege it was to meet and be taught by Rev. James Lawson. He had actually marched with Dr. Martin Luther King, Jr. during the Civil Rights movement of the 1960s and was part of King's intimate circle of confidantes and strategists. Our homework on Saturday night was to read *The Letter from the Birmingham Jail* written by King when he was jailed for his Civil Rights activism.

True to form, I got home late and only started my homework at about 11:30 p.m. almost falling asleep over the page. As I began reading, intending to simply skim over the material so that I would be familiar with the basic content for the next day,

something happened that I have never experienced before or since: my consciousness was split down the middle.
To the right of me and slightly above my head, I heard the voice of Dr. Martin Luther King Jr. reading the letter to me in his southern American drawl. I had never heard any recordings of him speaking but I knew immediately and intuitively that it was him.
To the left of me was my human consciousness reading the letter for homework.
I could move between both dimensions at will. I was startled when I heard the Voice, and fascinated that I could switch it on and off voluntarily, depending on where I chose to focus my attention. The Voice was compelling and yet I flipped back and forth between belief and unbelief. Was this really happening? How did it come about?
The Voice moved me. It got under my skin. I began to shake and cry. I could not continue reading. There was a cement mixer in my gut and in the midst of the churning I heard what seemed like a different Voice inside me say:

"It's time to go home now."

Martin Luther King had been speaking to me from the field outside my body. This Voice, which was telling me to go home, came from my centre, my gut. I knew what it meant:
"Go back to South Africa, start the ministry, Green Card or no Green Card, like it or not."
I was in awe, in fear, in trembling. Without feeling any sadness, my body got taken over by loud unrelenting sobbing.
This thing that was happening to me was too big to keep to myself. I had to tell someone. But who? Who do you call at midnight on Saturday, who will be happy to talk to you, who will understand the enormity of the experience and who will not judge you as an attention-seeking religious drama queen?

Rev. Carole Traylor (deceased 2007) was my woman. Rev. Carole was an African priestess living in flimsy disguise as the Youth and Family Minister at Agape, a teacher at the Holmes Institute and also my personal spiritual counsellor. I knew there was a God when she picked up the phone. I do not remember what I said or what she said. The important thing was that she was there as a witness. She believed me. She made the experience real. I slept peacefully, knowing I would follow the Voice, come what may.

The next day, Sunday, right before Day 2 of the workshop started, I was standing in the queue for coffee in the Holman Church, thinking that I would tell Rev. Dr. Michael Beckwith about my experience. In that moment, I turned around and, miraculously, there he was right behind me in the queue! Without so much as a "Hi," he abruptly asked:
"Stephanie, when are you going back to South Africa?"
"I don't know exactly." I replied. "But I had my call from Dr. Martin Luther King last night."
"Yes," he said knowingly as if he had been there.
Then he walked away, and left the church. He did not come back for the rest of the day. It looked as if he had simply touched down for a moment to get the confirmation of something he had already intuited.

Later that day, when the workshop had finished, I raced the forty miles over to the Santa Anita church, where I had completed my first ministerial training, in order to attend the Memorial Service for Dr. Roger Stevens who had been a teacher of mine at Ministerial School. Dr. Margaret Stevens, the former Minister of Santa Anita, who had interviewed me in South Africa in 1989, had flown down from Ashland, Oregon, especially to officiate at the Memorial Service for her ex-husband.

I felt such gratitude to the Santa Anita community. The members had embraced me when I first came out from South Africa even

though most of them had not understood a word I said, divided as we are by our common language....
After the service, many old friends came up to me and asked: "When are you going back to South Africa?"
It was a simple enough question, but I had never been able to answer it properly until that very day.
"In December," I replied confidently.

A plan had already begun formulating itself in my mind over the course of that day: I would fly back to South Africa in December 1999, and attend the Parliament of the Worlds' Religions in Cape Town just the way I had wished it. After the Parliament, at the beginning of the New Millennium, in January 2000, I would go back up to Johannesburg to start my multi-racial ministry.

God's timing, not mine.

Chapter 15

The Windows of Heaven

Bring all the tithes into my storehouse.... and I will open the windows of heaven for you and pour out blessings for you until you shall say, It is enough.

Malachi 3:10

Give, and it will be given unto you; good measure shaken down and running over they will pour into your robe. For with the measure that you measure, it will be measured to you.

Luke 6:38

Interpretation
Both of these verses are about the abundant generosity of God but God is not to be understood as a power outside of ourselves. The Spirit is within. Giving and receiving are one and the same thing. This might not be an easy concept to grasp because our conditioned thought tends to project power outside of ourselves and make the outside world the source of our experience including our financial supply or lack of it.
In each Bible verse above, it is clear that we have to give something before we can receive this abundant flow. In the act of giving (without thinking of getting a reward), we open up the conduits that we are for the power of the universe to flow through us and show up as abundant supply in our world of experience. Giving a part of our good back to the source of our spiritual food (tithing), and sharing our good generously, unleashes the Inner Storehouse of Abundance.

Note: "They will pour into your robe" refers to the ancient tradition amongst the Middle Easterners of wearing long, wide and loose robes which they would lift up to create a container. Then the things they could not carry in their hands could be poured into this fold in their robe.

My Story
After Martin Luther King Jr.'s "call" in January, 1999, I began asking friends and colleagues in the Agape Community to help me vision for my South African ministry.

Let me briefly explain here the difference between "Visioning" and "Visualisation."
Visioning is a term coined by Rev. Dr. Michael Beckwith to describe an inner process in which an individual or a group meditates on a particular question, project or idea for approximately 30 – 45 minutes. After the silent process, the group members share their revelations and insights. Usually

someone takes notes so that there is something to refer back to when the vision starts to manifest in the physical realm. In the visioning process, we open up, in a surrendered way, for the Divine Idea to be revealed to us.
Visualisation is more prescriptive than visioning. The individual or the group deliberately imagines what they would like to manifest and experience. They consciously paint the mental pictures of their desired outcome, they imagine hearing the words and feeling the feelings that are directly associated with the result in the physical world that they are attempting to achieve.

At the end of the monthly visioning sessions for the new ministry in South Africa, when each group member shared what they had received from Spirit, the consistent message was that the ministry was already successfully established, that the right people would be there, that I would be guided and protected, that I would get help and that I was not alone. That was all very well but my private reaction was:
"Hrmph! Fine for them to say!"
But they were right and I truly *was* being carried.

I remember, just before our final exams at Ministerial School, Rev. Carole Traylor, my teacher, asked me:
"Do you feel ready to graduate?" To which I replied:
"It does not matter whether I feel ready or not. I have the sense that an invisible gate has opened and I am being moved through it. I feel like I am being lifted up on a tide of energy and all I can do is ride it."
I must have been feeling the way women feel when they are birthing. To resist would not only have been mad but impossible. And so it was that 1999 became the year of my "pregnancy." There were just over nine months from the time of my "call" until the date of my departure from California, which was set for November 11, 1999. I was giving birth to a vision and I moved into high-level action.

The Parliament of World Religions was still accepting proposals for lectures and workshops. Two of mine were included in the programme: "The Art of Creating Ritual" and "Compassionate Communication." One of my students at Agape, Michal Golan, with whom I had had a special bond, also had two proposals accepted which was wonderful. It meant we would be in Cape Town together.

More unexpected support came from Marshall Rosenberg, a global teacher of Nonviolent Communication. I had approached him at the end of a Nonviolent Communication (NVC) workshop at Agape in March of that year and told him of my vision for South Africa. I asked him for support to get some NVC training so that I could facilitate conflict resolution sessions between blacks and whites. He immediately offered me a scholarship to participate in his 10-day NVC training at Glenivy Hotsprings, California, in the coming June. I was delighted. And then he offered to give me another scholarship to cover accommodation and meals. All I had to do was get myself there. Bless you, Marshall. You were ahead of your time. Your training was something that prepared me for the challenging dynamics with my South African congregation in a way that no academic courses could ever have done.

As a result of my energy and attention being devoted to my big move, my Practitioner Counselling business and my income really suffered. By September, I was limiting myself to two meals per day. It was all I could afford. I had no idea how I was going to pay for the airfare from Los Angeles to Cape Town or for shipping my possessions across the world, let alone the start-up costs of a new ministry.

Fortunately, in late September, I was able to secure a nearly-impossible-to-get counselling appointment with Rev. Dr. Michael Beckwith. He advised me to live, breathe and speak about my vision in order to get others enrolled. He cautioned me that requests for money to pay for running costs, e.g. the church's light bills, inspire no-one; people wanted to know how my vision would make a difference on the planet and how they could make a difference by contributing funds and resources to that vision. He informed me that there are very few people in the world who are in a position to follow the Spirit and head up a visionary project like mine. Nevertheless, those who cannot be leaders but who still want to be a part of a grand vision, can contribute by donating funds.

Only because I was desperate, I took Rev. Michael's advice. I went straight home from the session and started writing. I produced letters to potential supporters; I started talking to friends and acquaintances about the possibility of an interracial ministry in South Africa that would heal the wounds of Apartheid. I got myself fired up and then offers of assistance started flooding in.

Agape friends, students and clients were magnificent. One organised a make-up artist and a photo-shoot for me so that I would have a professional headshot for a 3-fold brochure I wanted to create, outlining my vision. As I was driving home from the photo shoot, I was stressing because I did not know who was going to write the copy or do the graphics for this brochure. Then I caught myself and I shifted gears in my mind. I started to affirm, "The perfect copy-writer and graphic artist are within me now!" When I got home, there was a message on my answering machine from my friend, Wendy Taylor, offering to help me with any copy-writing I needed for my promotional literature. Her talented new business partner would help me with the graphic design.

On 3rd October, 1999, one of my dear friends, Feliza, organised my first fundraising event at Agape. There was a huge turnout. When I walked into the sacred space that had been prepared for the event to see a host of angels smiling at me and loving me, people who had been a part of my life during my ten years in America, I felt as if I had stepped across the threshold of Heaven.

Rev. Nirvana Gayle led a sacred ceremony with music and prayer and uplifting words to massage me through the birth canal into fully fledged ministry. Rev. Dr. Michael Beckwith spoke a blessing over me and donated $1,000.00 on behalf of Agape. Then the floodgates opened. The guests at the event were exceptionally generous with their funds and their prayers. $3000 were raised. That event was the transition into being completely visible in my commitment.
No more hiding.
No more playing small.
No going back.

As the time for my departure drew nearer, I attended one of my last Wednesday night services at Agape. Before I left my flat that evening, I had a strong hunch that I should change my clothes. I was "told" to wear a particular grey dress that had very large pockets. When I got to Agape, Rev. Dr. Michael invited me to address the congregation at the end of the service. So I sat in the front row near the stage and when the service was over Rev. Dr. Michael introduced me to the congregation and told them I would soon be going back to South Africa to start a multi-racial ministry. He asked me to come on to the stage and share my vision. Before I began to speak though, he made it clear that everybody was welcome to come up afterwards and meet me personally and offer me their support, financial or otherwise.
My short speech was loudly applauded and suddenly there was a long queue of people in front of me, each one hugging me and "pouring into my robe" so that the pockets in my dress literally overflowed with dollar bills.

Support kept pouring in. One of my fellow students at ministerial school, Rev. Marsha Megdadpour used to work for American Airlines and she organised a free ticket for me to London where I would change planes for Cape Town. Great - I was half way home!

My practitioner colleagues, clients, students and friends organised huge fund raising events for me. (Thank you Adoley Odunton RScP, Taffy Wallace RScP, Rev. Nancy Zala, Deborah, Feliza, Mark, Roo and Robin for all the organising. And thank you to Lynn Rose and Brenda Lee Eager for inspiring the guests with your singing.) The dollars were rolling in from my Agape friends and from others I knew outside the Agape community. Many friends came to help me pack, all wanting to share in the unfolding of this vision. This was no normal pregnancy. I felt as if I was carrying the Holy Grail inside me, protected and moved by Spirit.

Finally the day came, 11/11/1999 – deliberately booked, 11 being the number of initiation. A precious group of dear friends came to midwife me through the birthing canal - the departure gate at Los Angeles airport. We knew there was some finality about our kisses and hugs; I would not be let back into the U.S.A. for at least ten years and I might never see them again in this incarnation. But I could not cry. Horses ready to bolt don't cry. Adrenalin mixed with a compelling vision had been sustaining me with endless energy during those months of pregnancy since the January "call" and now it was finally time to fly – literally and figuratively.

Once on the plane, I found my seat and chatted to my neighbour while we waited for take-off. He was none other than Rev. Mvume Dandala, the black Methodist Bishop, who had performed the wedding ceremony for Nelson Mandela and his third wife, Graça Machel! It was a sign.
Then the air stewardess came round with a souvenir brooch of American Airlines—a pair of wings. Another sign.
After a long wait and no movement, we were told by the captain to disembark from the plane because of engine trouble. The airline ground stewardess who had checked my boarding card at the departure gate, was waiting to welcome us back into the lounge. Smiling, she commented on the number of friends who

were seeing me off. She had been touched to witness how much they loved me. When my friends heard that there was engine trouble, they had told her:
"Either the plane will be OK or else there will be a replacement, but no plane carrying Rev. Steph will be going down!"

Indeed, we did get another plane to fly us to London where, after three weeks of reconnecting with U.K. family and friends, I boarded my next flight for the last leg of the journey home to South Africa. As the plane circled above the city of Cape Town before landing, I had tears in my eyes, moved by the beauty of the mountains, the two oceans that converged at Cape Point, the intense light of the early morning sun, and by the power of Spirit that had brought me back to live my mission.

When I got off the plane, shaking with emotion, I kissed the African ground.

Part 7

SOUTH AFRICA:
Post Apartheid
1999-2005

Chapter 16

The Heavenly Treasure

19. Do not lay up for yourselves treasures buried in the ground,
a place where rust and moth destroy and where thieves break through and steal.
20. But lay up for yourselves a treasure in heaven,
where neither rust nor moth destroys and where thieves do not break through and steal.

Matthew 6:19-20

Interpretation

What are your treasures? What do you value - people, things or qualities? In this Bible verse, the treasures buried in the ground are material treasures. The ground signifies the earth plane. Anything physical must ultimately die or disintegrate or change form. Similarly, anything that we use to try to build up our false human sense of self, e.g. a job title, a car, an address, qualifications, a beautiful body, a library full of spiritual books etc. will fail. These things are superficial, they are bound to the 3-dimensional world of change.

The heavenly treasures are the infinite qualities of Spirit: Love, Humility, Wisdom, etc. We can cultivate these qualities and no-one can take them from us. If we make the choice to pray without ceasing *(Pray without ceasing. Ref.: Thessalonians 5:17),* as the Master Jesus advised us, to bless others, to be grateful, to fill our minds and hearts with uplifting thoughts, words and ideas, to build character, rather than be comfortable or be popular, we are ultimately wealthier from the spiritual perspective. This sense of spiritual wealth converts into enough of everything we need to live and flourish on earth as we already are living in Heaven. *(Thy kingdom come. Thy will be done, as in heaven so on earth. Ref.: Matthew 6:10.)*

My Story

Returning to the new South Africa, after ten years away in the U.S.A., was a culture shock of proportions that I had not expected.

Under Apartheid, I had felt safe most of the time. As you know, I had even done strange or risky things that most white people would never have dreamed of doing, such as:

- riding on the black buses;
- hitching around Johannesburg and accepting lifts from black men;
- meeting black friends in public;

- inviting black friends to my home;
- teaching in a school for black students;
- driving into the Soweto township with black friends to visit them in their home.

On these trips into Soweto, I had to keep my head down in my friends' car as soon as we crossed the boundary line between the white northern suburbs and the township. This was to protect my black friends. If I had been seen by their neighbours, my friends ran the risk of being persecuted by the township vigilantes for fraternising with the enemy.

However, now that Apartheid was officially over, and the new national government (the ANC) was in power, it seemed that the law of the African Jungle prevailed.

I had never imagined that there would be a black president in my lifetime and that the transition would be so peaceful. Nelson Mandela had been elected President in April, 1994, and did his best to right the tragic wrongs of Apartheid during his five years in office. Archbishop Desmond Tutu had set up the Truth and Reconciliation Commission in 1996 so that restitution could be made for the crimes committed by white people towards black people under Apartheid and so that the white perpetrators could request amnesty. What neither of these great statesmen could overcome was the crushing poverty of the masses of black people, coupled with widespread AIDS, starvation, lack of education, unemployment, inadequate health care and shelter. Pervading all the social problems was the deeply embedded anger and hostility of blacks towards whites and the fear and contempt which whites felt in relationship to blacks.

Naturally, now that the pendulum had swung in the opposite direction, the black people who had been so abused and exploited by Apartheid wanted to have some justice, but on their terms. If I had walked in their shoes, I am sure I would have thought and felt the same, but as it happens, I took on a white skin in this incarnation. I belonged to the nation of oppressors during Apartheid and after ten years away in America, I returned to the Beloved Country to find myself crying as a member of its unbeloveds.

As I flew to Cape Town on December 1, 1999, in order to present my two workshops at the upcoming Parliament of the World's Religions, I got chatting to a fellow passenger who was on his way to visit his aging mother. He was originally from South Africa but had chosen to emigrate to Canada along with hundreds of other wealthy, white, professional people during the "brain-drain" of the Apartheid years. They all suspected that eventually the lid would blow off the political pressure cooker and the forty million black people would rise up against their four million white oppressors and give them a blood bath.

Witnessing my exuberance at returning "home" and realising that my naivety was going to make me extremely vulnerable, my fellow passenger warned me:

- Never carry cash;
- Always use credit cards;
- Keep your card in your pocket;
- Don't carry a handbag;
- Don't wear expensive jewellery;
- Lock your car and keep your windows up;
- Never leave your car with anything on the back seat;
- Don't put your handbag on the passenger seat - put it by your feet while you drive;
- Don't go out at night if you can avoid it.

The excitement I had felt turned to terror. Suddenly I was paranoid about being out on the street by myself even in broad daylight. I had been used to the nights being out of bounds during Apartheid but not the days as well.

Only two suitcases did not show up on the luggage belt after our plane landed in Cape Town. One was mine. The other was my fellow passenger's. He was not even slightly fazed; he had often experienced missing luggage on his frequent flights from Vancouver to Cape Town and he was confident that our cases would arrive the next day.

My fellow passenger showed me the way to the Lost Luggage office where we filled out the necessary claim forms and then offered me a ride to my hotel in his rental car. He did not want to leave me to the mercy of the taxi drivers at the airport. Who knew what would happen to me if I got in a taxi alone, especially as I was wearing my bum bag around my waist, thereby advertising that I had valuables inside?
"Surely," I argued, "no-one would try to take this off me? It is close to my body. It would be hard to steal without me noticing, wouldn't it?"
Cynically, my fellow passenger reminded me:
"Your life doesn't matter in the new South Africa. You could easily be knocked unconscious or killed for that bumbag."

Like a docile pet, I followed him to the car rental agency and waited while he picked up the keys. We drove around for ninety minutes trying to find my hotel, which gave me plenty of time to share my vision of my multiracial ministry. My fellow passenger asked me about my religion. He had never heard of Religious Science or New Thought. What did I believe about God and Jesus, heaven and hell? I shared freely. When I said that I did not believe that hell existed as a place that we go to after death, his listening skills took a back seat and he girded up his loins for a spiritual battle - and a sexual victory. *(Gird up now thy loins like a man. Ref.: Job 38:3.)*

My fellow traveller was a born-again Christian and, as I later found out, he felt it was his duty to save me. During that 90-minute journey, while he had been deliberately leading me astray in order to keep me in the car, he had begun to concoct a devilish plan to seduce me and convert me to his beliefs in the process. (Note: as a minister, it is important to know your audience before holding forth.)

Eventually we "found" my hotel, but the receptionist would not let me into my room until after 2 p.m. Aaagh, it was only 11 a.m. I was exhausted after the overnight flight, no sleep, the inconvenience of the lost luggage, the detailed warnings about the dangers of life in the new South Africa, the recent religious battle in the car, the long search for the hotel and the African sun that was burning through the winter clothes I had been wearing in icy cold London the day before.

There was only one thing for this dilemma... Lunch.

We found a restaurant and over food, my fellow passenger suggested taking me shopping for clothes. By this time I had realised that I was not going to be able to manage a simple shopping trip to downtown Cape Town, tired and unstreet-wise as I was. I let my fellow passenger take charge.

First we drove out to his accommodation in the Tokai forest, a self-catering cottage where he checked in. Then he took me to a local mall that was fairly small and where he knew his way around, thus lessening the dangers. While he shopped for groceries in the Food Department of Woolworths, I headed for Ladies Clothing. Under the watchful eye of the store security guards standing by every clothes rail, I found some smart black shoes, a lightweight pale-green jacket and skirt, a black camisole, some underwear, toiletries and make-up.

Shopping completed, my fellow passenger invited me back to his cottage in the forest "for a cup of tea," he said. It was on the way back to my hotel.

"Yes. Okay," I said, remembering from my childhood in Britain that a cup of tea had the power to cure all ills and heal any adverse situation.

Colonially, we sat at the table outside his cottage to take some afternoon Earl Grey tea while we listened to the breeze rustle

through the trees of the forest. After a couple of sips, I impulsively lay down on the earth, wanting to reconnect with the South African soil, to smell the land, to feel the pulse in the heart of Mama Africa. My host watched and smiled, his devious plan unfolding nicely. He enjoyed me enjoying the earth as well as the spontaneous random weirdness of my life (this was not what I had imagined for my first day back in South Africa, but it had its own charm,) and he spontaneously lay down on the grass with me.
Reader, do you know this Rumi poem? It captures the moment...

Out beyond ideas of wrongdoing and rightdoing,
there is a field. I'll meet you there.
When the soul lies down in that grass,
the world is too full to talk about.
Ideas, language, even the phrase each other
doesn't make any sense.

(Excerpt from Soul, Heart, and Body One Morning,
by Jalal Al-Din Rumi, translated by Coleman Barks.)

My fellow passenger invited me out to dinner. He offered to take me back to my hotel first where I could shower and change or, alternatively, I could shower and change at his place and he would take me back to my hotel after dinner. I was hungry and chose the second option.

Well, in case you had not seen it coming, his cunning plan worked and he had his wicked way with me. And in case you are shocked at my lack of ministerial morals, may I reassure you that we did, at least, have dinner first.
The following night, to make it fair, I had my wicked way with him.
Now that the issue of morality has raised its head, we should penetrate the subject more deeply before continuing with the story.
In Ministerial School, our teacher of Ethics, Rev. Charles Rose, was very clear about the acceptable standard of moral behaviour

once we had become qualified ministers. He stated unequivocally that if we wanted to be sexually active, then we had to choose partners who were at least 50 miles (80 km) away from our church community or else get married. Another teacher in Ministerial School put it more bluntly: on no account were we to "f*** the flock!"
Considering that my fellow passenger lived thousands of miles away in Vancouver, I could satisfy myself that I was strictly adhering to the moral code. So you can see that I was not sinning – well, except perhaps for being a tad smug.

Did my fellow passenger fulfil his Christian duty and save me from the sin of my non-traditional religious beliefs? No, but he did his best with the "tools" he had available and, as outlined above, there was really nothing to save me from. "Sinners" have to feel guilty about sinning and desire salvation before they can be saved. I did not feel at all guilty about the "missionary position" I found myself in and even if I had, I do not believe that anyone can save me from myself. It is an inside job.

The following day, my fellow passenger kindly dropped me off at the registration desk of the Parliament of World Religions. We had arranged that we would stay together for the few days that he was still in Cape Town and he had also asked me to join him when he came back to South Africa in February, 2000. More about that later....

The Parliament Programme included a comprehensive list of warnings about how to protect myself from violence and theft in the new South Africa. The list reinforced everything my fellow passenger had told me about and there were even more warnings about taxis and ATM machines. Fortunately, there was very tight security around the world's religious leaders at the Parliament. This meant that I could relax and feel safe inside the various buildings where the lectures and workshops were being held. Any potential danger at the Parliament would be more likely to come from the friction between certain religious groups, particularly the Jews and the Muslims, in such close proximity to one another, rather than from any lingering hostilities towards whites in post-Apartheid South Africa.

Half way through the 8-day Parliament, I took a taxi out to Cape Town airport to meet a South African friend who was arriving from the U.S.A. I asked the taxi driver how life was for him now that Apartheid was over and how he felt about white people. He was a "Cape Coloured." The Cape Coloureds belong neither to the blacks nor the whites, but are a unique race of people whose origins stem back 400 years to the time when the European sailors first started coming to South Africa and fraternizing with the indigenous black women. The European settlers, predominantly the Afrikaners from Holland and the British, also fraternised with the slaves who were brought to South Africa on slave ships from the Dutch East Indies (present day Indonesia). Their offspring became known as the "Cape Malays."

My taxi driver shared that his life was much better now and that Mandela was an example for him. He asserted that if Mandela could forgive the white prison guards on Robben Island and all the other government officials who had persecuted him, then he, a humble taxi driver, had no excuse. Wow! I was impressed. He meant it. He was clearly trying to live his life along spiritual lines. I wanted to believe he was the rule. Sadly, as it turned out, he was the exception.

When I finally arrived in Johannesburg in January, 2000, I moved into my sister's home and stayed with her and her family for four months. There I saw adverts on TV warning the public to watch out for crime at the ATM machines. Every person I met had a personal story of a violent crime. In an attempt to warn me of the dangers, as well as process their traumatic memories, my family and friends overwhelmed me with horrifying stories about their experiences at the hands of desperate black people:

- My sister's home had been robbed;
- My 10-year-old nephew had had a gun held to his head and been tied up;
- My 5-year old niece had been threatened at gun-point;
- One friend had been car-jacked as she was entering her driveway;
- Another friend was robbed in a mall car park by a thief who had been hiding under her car while she shopped;
- Yet another friend had been gang-raped in her home and been left for dead.

In my ten years away, the white South Africans, (and increasingly the wealthy black South Africans), had become gradually used to increasing and random violence. They were calloused and they were alert. In contrast, I was full of idealism, remembering that I had always had a good relationship with black Africans in the Apartheid years, remembering that my friends in Los Angeles were black and I had had no qualms about going to visit them in the "hood" of South Central Los Angeles even late at night. At Agape mixed-race relationships were very common. There I had seen what was possible between people who were joined in a common spiritual intent; skin colour simply did not feature. In South Africa, colour determines everything - at least everything that pertains to our human lives.

One Saturday afternoon, just a few weeks after getting back to Johannesburg, Jack, a former student of Rev. Gladys' whom I had serendipitously been introduced to via a friend of a friend, was driving me home from a meeting and I asked him to come with me to the ATM because I had to withdraw a large sum of money and I felt too vulnerable on my own. I was afraid of being robbed but I believed that if he were there looking out for me, I would feel safe. Jack agreed and decided to take me to Rosebank Mall.

Reader, Rosebank Mall is in the former white northern suburbs of Johannesburg. I used to work in the office building across the street from the Mall during the days of Apartheid. Since 1994, more and more black people have moved into the area as their wealth has increased and they are no longer subjected to living in poor conditions, characteristic of the Johannesburg townships, Soweto and Alexandra.

Jack thought that it would be safer to use an ATM inside the mall rather than outside on the street. Having parked the car and located the ATM machines in the mall, Jack stood behind the painted line on the floor, a respectful distance away from the ATM machine, from where he could see me while I got my U.S. Bank of America card out and began making my two transactions.

Suddenly two young black men, very shabbily dressed, were standing either side of me. They were telling me the machine was not working. It was not true but they were trying to confuse and distract me. They had already seen me type in my pin. They managed to take my card and run off. Jack *had not even noticed* even though he had been there all the time! Such was the thieves' deft brilliance. The mall security guard on duty was nowhere to be seen, but that was not surprising - he could have been in a syndicate with the thieves. It happened in a split second and with such finesse that no-one even realised anything was wrong. By the time I had figured out what had happened and put a call through to the Bank of America in the U.S.A. to block my card, it was too late. Within minutes, the two men had raced over to another mall and had used the card to withdraw 1,000 rands, (approximately £100 or $150 in U.S. dollars in the year 2000). They then went on to use my card to eat out at restaurants, buy furniture etc. This was in the days when forging the signature on the back of the card was all that was required to make a purchase. Thankfully, all their further attempts to withdraw cash at the ATMs were blocked.

I arrived home at my sister's feeling shocked and violated. But I had to accept that I had been so afraid of someone stealing my money at the ATM that I had actually manifested the very thing I feared, even though I had tried to protect myself by asking my male friend, Jack, to accompany me. The Law works on the unseen levels and always responds exactly according to belief. Furthermore, the Law works regardless of the protective measures we put in place on the outer levels to guard against the consequences of our fear.

My friends told me to be grateful that it was only money that had been stolen and that I should consider myself lucky that I had not been the target of a violent crime. After all, people they knew had been murdered for an ATM card or a cell phone.

I was, indeed, grateful that I had not been harmed, but more grateful that I had been given such a clear message about the power of my thoughts so that I could be more vigilant at the doors of my mind. I blessed the thieves for stealing my card. They had acted out my belief perfectly for me to see. And I still had my treasure in Heaven. I had the capacity to think new thoughts and choose where I placed the focus of my attention. In short, I still had my consciousness, the Spirit within that cannot be hurt, harmed or endangered. This is the inner treasure that no-one can touch.

Interesting Footnote:

My fellow passenger and I met up again during his next trip to South Africa in February, 2000, during which time we decided not to pursue our romantic relationship. However, he begged me, as a friend, to lend him my large tote bag for his extra luggage, promising to return it on his next trip. Reluctantly, I agreed. It was a special gift from a dear friend when I left Los Angeles and I sensed that I would not see it again. The Law works and I proved myself right as you will see.

Almost two years later, in December, 2001, I was at Heathrow Airport in London waiting for the train to Terminal 3 for my

onward flight to Egypt where I would spend a few days before returning to Johannesburg.
What was I doing in the U.K.?
Well, my father had just died and I had flown back to London to lead his memorial service and then sort out his possessions and sell his flat. From London I made a spontaneous decision to fly to Amsterdam for a few days to visit friends while I was in Europe. I arrived in Holland with two huge suitcases, full of personal items belonging to my dad. When I checked in at Amsterdam airport for the return flight, I prayed quietly for this burden of heavy unwieldy luggage to be removed from me. At the check-in counter, I asked if my luggage could be sent through to Cairo directly even though I had to change planes in London. Sadly this was not possible because of separate ticket bookings. I surrendered to the imagined task of picking up my luggage at Heathrow, pushing it for miles through underground passages to the relevant terminal and checking it in again for the flight to Cairo.
Three hours later, there I was at the Heathrow luggage carousel waiting, waiting, waiting for my two huge cases. After thirty minutes, my name was called out and I was told to report to the Lost Luggage Department. There I was informed that my luggage would be on the next flight and would be sent directly to Cairo for me. Ah, right, prayer had been answered. Spirit had lifted the burden from me.

As I stood on the platform at Heathrow, I mused about the last time my luggage had not arrived with me on the same flight. It was that flight to Cape Town in December, 1999, when I had first met my fellow passenger. Then I started wondering,
"What happened to that tote bag of mine? I need to get hold of my fellow passenger and I can't remember where I put his address...."

Just then the train pulled up. And who should get off the train where I was standing? Yes, my fellow passenger, of course! Can you believe it? If he had been sitting in a different carriage or if I had been standing in a different place on the platform, we might never have even noticed one another.

As if it were the most natural thing in the world for us to meet, he asked me where I was flying to and when.
"Cairo," I told him and gave him my departure time.
He was flying to Vancouver. He calculated that we both had at least a couple of hours before check-in and he invited me to lunch before my flight to Egypt. I accepted and with that, he gallantly picked up my "hand luggage" consisting of a small but extremely heavy back pack and a large, extremely heavy shoulder-bag and he strode ahead in the direction of lunch. As I walked with him to the restaurant, carrying my bum-bag around my waist, the only item of luggage that was left to me, I realised with a smile that Spirit had answered my prayers to perfection.

In contrast to how deeply impressed I was with Spirit, I was not at all impressed with my fellow-passenger's rather pathetic story about why he had not been able to return my tote bag to me. Of course, he renewed his promise to bring it to me in Johannesburg but I never saw him or the bag again. The bag was an earthly treasure I had to let go of. And the fellow passenger? Let's pray for him that his god saves him from the sin of seducing more ministers as well as "borrowing" their tote bags under false pretences.

Chapter 17

The Early Church of the New Millennium

And I will bring the blind by a way that they knew not,
I will lead them in paths that they have not known:
I will make darkness light before them, and crooked things straight.
These things will I do unto them, and not forsake them.

Isaiah 42:16

Interpretation

This verse seems to be about God leading us on our life journey when our physical vision is limited and we have no previous memory of the road we are on, or when we are struggling in the dark and have obstacles to overcome. It is bad enough that we cannot see and it is dark, but added to that, even the path is crooked so we cannot confidently put one foot in front of the other and expect to reach our destination. The Spirit leads us safely on and clears the path ahead of us.

Let us, however, interpret this verse metaphysically as a metaphor for the journey inwards.

"Blind" means "those who cannot discern the Spirit."

"Paths they have not known..." means "the inward journey that cannot be figured out by the intellect or remembered from previous experience." The inner path is through stillness and quiet rather than the busy mental and physical activity of our human experience.

The "darkness" means our ignorance of spiritual truths and the spiritual nature of our being.

The "light" means the dawning of awareness, which occurs when we contemplate the things of the Spirit.

The "crooked places" are the old beliefs we have been conditioned with that act as obstacles to our journey - maybe pride or fear, or mental concepts that would hold us imprisoned in our false identity of humanhood.

On this journey, the Spirit eternally accompanies us. We are forever surrounded by this Presence of pure energy that responds to our thought. Our sacred intention to know God brings us both inner sight and eternal light and we are guided, governed, directed and protected.

My Story

How in Heaven does one start a church? Goddess knows because I certainly did not.

The first week of being back in Africa was intense, hot, dangerous and filled with overwhelming images of crushing poverty, side by side with extreme wealth, against a backdrop of raw and exquisite beauty. This was "home" and yet everything was unfamiliar. I felt lost and anxious and wandered through the Parliament in a state of spiritual shock.

Thankfully, there were some amazing highlights which interrupted the Committee of Terrorists in my head. These included delivering my two workshops and participating in profound meetings and joyful celebrations as all the religions of the world came together in one accord to celebrate the human spirit.

One of the profound meetings was on 5th December, when I met Ahmed Kathrada, a former prisoner on Robben Island and a close friend of Nelson Mandela during the years of incarceration there. The Island had recently been declared a World Heritage Site as well as a Peace Site. Ahmed had been chosen to accept the Peace Pole in a special ceremony. As part of its programme, the Parliament had arranged a boat trip to Robben Island for delegates to ceremonially plant the Peace Pole along with Mr. Kathrada.
So very early in the morning, we gathered shivering at the V&A Waterfront ferry point and took the 30-minute boat ride across very choppy waters to the Island. Looking back at the silhouette of Table Mountain overshadowing Cape Town Harbour in the early morning mist, I tried to put myself in Mandela's shoes when he was taken to the Island for the first time. He had been given a life sentence. He could not have known then that, one day, he would not only be released but also become the first black President of South Africa. Or did he always have a sense of a great destiny?

Ahmed addressed the crowds, urging us to think of Robben Island as a place where the human spirit was victorious over the forces of evil rather than a place of suffering. After the ceremony, we were taken on a guided tour of the Island and also around the prison, culminating with a visit to Mandela's former cell. That tiny cell, where Mandela slept on the concrete floor for eighteen years, put my fears into perspective. Really, what did I have to worry about?

Later in the week, I had the thrill of seeing Mandela make a special guest appearance during the Parliament. Mandela was truly a living legend. When he walked on the stage, people spontaneously rose up from their seats as if attached to the strings of a giant puppeteer, and broke into loud cheering and thunderous applause for what seemed like many minutes. Mandela stood there smiling, letting it all in. He asked us not to take flash photography as his vision had been damaged by long years of working in the limestone quarries of Robben Island where there was no shield from the intense glare of the African sun as it sizzled blindingly on the white rocks.

After Mandela's speech, I watched my beloved minister, Rev. Dr. Michael Beckwith, present him with the Ghandi-King award, just like I had wished, dreamed and intended exactly a year before when I believed there was no possibility of my being there to witness this grand event.

So you see, on the outside, it was all good. But I was left with the constant question:

"Steph, what in Heaven's name have you done?"

As I sat drowning in doubts and recriminations, God sent me Michael, a young man who had read *Conversations with God* by Neale Donald Walsch and was so inspired by it that he had stepped up as the representative for *Conversations with God* (abbreviated here to CWG) in South Africa. His work was to coordinate the fledgling groups that wanted to start up by putting CWG fans in touch with each other. We agreed to meet up when we were both back in Johannesburg and talk about starting a CWG group together. Great, so I had one tiny connection.

Lucille Kent Lückhoff in Cape Town

As I mentioned, Michal Golan had been one of my students in practitioner classes at Agape who had also been accepted as a workshop facilitator at the Parliament. After her workshop, one of the participants, a beautiful middle-aged woman with green eyes and shoulder length grey hair, approached us both and invited us to stay at her guesthouse in Rondebosch, a suburb of Cape Town. Her name was Lucille Kent Lückhoff. We refused her invitation because we were already booked to stay in a local youth hostel for two nights after the Parliament was over. We both automatically assumed that she was touting for business. I found out much later that this was the furthest thing from her mind.

The Parliament finished. The Agape crowd went back to California leaving Michal and me to explore the Cape together for a couple of days before she, too, returned to Los Angeles. Michal refused to drive stick shift on the left hand side of the road and, alluding to the fact that I was born in Britain and was, therefore, already trained, handed me the keys to our small rental car. Goddess bless Michal. She helped me make the psychological transition from being completely surrounded and upheld by the Agape community to being completely, alone in South Africa and having to now start my own community AND drive on the left hand side of the road.

Interesting Footnote:

Michal and I lost touch from the time she left South Africa in December 1999 until the Sulha of August 2007 an annual nonviolent conflict resolution gathering between Jews, Palestinians and Christians held in Israel. The event was hosted by my friends on the Inter-Faith leadership committee in the Holy Land and took place on the grounds of a Trappist monastery on the outskirts of Jerusalem.

One evening, during the musical entertainment, I was dancing under the stars amongst friends of all religions and nationalities, feeling supremely connected to the Universe, when I turned around and who should I see dancing behind me but Michal! She smiled knowingly as though it was the most normal thing on earth for us to meet up in Israel after an eight-year gap.

The Cape Town angels sent me some comfort to ease the transition in the form of Avril, my previous landlady in Johannesburg and tenant in Los Angeles. I looked her up online and discovered she had moved to Cape Town and opened the Cape Town Music Academy. We were able to reconnect and share our journeys. Avril had left Science of Mind and become a traditional Christian which I found fascinating. Our strong friendship remained unaltered and she whole-heartedly supported my mission to start a Religious Science Church.

Then there was Milly Churchill. She had been a Science of Mind student at the Port Elizabeth A.C.T. (Association for Creative Thought) Centre with Dr. June Jones and then moved to Cape Town and joined a spiritual community called the *Emissaries of Divine Light*. I had dated her ex-husband for a while in Johannesburg in 1988 and he had put us in touch with each other because he thought we would get along. He was right. We became good friends all those years ago and, through a young man I met fleetingly at the Parliament who was connected with the Emissaries, I got Milly's telephone number and we were able to reconnect. She even hosted me for a few days in her home at Fish Hoek Beach where the sea, the sand, the salty air and Milly's kind and humble heart helped me to re-ground in South Africa.

A few days later, my sister and her husband arrived in Cape Town with my niece and nephew. We met up in Hout Bay where they had rented a holiday home. Thank Goddess for the kids and the perfect distraction they created for me. Rael was 10 and Sandra was 5. They happily let me devote myself full time to being an auntie and to making up for the ten lost years of auntiehood while I had been studying in America.

A few days before Christmas, my sister and I were shopping in Claremont, a suburb of Cape Town with a large mall. Suddenly I saw someone walking in front of me whom I recognized. Well, actually, I recognised her striking long blonde hair. I stopped her and said,

"I know you!"

She turned around, took one look at me and said:

"Yes, you're Stephanie. I am Marcia. You went to live in America. We did not think we would ever see you in South Africa again."

Bless Marcia for her superior memory.

Marcia and had I met towards the end of my time in Johannesburg in 1988. People in the local metaphysical circle had been telling us that we needed to meet long before our paths crossed. When we did finally meet, we proved them right. We became fast and firm friends but in the days pre-email and Skype, we had had no contact during my 10-year absence in America. Marcia was delighted that I was back in South Africa and excited about my plans to start a ministry. She gave me her number and invited me over after we got back to Johannesburg.

A few days later, one of my practitioner clients from Los Angeles, Mel, showed up to celebrate her 40th birthday in Cape Town. An American friend of hers who was studying in Cape Town organised for her to stay in a centrally located guesthouse called *Ivydene* in Rondebosch. At the time, I was staying about 25 minutes drive away from the centre with my family in Hout Bay. Mel invited me to come and spend New Year's Eve with her. She said the guesthouse owner was "cool" (American for "laid-back, flexible, accepting, kind, generous and understanding") and did not mind if I stayed the night.

Ivydene, being such a mystical place, was not easy to find. It is located in a quiet suburb at the end of a private road and, if you do not know it is there, you would never see it or be able to find it. The guesthouse is actually a charming 100-year old, sprawling,

Old Cape farmhouse which has been turned into a number of guest flats as well as private living accommodation for the owner. However, it is a dimension apart.
I arrived at 11:45 p.m. Mel and I meditated and prayed as the clock struck midnight and the new Millennium was birthed. Then we fell asleep, respectful of each other's space on the opposite sides of her huge king-size bed in the Mountain Flat at Ivydene.

On New Year's Day, the "cool" guesthouse owner knocked politely on the bedroom door and came in bringing breakfast on a laden tray, complete with a small vase of flowers. She and I recognized each other immediately! It was none other than Lucille Kent Lückhoff, the lady I had met at the Parliament after Michal's workshop!

Even though Lucille ran a business as a guesthouse owner, she confirmed that her offer of accommodation at the Parliament had been absolutely genuine, not a business proposition. She went on to say that it was her privilege to host monks and other spiritual leaders who were attending the Parliament and not to charge them if they did not have the means. Michal and I had turned her down, never suspecting that Lucille meant for us to be the recipients of her generosity. Clearly though, Lucille and I were supposed to meet and Spirit organised Plan B on New Year's Day 2000 with the kind assistance of my former client, Mel.

By this time it was about 9:30 a.m. on 1st January, 2000 and, since I could feel a workshop coming on, I invited Lucille, Lucille's friend and Mel to participate in my *Happy New You* workshop which I have been running every year since 1985. Amazingly, all three ladies were available and keen so we created sacred space in the Mountain Flat and sat around the table there to reflect on 1999 and set our intentions for 2000. Lucille really appreciated the workshop and afterwards she said to me:

"I want you to know that you always have a home here in Cape Town at Ivydene."
That was a turning point for me. I could see that I was being taken care of and I started to feel not alone. Lucille has been true to her word ever since and always hosted me on my trips to the Mother City.

Return to Johannesburg
In the first week of January, 2000, my brother in law, Josh, drove the whole family from Cape Town back to Johannesburg, which was a long dry 1700 kilometres, mostly through the Karoo desert. Once the Johannesburg skyline came into view, my heart leapt and then sank. Accusatorily, I reminded myself that I did not know how to start a church. Of course, we had had a course on *Your First Ministry* plus another course on *Church Management* at Ministerial School. We were given instruction on how to do the C.E.O. part of our job, manage the Board, the finances, the church building, the volunteer teams, communications etc. etc. Regrettably, I was not paying attention. Those classes meant nothing to me at the time because I could not see myself in the role of a pulpit minister with a traditional church. Instead I clung to the fantasy that I would somehow come up with a valid alternative to church before I left America. But I didn't.

So, since I was making it all up from scratch, the first thing I thought of doing was to contact Rev. Gladys' daughter, Sally, to get the names and numbers of the former members of the Church of Religious Science in Johannesburg. She kindly provided me with about 43 names. I worked down the list of phone numbers, reconnected with old friends and introduced myself to people whom I had not met before I left in 1989.

At the same time, I looked up old friends who were not connected with Science of Mind. From these two groups of people, I picked a handful and asked them to vision with me for the new ministry. They agreed. The only problem was, they lived in far-flung parts of the city and we needed a central place to meet. Marcia provided the solution and generously offered her home near Hyde Park even though she was not available on our visioning meeting nights to vision with us.

Then, fortuitously, through a friend of a friend, I met Jack (my ATM security guard in the previous chapter) and his wife, Maggie, a Scottish couple who had been Rev. Gladys' last private students from the time she closed her church in 1995 until her death in 1998. (Sally knew of them, but did not have their phone numbers or addresses because they had not been members of the church.) They had continued their study group and had turned it into a weekly mastermind group so that they could manifest, among other things, greater financial wealth.

Jack and Maggie invited me to come and meet them at their Saturday morning Mastermind Group and give them an introduction to the ministry I was starting. Happily, I accepted and experienced my first failure. I am not sure what their expectations were but it was clear to me that I did not fulfil them. I was not a younger version of Rev. Gladys and I was not going to be carrying on where Rev. Gladys left off. She and I were completely different despite the fact that we represented the same teaching. In any case, they did not ask me back but a few of them did come to the classes and groups that I later established.

Jack and Maggie were firm believers in tithing as a means of growing a prosperity consciousness and they continued to support my spiritual work financially even after they left South Africa and emigrated back to the U.K. Thank you very much, Jack and Maggie, for all your kindness.

Michael, from the *Conversations with God* group, and I often met for coffee during my first few weeks back in Johannesburg. With his support, I designed and started my own six-week CWG group. CWG was enormously popular in South Africa at this time and I decided to use it as my spring-board to reach those interested in the non-traditional approach to spirituality.

Ernest Holmes and the Science of Mind were little-known concepts in South Africa in those days. Louise Hay had done a lot to popularise the teaching. Her books were widely available in the Central News Agency (CNA), a South African chain of stationery-and-book stores. Yet, hardly anyone knew that Louise Hay was a Religious Science minister, just like me, and that she was teaching Science of Mind in all her writings. Most people thought it was her own teaching, whereas she was simply a very successful mouthpiece/scribe for the Science of Mind principles and had a special gift for making the teaching relevant and applicable to our modern lives.

The only drawback with the CWG group was that I did not know where to run it. My friends in Johannesburg all knew I was looking for a space to rent and on the same day, three different people told me about the Masonic Hall, which was just around the corner from my sister's house in Parktown North. I could take a hint!

Renting the Masonic Hall

I inquired. The hall was available. There was a large hall in the front of the building and a smaller hall in the back. The smaller hall had a long narrow adjoining area with a small kitchen and long tables with benches where we could have fellowship after the meetings. It was very reasonably priced and the two care-takers doubled up as guards for the parked cars during services and classes.

In early February, 2000, we started our six-week CWG course. The word had gone out and more than twenty people came to the first session! They loved having a forum to meet with like minds. I told them that I did not have a fixed idea of what ministry had to look like in South Africa; I wanted it to be something that would serve the people. Did they want to do Sunday services in the traditional way? Or did they want to have a service at a different time in the week? Did they want to have a service at all? Yes, they did and they preferred Sundays.

Sacred Gathering at Claire Dalton's

My three-month tourist visa in South Africa was going to expire at the end of February, 2000. I would have to leave South Africa and then re-enter to get another three-month visa. Where would I go? My grandmother provided my answer; she made her transition in the U.K. and I flew back to be with my dad and my sister and attend Grandma's memorial service.

Before I left for the U.K., I sent my first official mailing to the people on Rev. Gladys' list, sharing with them about my vision for the ministry in South Africa and inviting them to come and transmute the energy of the old ministry under Rev. Gladys and set the tone for the new one with me. The first official gathering was scheduled for March 12, 2000. It would be held at Claire Dalton's beautiful farm/seminar centre in Zwartkops near Muldersdrift, about a 45-minute drive from downtown Johannesburg.

Do you know how I met Claire? When I first visited South Africa in 1985, mum had introduced me to her next-door neighbours: "Toni the Greek" and "Hildegard the German." Mum and Toni used to meet at the local bus-stop each morning and take the same bus to work in downtown Johannesburg which was the Central Business District during the days of Apartheid.

Before I arrived on holiday, mum warned Toni that I was "a little bit different" and that I enjoyed spiritual pursuits. Toni said he had a colleague called Claire who was "a little bit different" too and always talking about spiritual stuff. He thought Claire and I should meet and he would try to arrange it. However, he was too slow. I started attending Rev. Gladys Harrison's church in January 1986 and it was there that I met Claire Dalton and her husband, Bazil.

By the time I came back to South Africa in 1999, Claire, bless her, had been widowed. She was being squeezed out of her huge property by the Spirit (although it looked like a financial downturn) and was on the brink of moving down to Cape Town to start her own healing practice. She offered to host my gathering when we first reconnected on the phone. It turned out that 12th March was her very last day on the property and on 13th March she left for Cape Town. Thank you, Claire. I hope we blessed the land that you loved so much.

The day dawned full of anticipation. A dear friend, Laurette, with whom I had shared the *Firewalk* experience in 1989 right before I left for the USA, picked me up and, together with Claire, we three created the sacred space with an altar, flowers, candles and incense.

As I stood outside the entrance watching my guests walking down the path towards me from the parking area, I felt a massive lump in my throat. This was it. It was happening. I had called. They had answered. It sounds corny but I felt like a shepherd with my sheep returning home. I had not seen these people for over ten years; I did not know that I would ever see them again when I left for America. What I would be offering was very different to what Rev. Gladys had presented. How would they respond to my new-fangled American ideas? I need not have been concerned as the Spirit took over when we gathered in prayer. They responded beautifully, fully engaging in the rituals to release the past and bringing their wise contribution to bear on the formation of the new work. When they read the Vision Statement I had created in America for the South African ministry, they suggested that I change the word “Apartheid” to “separation” and the word “inter-racial” to “multicultural.” These were two very expansive changes which I welcomed.

When the name for our community, *Soul Home*, came to us a little further down the line, we incorporated it in the Vision Statement as follows:

Vision Statement

Soul Home is a multicultural spiritual community where all traditions and religious viewpoints are honoured and included. This ministry is a sacred space where the wounds of separation are consciously addressed and healed. Soul Home is a prototype for harmony and spiritual partnership in South Africa and the world through the teaching of universal spiritual principles and the practice of nonviolence, forgiveness and compassion.

When the ceremony finished we had a most joyful fellowship with lovely strands of connection being rethreaded after ten or more years of being apart. Nearly everyone had gone their separate ways when Rev. Gladys' church was closed and they were all delighted about the opportunity to reconnect.

Ze and Zoo Lake Sessions

Only one person showed up whom I did not recognise, Ze. A friend had told her about the gathering. Said friend did not even come. Said friend did not explain to Ze that it was only for people who had been a part of Rev. Gladys' ministry. Ze participated fully despite the fact that she did not know what was going on.

At the end of the afternoon, Ze asked me if she could come to me for counselling. Of course, what an honour! But where would we work together? We could not work in my brother-in-law's Jewish home where I was staying. I did not have a car and could not drive to her home. Where then? How about the park at Zoo Lake? Yes, we could sit there and pray together.

So Ze picked me up and we found a seat near the Lake in a fairly secluded spot, which is an advantage for prayer, but makes you a bit vulnerable if anyone wants to come up and attack you and steal your handbag while you have your eyes closed. Hmm, we stepped out on faith. Nothing happened. We were safe.

Ze came regularly and responded to the prayers. She gave up her failing business and moved back into work she was passionate about - language teaching. She started clearing up her life and became one of the most loyal members of the congregation, eventually steering her nephew and then her son, Mark, to me to perform their respective wedding ceremonies.

Easter Sunday

23rd April, 2000, the first Easter Sunday of the New Millennium, was the date for my first-ever proper church service. On the Saturday evening before, Rev. Gladys' daughter, Sally, and her husband, Kevin, came over to help me set up the hall. I had two other little helpers too - my young Jewish niece and nephew were very curious about Auntie Steph's activities and asked their parents if they could come and help me. Surprisingly, my sister and brother-in-law consented. The children helped me carry in bunches of flowers, altar items, CDs, coffee, tea, milk, sugar and biscuits. Kevin tested the sound equipment and while the rest of us set up the chairs in a circle, I played Agape Choir CDs.

Sally gave me a thick blue cloth that Rev. Gladys had used for the altar in the old church of Religious Science, plus the original heart shaped basket that we always used for the offering. My eyes were moist as I decorated the altar, now covered in the blue cloth, with symbols of all the major world religions. I could not help remembering the early days in Apartheid Johannesburg and my vision to start a multi-racial ministry. Here I was, doing it. It was a profound moment.

The new day dawned and I was awakened early by Spirit to prepare myself inwardly and add the finishing touches to the ceremony that I had planned. I wanted the service to be meaningful and to give whomever showed up their own experience of the death of the ego-self and the resurrection of their inner Spirit. There was to be very little sermonising and plenty of meditation, music and guided processes. And so that I could disabuse people of their old concepts of "minister," I naturally wore a very bright pink mini-skirt suit with lips and nails to match, plus black stiletto heels and, of course, black stockings!

Thirty people attended. Thirty people! Amazing. As well as putting the word out at my CWG group, I had advertised the event in *Link Up* magazine, the very same publication, in which fourteen years previously I had found the advertisement for Rev. Gladys' church, then known as *The Abundant Living Centre*. Twenty-five members of that pioneer congregation were white and five were black. They all participated equally and chatted easily with one another afterwards over tea. Joy and gratitude suffused the whole event. It was a total success. Best of all, they wanted more. They wanted regular Sacred Gatherings and spiritual community—just like me.

After I had packed up and paid the car guards, I drove back to my sister's home feeling completely deflated, empty and alone. Adrenalin had stopped pumping and the high was over. I had made no plans for my life after the service because I simply could not think that far ahead. So, there was no-one to have lunch with, no-one to do the post mortem with, no-one to get feedback from. Just me, feeling sorry for myself and hitting an anti-climax of note. My sister's house seemed empty when I came through the front door, but then I heard music coming from Rael's bedroom.

I should tell you that Rael was born with Prader Willi disease, which means he is "lower functioning" and constantly hungry. The fate of many Prader Willi sufferers is to die of obesity in their mid-thirties. Rael and I had always had a special soul connection. He has a huge heart, a brilliant sense of humour and an intuition that astounds me.

On that Easter Sunday, Rael was sitting by his desk with the autumn sun streaming in through the window behind him. Next to him there was a small round table, covered in a cloth, upon which he had placed a jam jar containing some rather droopy flowers from the garden and some china ornaments. He was listening to a radio station playing religious music.

"What are you up to, Rael?" I asked, to which my dear Jewish nephew replied, as if it were obvious:

"I am having church, Auntie Steph."

Chapter 18

The Enemy Is Within

.... A man's enemies are the members of his own household.

Micah 7:6

Interpretation

This saying is mostly interpreted to mean that your family members or the people you live with are your enemies. This is strange because they are the ones you are closest to, the ones you would least suspect. To understand the metaphysical meaning, however, change the word "household" to the word "consciousness." This means that our enemies are all within us.

Who or what are our enemies then, if not people per se? Metaphysically speaking, our enemies are our

- fearful thoughts;
- negative thoughts;
- attacking thoughts;
- victim thoughts;
- resentments;
- prejudices;
- old encrusted attitudes and opinions;
- long-nurtured conflicts;
- bad memories;
- the seven deadly sins.

It is difficult to see the content of our consciousness on the internal invisible level, but if we are out of alignment spiritually, our negative thoughts will certainly show up as people who are seemingly operating against us, or as conditions appearing as unfavourable. As soon as we take responsibility for the unconscious beliefs that appear to be manifesting so-called "enemies" in our lives then we have the power to make changes and get free of the trap of victimization. You see, these "enemies" are essentially actors in the plays that you and I are directing on the stage called our life. They are reading their lines and playing their part perfectly in the script *we unconsciously wrote*. Our job is to rewrite the script consciously which causes our enemies to either disappear or appear to change.

My Story

When I returned to Johannesburg in January, 2000 and contacted Rev. Gladys' daughter, Sally, I learned that Rev. Gladys had retired from full-time ministerial work in 1995, and had died peacefully in her sleep in November, 1998. Her transition was just two short months before I got my "call" in January, 1999, at which time I tried to phone her from Los Angeles to share the happy news that I was finally coming back to South Africa to serve as a fully qualified United Church of Religious Science Novitiate Minister. This was exactly what Rev. Gladys had intended for me eleven years previously. But when her phone kept ringing and no-one picked up, I "knew" deep down that she had left her body and "gone home" to the spiritual realm. And from her elevated perspective beyond the body, I suspect she already knew that I was on my way home too - home to the Beloved Country....

Rev. Gladys

From my earlier story, you might have been misled into thinking that Rev. Gladys and I were still enemies when she died. I am delighted to reassure you that this was not the case. Yes, it is true that we did not see each other again after I left for America but I did write to her when I graduated as a minister at Santa Anita and she wrote back, congratulating me on my achievement.

A few years later, in March 1998, I was about to enter my final term at the United Church of Religious Science Ministerial School, Holmes Institute at Agape, and I had no money to pay my debts to the School, nor my tuition fees. Graduation and licensing expenses would be due in May but they could wait. At the 11th hour, the evening before the deadline for registration, I was desperate and, in my desperation, I got humble enough to reach out to Rev. Gladys. I knew if anyone could wreak a miracle with a Spiritual Mind Treatment, she was the One.

When I called Rev. Gladys from Los Angeles in March, 1998, miraculously she picked up the phone. Squirming spiritually, I

told her about my situation and why I needed prayer. She was as deprecatingly blunt as ever:
"You sound very confused, dear." she said. "You just have to get clear on what you want and everything you need will manifest."
Duh!
Why didn't I know that?

Poor Rev. Gladys could not believe that I was about to graduate as a Religious Science minister and still had not got my financial act together. Nevertheless, turning aside from the human condition of lack and fuzziness, she prayed to know the Truth about me spiritually and about the completion of my ministerial studies. And that was the last time we spoke in this dimension.

I went to bed feeling like a worm in the dust. *(They shall lie down in the dust, and the worms shall cover them. Ref.: Job 21:26.)*
The next morning, the day of the deadline (or "dreadline"?), I remembered a lovely African-American woman whom I had "coincidentally" sat next to in the dining room at an Asilomar Religious Science Retreat on the Californian coast a few years earlier. When I shared my vision with her of a multi-racial ministry in South Africa, she told me that she believed in what I was doing and invited me to call on her for support, financial or otherwise, whenever I needed it. So I called on her a few days before my registration deadline but she did not respond. I gave up. On the morning of the deadline, the Voice said,
"Try her again."
No answer.
I left a message.
And gave up again, irritated with that stupid Voice.

But then a miracle occurred. She called me back, apologising for not responding sooner. She explained that she had recently moved from the Mid-West to California and only rarely checked her answering machine at her old address. But on that very day, she "happened" to check! She said "Yes" to my request right away. It was a matter of about US$1,500.00. Since it was already late in the day, she offered to liaise on my behalf with Rev. Nirvana Gayle, who was the Dean of Holmes Institute at Agape at that time. Rev. Nirvana was willing to let me register for the new term and wait a few days for my benefactor's cheque to clear. Phew!

When the time came to pay my graduation and licensing fees, I got humble again and called my mum in South Africa to ask if she could help me. Very generously, she agreed to pay the whole amount as a 40th birthday present.
Thank you, Mum.
And thank you, Rev. Gladys.

The Former Congregation

Of the 43 names on Rev. Gladys' contact list who had belonged to the 1st Church of United Religious Science in Johannesburg during the 1990s, only five were willing to join me in the creation of a new ministry. Of these precious five, three were my personal friends! That was fine with me. I did not take it personally. We had been taught about this particular syndrome in Ministerial School whereby, even if the exiting minister had been a crabby demonic fascist and the new minister an angel of mercy, the old congregation would have still been loyal to their former minister and judged the new minister to hell. Rev. Gladys was not a crabby demonic fascist; I was not an angel of mercy, but the congregation knew their loyalties. Many of them belonged to the older generation of white South Africans and were not bubbling over with enthusiasm about a multi-racial ministry.
Over their dead bodies, actually.

Oh well, my spiritual teacher in Los Angeles, Zuriel, assured me it was a good sign when the potential flock started running a mile in the opposite direction:
"The Christ within is not neutral," he warned me. "Once you start preaching the Truth, people will either love you or hate you."

He got that right!

My very own rebellious nature

As you will have no doubt noticed, I was always keen to disabuse people of the notion that female ministers have to be unfeminine or asexual. My thinking was:

"Why not make myself attractive? Why not use the Law of Attraction to the hilt?"

So, interpreting and using the Law as effectively as I could humanly, I always made sure that I wore something attractive at Sunday gatherings; perhaps some flamboyant African priestess gear complete with turban or else a business suit with a mini-skirt or else a top showing an eensy-weensy bit of cleavage. I would never wear a mini-skirt and show cleavage at the same time. Obviously, that would have been smutty....

Usually women constitute the larger percentage of a congregation in a New Thought church and so, to attract the men, mini-skirts were my divinely inspired idea. I knew that while the men were looking at my legs, Spirit would be doing a number on their consciousness. In fact, one former Catholic Priest who started attending my Sunday services commented as he shook my hand upon leaving the church:

"Reverend, I am sure that your sermon this morning was very interesting but by the time I had stopped looking at your legs, you had also stopped talking and I realised that I had not heard a word!"

I lost a lot of weight after I returned to South Africa and was amazed when I went clothes shopping one winter's day in July and found that I was able to fit into a very tight, black, leather pants suit. The pants were tapered to the ankles and the jacket was shaped into the waist and did up with a full length zip. It was definitely not designed for biking, more for attracting. The black high heels I wore with it added to the allure. The vibrant red

lipstick played its part too. Look, I did not buy this suit with a Sunday Service in mind but then I got to thinking:
"Why not?"

So I wore it. The congregation were agog but most of them loved it, except for Steve's wife, that is.
Steve was a tall, middle-aged man who had been attending regularly since I started my Sunday Gatherings. He was a wonderful person with a great sense of humour and always keen to participate in our Sunday conversations about God. It saddened him that he could not share his spiritual pursuits with his wife. She did not mind Steve attending church without her but she was anti all forms of church and organised religion. Steve must have persuaded her though, because one Sunday in August, she came to Soul Home for the first time. It happened to be the very Sunday that I decided to wear my leather suit. Oh dear. Steve's wife was stony-faced all through the service. Steve looked awkward and embarrassed and did not speak up when I asked my audience for input on the theme that morning. After the service, Steve and his wife hurriedly disappeared and I never saw either of them again. It was a sad loss and a wake-up call for me. I learned that if my public image detracts from the spiritual message or conflicts with it, then I am not serving in the highest way. Needless to say, I never wore my leather suit in church again. The mini-skirts, however, were de rigueur.

My Mother and Stepfather

The other "enemies" I encountered were my family members. My mother and my stepfather could not fathom how I would support myself without a regular stream of income from an employer. They thought I should "stop messing about with this religious stuff" and get a proper job. Of course, they were worried that I would fall flat on my face and come to them begging for alms. *(And they recognized that he was the beggar who had sat daily and asked alms at the gate which is called Beautiful. Ref.: Acts 3:10.)* They perfectly articulated my ever-present fears of failure, particularly financial, in my mission. My fears dissipated, however, as soon as I began the work of focusing my attention on serving my spiritual community. The funds flowed and I never had to beg my stepfather for a sub or a loan or an alm.

My Sister and Brother-in-Law

My sister, Hannah, who had also immigrated to South Africa in the early 1980s, soon after my mother, converted to Reform Judaism so that she and her boyfriend, Josh, could marry and have a family. After ten years of marriage, they had decided to convert to Orthodox Judaism and were busy preparing for that next step when I arrived from America.

My Jewish brother-in-law, Josh, generously agreed to let me stay in the family home with him, my sister and their two children, two dogs, two cats and a parakeet until I re-settled myself in Johannesburg and found my own place to live. This was truly a generous gift and, I only understood much later, what a grave conflict it had been for my brother-in-law to have a "Christian" minister in his household who was starting her ministry under his roof. The entire family's standing in the local Jewish community could definitely have been tarnished.

To make matters worse, I religiously, but insensitively, wore my huge ankh around my neck all the time. It was my only piece of jewellery. To me, it symbolized the Divine Power of the Pharaohs. To Josh it was a cruel reminder of how the Egyptians had enslaved the Israelites before Moses led his people to the Promised Land. I took it off for the Friday night Shabbat dinners in my family's home once I realised what a hateful symbol it was for Josh. It cannot, however, have been easy for him to see me wearing it every day while I laid the foundations for my church in South Africa.

We were all relieved when I found my own cottage nearby and moved out. Still, I admire Josh for his principles. He put his family before his religion and that was both a brave and generous act.

Was Josh an enemy? Not really. In fact, he was a stellar example of how the principle of love can transcend religious differences. But he did symbolise my beliefs in the lack of understanding between the world's religions and my fears of public suspicion and misunderstanding towards my "unorthodox" New Thought teaching.

Technology

My other enemy was "technology" or, rather, my belief that technology was against me. My laptop had worked perfectly when I bought it in the U.S.A. When I got to South Africa, I could not get online for the first nine months with that laptop! The accursed machine was pulled apart by various technicians at various costs. Finally, after my new friend, Karen, a Joel Goldsmith student, reminded me that the true connection was within, i.e. with God and not with the world wide web or the Internet, I let go. I prayerfully set about the business of getting connected on the inside with my own indwelling Spirit. How do I do that? I have to turn aside from the outer problems and realise that there is only One Power and I am naturally in constant communion with It since It is Who I am. My intention was to get conscious of that communion by putting my attention on It instead of on my problems. Immediately after I began the work of going within, one of my friendly technicians had the divinely inspired realisation that the modem was faulty. He replaced the modem and Hey Presto! Rev. Steph was finally online.

The Department of Home Affairs

Another enemy was the Department of Home Affairs, specifically the Immigration Department. This government body was the perfect reflection of my old belief that "I am an alien." My residence permit that I had had under Apartheid had expired and I had no right to live or work in South Africa when I returned in 1999.

A friend of my mother's knew someone at the local passport office in Edenvale who would help me get a new residence permit. I met her in January, 2000, and we started the application. It was a long wait while the wheels of the bureaucracy turned and my status was checked in the immigration archives.

Finally a government letter arrived a few months later on September 7, 2000. That very evening I was due to start teaching my first ever three-month Science of Mind Foundations course in South Africa. I had fourteen students registered. Eagerly I opened the letter but was horrified to read that my status as an illegal alien had been verified and I needed to leave the country within the next two weeks! The letter went on to threaten that if I was still in South Africa after that time, I could be arrested. I was advised that if I wanted to submit my application for permanent residence, then I would have to do it outside South Africa—a process that would take a minimum of eighteen months which really meant "a very long indefinite period."

I prayed. I knew I had not been brought this far to get stopped. I stepped out on faith and taught the first class of the Science of Mind course that evening, electing not to tell my students that I might only be there for the first two weeks of the three-month course.

In answer to my prayer, a new American friend in Johannesburg referred me to an immigration consultant who had helped him get his residence status in South Africa. God bless Julie! She was a dyed-in-the-wool Afrikaner and a committed Christian who had worked in the Immigration Department before the change of government in 1994. When she realised that all the jobs the white people had held would now be going to black people, and when she saw the inefficiency and the corruption creeping in, she left the Department of Home Affairs at the age of 59 and began an independent consultancy. She had friends in High

Places, i.e. God and His Heavenly Host, as well as ex-colleagues in the Immigration Department. And what a formidable team that was!

Julie was committed to getting my status sorted. Even though our teachings were wildly different, she embraced my mission to start a church in South Africa and had the inspired idea to get my old permanent resident status reinstated.

"The process should only take three months," she said confidently. Plus, I did not have to leave the country to apply. We only had to prove that I had never left South Africa for good, but solely to study in America because there was no ministerial school in South Africa. Since it was the truth, it was easy to prove. We set about getting letters from my teachers and associates in the U.S.A. who could vouch for me, and from friends in South Africa who had been part of Rev. Gladys' ministry and who knew my vision.

We submitted it all and waited. Three months passed, then six. I had already successfully completed my first Science of Mind Foundations course. Word had spread and many more new students had already begun the second Foundations course.

Julie called the Department. They could not find my application. Would I resubmit the documents? We resubmitted. We waited. Months went by. Julie put in regular gentle reminders not wishing to irk anyone who might "accidentally" tear up my application and throw it in the bin.

Through her dear friend and ex-colleague at the Department, Julie found out who had the responsibility for my application. It was a young African and since we had not received any communication from him, Julie asked her friend to try to give us an update. Said friend found my application at the bottom of the pile on the young African's desk. She assumed that the first set of documents had been simply thrown in the bin. Other applicants, whose skin had more melatonin in it than mine, were on the top of the pile. Hmm....reverse racism?

On 14th June, two days before my 44th birthday and eighteen months since we had begun the process, I wrote in my diary that what I most wanted for my birthday was my residence status. And, in answer to my prayer, it was granted on that very day – only I had no knowledge of it. Why? The approval letter had been sent to the wrong office for collection and was only discovered two months' later in mid August! It was stamped "14th June." I can't help noticing that this entire process took eighteen months. Obviously, I had made a definite mental note about the expected time frame for processing based on what I was originally told about a Permanent Residence application. The only difference was that I had spent that eighteen months in South Africa instead of applying from overseas.

You can imagine how ecstatic I was to have the letter in my hands with a Department of Home Affairs' big blue and gold logo on the top and the signature of the Immigration Department official on the bottom. Julie was stern with me:
"This is not your residence permit," she cautioned me. "It is simply a letter authorizing your passport to be stamped with your real permit. But it is as precious as gold dust. You must lock it in your safe. A photocopy of the letter will not be considered valid."
OK, I got it. I should not lose this letter.

Julie advised me that to complete the process, I would have to go down to the Police Headquarters in Johannesburg city centre and get myself finger printed, photographed etc., and only then could I get the official stamp in my passport. Since there were only a few days left before a trip overseas to the Ukraine, and I was afraid of getting mugged or carjacked if I travelled alone to downtown Johannesburg, I decided to take the letter with me in my passport to show to the immigration officials when I landed back in South Africa. I would organise the stamp after my return.

Elizabeth, my cleaning lady

A couple of days went by. My cleaning lady, Elizabeth, came over to clean for me. The next day I started packing for my trip.
Where was my letter?
Surely I had left it on my desk amongst a pile of other papers that I needed for my trip?
Or had I put it in the filing cabinet with my other important documents?
Or had I misfiled it?
Had it slipped down between the files?
I hunted obsessively. I took every piece of paper out of every file, turned it over, checked twice before putting it back and then went through the entire process again.

No letter.

Only a year later, when I caught Elizabeth in the act of stealing one of my dresses, did I realise the fate of my leather jacket, my suede shoes *and* my immigration letter. She would have made thousands of rands for that document on the black market. It truly was gold dust for all those who were trying to enter South Africa illegally across the border from Zimbabwe. There was no photo. No gender was mentioned. Simply the words:

S. Clarke has been approved for residence status.
Elizabeth was the perfect embodiment of the common belief amongst many householders in the white communities in South Africa, that "all African maids steal." Clearly, I had unconsciously adopted this belief for myself so I had to prove it out in my experience. My apologies for my ignorance, Elizabeth. I wish you well.

Julie and I resubmitted all my documents with a letter explaining the theft. It took me another year to give up my belief that I was a victim of the new South African bureaucracy. Instead of waiting for the "powers that be" outside of myself to grant me approval, I had to come to terms with my own inalienable right to exist on earth. As soon as I acknowledged there was a right and a reason for me to be on the planet and a clear purpose for me to fulfil in South Africa, we received a signed copy of the approval letter. Finally, I had become grounded and a legal resident of planet Earth. My alien days were over.

Interesting Footnote:

Since all our enemies are within our own consciousness, once we change our internal false beliefs, those outer "enemies" disappear or transform.

After I let Elizabeth go, I asked around amongst my friends if they could recommend a trustworthy maid who could work for me one day a week. That is how I met Margaret. Margaret was a love, a tireless angel, joyful, willing, punctual and she always left a lovely atmosphere in the house at the end of a day's work. She cleaned with her whole soul.

I gave Margaret permission to play my CDs while she worked. Her favourite was Sade. On Tuesday mornings, I used to put Sade on for her when she arrived and often we would have a little dance and giggle together before we went about our business. I also used to greet her and say goodbye to her with a hug. This was a bit strange for her at first but gradually she began to welcome it. One day Margaret said to me:

"Madam, Tuesday is my favourite day of the week. When I come to work for you, I feel like I am entering the Kingdom of Heaven."

Thank you, Margaret, and bless you. But remember that you were the one who carried Heaven with you in your heart.

Chapter 19

Love Your Enemies

Love your enemies, bless anyone who curses you,
do good to anyone who hates you,
and pray for those who carry you away by force
and persecute you.

Matthew 5:44

Interpretation

In Moses' day, the "eye for an eye, tooth for a tooth" approach was commonly practised i.e. "Whatever is dealt out to you, make sure you do it back in the same measure." This is the selfish approach that, as Ghandi observed, would leave us all blind and toothless!

Jesus had a radically different approach to dealing with our enemies and it is the toughest lesson on loving that we will ever have to learn. It is easy to love the people whom you like and who agree with you but much harder to have compassion for the ones who seem to oppose you. Jesus wanted to protect us against judgement, revenge and retaliation towards our so-called enemies, knowing that that would only engender more of the same reaction towards us from the universe around us. The Law works like a boomerang, returning to the place from which it was sent out.

You and I are not required to approve of people who are actively hurting us. We do not have to condone violence or abuse in order to be spiritual. Our work is to behold the Divine in our attackers, to accept that everyone is seeking his or her good to the best of their ability and level of consciousness at any given time in their spiritual journey of development. If you had been born wearing your enemy's shoes, would you not be responding in exactly the same way right now? It is only through healing our relationships with others that we can end the sense of separation between ourselves and God. Remember, there is only One of us here.

My Story

The people who attended my Sacred Gatherings on Sundays in April and May, 2000, were mainly white. I prayed for a way to grow the ministry and attract black people in order to fulfil the vision for which I had been sent.

The answer to prayer came quickly when I was re-acquainted with Naledi Deane, a beautiful black woman from Soweto. She and I had been introduced briefly in Rev. Dr. Michael Beckwith's office during her visit to the U.S.A. a few years prior. For years, Naledi was one of the only two black women in South Africa who had received a licence as a Religious Science practitioner. She was, and is, a dynamo of love and power.
Naledi and I decided to create a special healing ceremony for Youth Day 2000 and began visioning together.

Youth Day is a public holiday in South Africa. It marks the anniversary of the uprising that occurred on 16th June, 1976, at a Soweto school. You might have seen the show or the movie, *Sarafina,* about the events on this pivotal day in South African history. The movie, based on Nelson Mandela's autobiography, *A Long Walk to Freedom*, also includes a short clip of the Soweto students' uprising.
On this particular winter's day in June, 1976, the students at this township school had reached the boiling point of their anger and were courageous enough to stand up and refuse to be taught in the language of their white oppressors—Afrikaans. They staged a peaceful demonstration whereby they started walking out of the school in protest. The white Afrikaner militia and police force were alerted and then rushed to the scene with their army tanks and guns and began shooting at the students in cold blood. Many young blacks died or fell to the ground wounded. The rest ran for their lives.

Under the white Afrikaner government, 16th June was acknowledged as Soweto Day but Mandela changed the name to Youth Day when he was elected President in order to honour the young people who had given up their lives in the noble fight against racism.

Naledi and I deliberated over where to hold this multi-racial event. If we had held it in the mainly white northern suburbs, the

black people would not have been able to afford the taxi fare from the township. If we had tried to hold it in the Soweto Township, the white people would not have come because it would have been perceived as too risky. Failing to find any neutral ground that would have been safe, affordable and within easy reach for all of us, we agreed to hold the event at the hall I rented for my Sunday services in the white suburbs of Parktown North. Naledi kindly offered to arrange transport for the participants from Soweto. She would invite family and friends who had cars and a small young peoples' choir. I would invite my fledgling congregation. It was an experiment.
Would it work?

As often happens at events such as these, the room is not packed with people but it is packed with the Spirit and feels full because the individuals who are there bring such an oceanic consciousness—willing to self-examine, willing to share vulnerably, willing to be transformed and let go of the past. Our Youth Day Sacred Gathering on 16th June, 2000, was an event such as this.

A few of the members of my congregation dared to follow me into the Unknown and showed up early to help me set up the sanctuary. Naledi arrived with her shy young peoples' choir. Everyone was cautious at first. This kind of gathering had never happened before in their previous experience where black people and white people had been so polarized.

Naledi and I welcomed everyone and said an opening prayer. The black choir sang for us, a moving African song and then Naledi and I asked for everyone to pair up with someone who had a different coloured skin. Once everybody had a partner, Naledi and I instructed the dyads to share their stories of 16th June, 1976—where they were, what they had been doing, how the experience of the day or the news of the day impacted them. The job of the person in the listening role was simply to listen and learn and extend compassion.

As the pairs began to share with each other, I noticed that one of the older women from Soweto was in tears as she told her story. I witnessed my white friend with her arms around her black sister, giving her comfort. In that moment of shared pain, they had become equals not enemies. This was unprecedented.

Naledi and I paired up so that we could participate yet still facilitate. Naledi allowed me to tell my story first.
I remembered that day clearly. Not because of what was happening in South Africa but because it was my 18th birthday, my symbolic coming of age and independence. I was in England, on the other side of the world, sitting in the gym at Rosebery Grammar School, Epsom, Surrey, taking my "A" level (final exam) in Latin. Poor me. Rosebery was a single sex girls' school. Very white-bred and famed for its academic excellence. Many of its pupils were the daughters of the wealthy elite of Great Britain. Could there have been a more opposite extreme from the school in the Soweto township?
Ironically, of the eight houses at Rosebery, all named after famous British people, the house I belonged to was Rhodes House. It was named after Cecil John Rhodes from whom Rhodesia took its name until the coup when it became known as "Zimbabwe." Even though the Afrikaner nation is infamous for legally establishing the Apartheid system, it was actually the British settlers and diamond speculators, under the magnate Sir Cecil Rhodes, who were responsible for the beginnings of separatist policies in 1872 by introducing the Pass Laws i.e. passes/identity documents were to become mandatory for the black and coloured workers so that the whites could control the movement of labour on the diamond mines.

Anyway, I clearly remember my "suffering" on 16th June, 1976; I was complaining to all who would listen because I was having to

do an exam on my birthday. Plus, my hay-fever was particularly bothersome on that English summer's day.
The events in South Africa did not even impinge slightly on my awareness. I did not watch the news on TV that night because I was undoubtedly cramming for the next day's "A" level exam. At that time in my life, I was consumed by my personal ambitions to get good grades and qualify for a place at the University of Oxford or Cambridge – the recognised pinnacle of English academic and social privilege.

On the other side of the world, in Soweto, Naledi had not been directly involved in the uprising at the school because she was already at college by this time, but she lived close by and was alarmed when she saw the tanks coming through the township and people being shot at randomly. She had just enough time to run home and hide under the table, praying the white police would not invade her home and find reason to shoot her.

"How did you get free of hatred for and fear of whites?" I asked. "Prayer," she answered. "I had to learn to find compassion in my heart for white people. I had to learn to see God in everyone – beyond their skin colour."

It is a testament to Naledi's spiritual commitment that she was willing to partner with me on the day of our ceremony and share her deep pain after I shared my experience of my ivory tower in Surrey and my ignorance of the suffering that was going on in the southern hemisphere. In her love for humanity, black and white, Naledi created the space for her friends and family to be there at our sacred event and to go deeper on their journey of healing too. Bless you, Naledi. You are a giant.

When the ceremony was over we broke bread together. In an atmosphere of intimacy, goodwill and curiosity, we feasted and celebrated together. The black people had the experience of sitting and eating at the same table as the white people and even being served by the white people. For some of the older black people, this was a little uncomfortable after being conditioned for years to be in a state of fear of, dependency on and servitude to the white bosses. Apartheid had been officially over for six years by this time but the mark of its branding iron would take many more years to fade.

A new community was built that day, a spiritual community, exactly as I had hoped and prayed for.
I love this line from the Course in Miracles:

The place where old wounds are healed becomes holy ground.

The vision that I had in 1987 of a racially integrated South Africa, with people of all colours praying and worshipping under one roof, was manifesting.

Chapter 20

Priestess of Sacred Ceremony

But as it is written,
The eye has not seen
and the ear has not heard
and the heart of man
has not conceived
the things which God has prepared
for those who love him.

1 Corinthians 2:9

Interpretation

This biblical verse reminds us that our physical eyesight, our physical hearing and our human heart will never have the capacity to conceive of the Good that is in store for those of us who love God. This is because, humanly, we function in the relative world of the five senses. Our attention is usually directed outward to where we experience our world according to the nature of our beliefs and sensory perceptions. Most humans have the experience of "not enough" when they are focused on the ever-changing outer world of effects. To compensate for the "not enoughness" of the human experience, many people tend to grasp, struggle, manipulate, lie and even steal to get their fill of their imagined "good." They can never, however, achieve satisfaction in the earthly domain.

People often say "I will believe it when I see it." Wayne Dyer, a well-known transformational author and speaker, wrote a book entitled *You'll See It When You Believe It.* He wanted to help us turn our consciousness around to focus on the inner planes of the Absolute, in order to experience life in a more joyous way. Through our five senses, we cannot grasp the full vision, sound and feeling of the Infinite Potential for Good that resides within us at our spiritual core.

God is not a person and, therefore, does not have a gender. although It includes both the Masculine and Feminine Principle. Loving "him" simply means that we consistently choose to devote our attention to the Invisible, Inaudible Spiritual Realm within rather than the outer world of effects. You and I can make a choice to put our attention on the inner dimensions of the All Good and the Infinite Possibilities for Wealth, Harmony, Love, Joy, Peace and Freedom. In the instant that we go within and become more convinced of the Reality of this Inner Realm as opposed to the seeming reality of the outer realm, there will be a shift in the direction of greater Good in our experience. And, as that Good is unlimited, the more attention we place on our

Indwelling Spirit, the more that Good can manifest Itself, revealing Itself through and as us, as a gift to ourselves and to the world.

My Story

Designing and facilitating Sacred Ceremony has been a passion of mine since I discovered its magic in 1991 with the help of Diana Kruschke, the wife of my former boss in the U.S.A., Doug. Together, Diana and Doug would often facilitate public rituals such as wedding ceremonies or memorials. They would also create rituals in their home to honour the change of the seasons, New Year's Eve or special events such as anniversaries.

With my scientifically superior left brain(!), I initially judged Diana to be a little strange with her love for ritual. Certainly, I could see no purpose to the empty rituals performed in churches but neither did I appreciate the transformative power of what she was trying to teach me, until I experienced it myself *in my own body*. Ritual involves the *whole* self in a creative, dynamic, energy field that leaves all involved changed forever. Thank Goddess, Diana remained persistent in exposing me to this sacred path of transformation and I remained open enough for the magic and the mystery to break through into my earthly consciousness. When I returned to South Africa as a new minister, rituals became a key component of my ministry.

Weddings

Symbolically, given my multicultural vision for my ministry, the first wedding ceremony I conducted was for a beautiful black couple who were yoga teachers. The groom came from Jamaica and the bride was part Indian from East Africa. On the evening of that very same day, I also officiated at a ceremony for a white couple. The bride was Afrikaans and the groom was Greek. After that many other soul-mate couples showed up at my front door to begin preparations for their wedding ceremony. Very few of

them were mainstream and by that I mean that they were from different religions or cultures or of different skin colours. It was always a privilege to witness the unconditional love that crossed social divides and to be able to guide and accompany these couples on their rite of passage from separation to Oneness.
There was one particular couple whose story I want to share with you here.

Bush Wedding

I was asked to perform a wedding for a couple who were both architects. The bride, Lisa, was a South African, with an Afrikaans background. The groom, Andreas, was a German immigrant. My first impression of them as a couple was not entirely positive. It was clear to see why they were so successful in their work; they were both very ambitious and competitive and very good at planning. In full work mode, both were extremely focused on the left-brain, logistical planning of the ceremony; organising the venue, the music, the altar and who would walk in from which side of the sacred space. It was challenging to get them to focus on the spiritual meaning of the ceremony and the life commitment they were about to enter. I was concerned that all that testosterone would not bode well for their intimate relationship. In hindsight I must admit that I am grateful for all the planning that went into the event, partly because there was no opportunity to do a rehearsal on-site and partly because ..... well, you will see why.

The couple flew me into the game reserve, where I was met at the landing strip and taken to the main lodge with its surrounding cottages. The bride and groom had hired a number of eight-seater game drive vehicles; green, mud-bespattered, open-topped land rovers, to transport the guests from the lodge to the wedding venue.
Everything was going to plan until a local leopard got an irresistible sniff of a local leopardess with whom he wanted to mate. Hot on the trail of the future mother of his cubs, the

leopard could not change his spots *(Just as a Hindu cannot change his skin or a leopard his spots... Ref.: Jeremiah 13:23)* and protect himself with his usual camouflaged cloak of invisibility. He was "spotted" when he dared to run right through the game lodge! Naturally, he had no appetite for human flesh in that moment but, the tourists and wedding guests did not know that. So they timidly stayed in their cottages, peeking through the net curtains, refusing to leave for the wedding venue with the leopard at large in the camp.

As soon as I arrived, the groom started herding the wedding guests onto the vehicles. He asked the safari drivers to move swiftly and to not stop to watch any game on the road. Meanwhile, the guests had a different agenda; the South Africans were keen to see the leopards mating from the safety of the vehicles and the groom's European guests were keen to see any game at all as this was their first safari experience.
The groom's mother, a German lady who had come from Switzerland for the wedding, made a point of sitting in the same vehicle as I did. She then announced loudly:
"Well, if anyone is going to see the leopards, it is going to be the metaphysical minister, so I am sticking close to her!"
I was deeply flattered that she had so much instant faith in my mating-leopard-manifestation abilities but, secretly, I set a firm intention to get to the wedding without delaying proceedings. I preferred to manifest the leopards after the wedding was over.

It was a 30-minute drive to the open-air bush "chapel" by the river, where everything had been prepared. However, on this occasion, the journey took 45 minutes as the Europeans insisted on taking photos of everything and kept asking the driver to slow down.
The vision that met us when we finally arrived was just like a scene from the movie, *Out of Africa*. Planted in the swaying yellow grass next to the trees on the bank of the river, were about ten game rangers, inconspicuous in their khaki uniforms,

standing in a huge circle around the chapel area. They were poised with their guns to scare off, and even kill, any uninvited guests of the four-legged, shaggy-mane variety. There was an altar table covered in a long white tablecloth, complete with candles in tall glass jars and a vase of roses and there were about 60 chairs, also draped in white cloth, set out in two sections facing the altar, with an aisle down the middle for the bride and groom to make their traditional entrance. Behind the guests, a friend was managing the music system, playing classical music while everyone waited for the bride.

Lisa arrived in a beribboned wedding car (no mud-bespattered vehicle for her on her special day), and when she stepped out looking ethereal in her long white dress and veil, the guests gasped in delight.

Considering the potential danger of a Bush Wedding, this one went off without a hitch. After the ceremony, the wedding party celebrated with champagne but I could not stay for that or for the dinner at the main lodge. I had to get back on the road to Johannesburg to conduct a Sunday Service the following morning.

One of the game rangers drove me to the entrance of the game reserve, where my rental car was waiting for me. And guess what we saw on the way.....? Well not exactly *mating* leopards - unfortunately, we had missed the Big Bang by a few seconds. But right there on the side of the road, in the long yellow grass, resting after extreme sexual exertion, lay the languid leopard and, a few feet away, his new missus in post-coital stupor. The male was so relaxed and satiated that he could not be bothered to run out of sight but rather preferred to conserve his strength for Round 17. The female was similarly resting in the aftermath of being waylaid. The ranger informed me that leopards mate many times per day during the mating season, with very little downtime.

Ironically, the purpose of a sacred wedding ceremony is to create the intimacy of a bedroom in which the guests can witness the unique love connection flowing back and forth between the bride and groom. And here we were, the ranger and I, as guests in the intimate domain of the leopards, privileged to be in their bush boudoir without fear. The male let us observe him admiringly, even allowing us to take photos as he observed us with his languorous emerald green eyes. It was a precious moment, suspended in time, of linking with that wildness eye to eye and without concern.

The light was fading fast by that time and I still had a three-hour drive through rural Africa in the pitch black night. Very reluctantly, the ranger and I left the couple to do what came naturally and pressed on towards the entrance and my waiting car. Both of us were in silent awe at the untamed majesty of those emerald eyes and felt privileged to have been permitted to share the intimate moment.

First Interesting Footnote:
In November 2010, when I was working in Europe and debating about whether I should try to book a ticket back to South Africa for Christmas and New Year, this same wedding couple contacted me. They had given birth to a baby girl, Sophia and asked me to do the Baby Blessing in their home near Pretoria. When I saw them with the baby, I was deeply touched by how much they had grown together as a couple and how well they parented. Not what I had expected but I was so glad to be so wrong.

Second Interesting Footnote:
In 2015, thirteen years after the bush wedding, I was invited to dinner by my friend, June Kraus von Trebitsch, an opera singer from New York, who had sung at one of my first memorial services in South Africa. On the way to the dinner, I randomly started thinking about Lisa and Andreas and I wondered how

they were. June asked me to bless our meal and when I finished praying, one of her guests spoke up and said,
"I have met you before but I only recognised your voice when you started praying. I was a guest at a wedding you facilitated for a couple of friends of mine who are architects. It was in the bush many years ago...."
No coincidences.

Baby Blessings

What most people might call a Christening, I call a Baby Welcoming or Baby Blessing or Naming Ceremony. I would rather call these ceremonies anything but Christenings as that title assumes that the child is born in sin and will consequently go to hell, unless s/he is first sprinkled with holy water and purified by the priest. No for me, the point of the ceremony is to honour the new life that has appeared in our midst, to behold the Innocence and the Infinite Potential that resides in the child, and to commit to raising that child in the knowledge of his or her Essential Spiritual Power and Purpose. It takes a spiritual community to raise a child.

Daughter of the Nile

The particular Baby Blessing I want to tell you about was requested soon after I had returned from my first pilgrimage to Egypt in May, 2001. When the mother came to our first preparation session, she informed me that the ceremony would be held at the home of the baby's godmother, Kim Lings. She assured me that Kim's house in Westdene would be easy to find as it had been painted and decorated to resemble a Pharaoh's tomb.

My client shared that she had visited Egypt with her husband when she was three months pregnant and had climbed inside the Great Pyramid to visit the King's Chamber. At that point, I figured out why I had felt compelled to fill a small cut-glass bottle with Nile water during my recent trip to Egypt. It was obviously meant to be used to bless this baby. Also, while in Luxor, on the East Bank of the Nile, I had invested in a beautiful full-length, cream-coloured cotton galabeya with rows of thick bright gold stitching around the neckline. Yes, it was designed for tourists but it definitely had the feel of priestess gear and would be perfect to wear for the ceremony.

In Kim I found a sister. She was an Egyptophile like me but a thousand times more committed to public visibility. The outside walls of her house were covered in huge bold hieroglyphs. There were ancient Egyptian artefacts in every room, including a large upright painted wooden coffin, which may once have housed a mummy. The ceilings had been painted dark blue with gold stars to represent the heavens and the afterlife for the departing Pharaohs' souls.
I learnt that Kim owned a travel agency specialising in tours to Egypt: *Nile Travel.*

The Baby Blessing ceremony was held on the patio. Kim and my client had prepared a beautiful altar table with a white cloth, decorated with white roses, Egyptian artefacts and the Nile water to bless the baby. Kim's Egyptian colleague happened to be there too. He was an historian and archaeologist and used to lead Kim's tours through Egypt. He was on a rare visit to South Africa to give lectures on Egyptology.

Well, all blessings to the baby girl for serving her spiritual purpose and being the catalyst to connect Kim and me. After this ceremony, I asked Kim to be my personal travel agent and she always did a stellar job of booking my group and individual pilgrimages to Egypt.

Memorials

Of all the ceremonies I perform, Memorials are my favourite. Why? Because in the face of death, people become real, raw and vulnerable. They have no control over their own or their loved one's mortality and their focus suddenly shifts to what matters: love, relationships, forgiveness, leaving this world a better place. During a Memorial Service, some will wonder what others will say about them when they are gone, while others will let the death of their loved one serve as a wake-up call, a reminder that they only have a limited time on this earth.

Within a few months of my return to Johannesburg, the ministry began to grow and I was constantly busy. My schedule was so full, in fact, that a Memorial Service was always a stretch to accommodate. From the time the call came in from the family, an intense three-day process would begin for me, in which everything else had to be set aside or creatively rescheduled to a later time. Usually, I would meet with the family immediately in order to discuss their loved one and how that person should be celebrated. Then, after they had left, I would prepare the script, doing my best to convey the essence of the deceased person through my words. Sometimes I would go and sit by my CD collection and just ask the deceased,
"What music do you want me to play at your ceremony?" Invariably, a song would start singing itself in me and I would find it on one of my CDs. When I performed the Service on the appointed day, the families were always happily surprised that the music so perfectly fit the bill, although one family was a little spooked by this:
"How did you know that Mum's favourite singer was Frank Sinatra? We did not tell you that."
I just smiled and mumbled something about a "hunch" or a "lucky guess".

As I conducted the Service, my intention would be to silently hold the space for the mourners, while they were processing all the other deaths and losses they had experienced in the past, as well as the current one.

On the day after the Service, I invariably had to lay low. Carrying the weight of the unfelt grief, mine and everyone else's, left me feeling drained but it was so worth it to be, for a short while, in that rarefied atmosphere of Heaven's antechamber.

Cremation in Cape Town

The Memorial I want to tell you about now took place in early January 2001. I had been back in South Africa for a full year and had just returned from a Christmas holiday in Cape Town. It was a relatively quiet period in Johannesburg before the New Year began with a vengeance in mid-January.

Very early one morning, my phone rang, at about 6:45 a.m. I immediately suspected a crisis. Philippa's voice trembled on the other end of the line. Her mother had just died. Could I help with the Memorial Service? The Cremation Chapel was booked for the next day at noon. In Cape Town.

"Yes, of course." I reassured her. I would have to fly down to Cape Town as soon as possible. That was no problem. Philippa quickly booked me on an afternoon flight.

Where would I sleep though?

Well, her mother's Cape Town flat was full with bereaved family members but her mother's bed was now empty. Philippa's mother had died in that bed the previous night but they had since changed the sheets....

Did I mind?

No, I did not mind.

Hurriedly, I got up and packed all my memorial notes. Before the shuttle came to pick me up, I took a look at my CD collection. Should I bring *Nessun Dorma* by Pavarotti? No, I did not want to carry CDs unnecessarily so I left it behind.

Note to self: Listen to your intuition, Steph.

At Cape Town airport, I was met by one of Philippa's daughters, and taken to her grandmother's flat, where Philippa was waiting for me with her other family members. We gathered in the living room and everyone shared their stories of their beloved "Ouma", Afrikaans for Grandma. It got late. We still had not planned the music but gradually, the family members all left to go to bed until only Philippa and I were left. Clearly the music was going to be our responsibility. Philippa told me that her mum had loved listening to opera music. In fact, *Nessun Dorma* by Pavarotti was her favourite. Philippa had bought the CD for her Mum when they saw Pavarotti live in concert together in Pretoria. But where was that CD? It was too late to call anyone and ask around. We could not find it anywhere in her mum's collection. You can imagine, I was kicking myself the whole time for not trusting my intuition. Nevertheless, Philippa and I had great fun playing all her mum's favourite music while we searched for *Nessun Dorma* and selected the recordings for the ceremony. Eventually, at about 1:00 a.m. Ouma led us to her favourite by Pavarotti. We think that *Nessun Dorma* was the last track Ouma had been listening to before she died.

The ceremony design was unfolding beautifully and organically and I was really getting a sense of the special soul we would be celebrating the next day.

Philippa was impressed that I had no qualms about sleeping in her dead mother's bed. Honestly, I was too tired to care. It was about 1:30 a.m. by this time. It had been a long day which had started in Johannesburg and ended unexpectedly in Cape Town and included holding the space for the family while they processed their grief. At that point, I would have slept anywhere.

The next morning, as I emerged from that state between the dimensions known as sleep, I had the strong sense that I was licking an ice-cream cone and thoroughly enjoying it. In fact, I could not get enough of it. The experience was vivid and very real. The only problem was, I could not taste it and I could not understand why. I felt that I was tapping into Ouma and I understood that she no longer had access to physical taste now that she was out of her body.

I went through to the kitchen, where I found the family making breakfast. I asked Philippa and her daughter if Ouma had liked ice-cream. Why, yes! She loved it like a child loves ice-cream! In fact, the family had managed to take their Ouma away on a holiday to Italy a few months before she died. Every day she had insisted on indulging herself with a huge Italian ice-cream. It had been the highlight of her trip.

I wish I could tell you that the service was ethereal, that we were all lifted up on the wings of angels and lost our fear of death. But no. Sadly, it was a cold, jarring experience. The old, bent, white-haired ushers in their three-piece pin-striped suits, had seen it all before. Their job was to keep the mourners' conveyor belt moving and to make sure that the body in the coffin dropped down into the "fires of hell" in the basement, at the appropriate time for maximum dramatic effect!

To my dismay, we had been allotted a mere half-hour slot in the chapel, minus five minutes for getting seated and another five for getting out. This left us with 20 minutes to honour a long life of love and contribution. 20 minutes to say "goodbye" and to process the grief and the loss. 20 minutes to shift into the sense of joy and privilege it was to have known Ouma and to commit to taking her legacy forward into the world.
My memorial script for Ouma was at least an hour long. We had planned readings, songs and eulogies. We were going to give Ouma a send-off of note. Once I realised that there was no possible deviation from protocol, I had 30 seconds to shave 40 minutes off my ceremony. It became clumsy and disjointed.

To make matters worse, after we had been rushed out of the chapel, one of the bent old men came up to our group and announced without a shred of compassion,
"The body will be burnt now!"
It was horrifying. Instinctively, we clasped each other's hands and then we stood joined in a circle as I said a prayer to release Ouma to her Greater-Yet-To-Be.

Thank Goddess, Philippa, her family and I had celebrated Ouma the night before with the sharing of stories and laughter and tears.
Thank Goddess, Ouma still lives in the family's hearts and in their memories.
And thank Goddess that Ouma is alive and well in her own dimension beyond the Veil where, I have heard from a Very Reliable Source, the ice-cream is absolutely Divine....

Chapter 21

No Death. Only Life.

It is sown a natural body; it is raised a spiritual body.
There is a natural body and there is a spiritual body.

1 Corinthians 15:44

O death, where is your sting?
O Sheol, where is your victory?

1 Corinthians 15:55

Interpretation

Metaphysically speaking, Heaven and Hell are states of consciousness as opposed to places we go to after death. You can be in Heaven and expanding your Good or in Hell and contracting your Good right now – all depending on the nature of your thoughts, feelings and attitudes.

The Bible verse in Corinthians clearly tells us that there are two bodies, not one. The physical body is sown. It is the result of the biological process of creation and has a limited lifespan as does any person, animal or plant. The spiritual body, however, is not sown. It is not bound to the realm of time and space. It animates the physical body during the earthly incarnation and it leaves the physical body at the moment of death and rises upwards. The spiritual body is more refined than the physical body. It vibrates at a higher frequency and naturally moves upwards. The spiritual body cannot become denser than the physical body at the moment of death and move downwards. It is energetically impossible for a spiritual body to go down to hell and burn throughout eternity regardless of how seemingly evil the person was in their lifetime. Without fail, every spiritual body rises upwards and receives exactly the spiritual assistance it needs for the next stage of its evolutionary journey on the other side of the Veil.

"Sheol" means "pit" or "abyss" in Hebrew. It describes a dark and hopeless place where one is distanced from God. It also refers to "the abode of the dead." So in this verse, it may simply mean "grave." However, Christians may interpret Sheol to mean hell. But why? There was a tradition in Jewish culture of burning rubbish outside the city walls of Jerusalem in the Valley of Hinnon, known as Gehenna, and also dumping dead bodies there to be destroyed in the flames. Typically, these burning corpses once belonged to people who had died without any hope of any salvation according to popular belief at the time. These were the tormented souls who had committed suicide.

In Truth, there is no death – at least not for the Spirit within each of us. The grave cannot claim the Essence of Who we are. If there is no death, then we cannot really talk about "life after death". There is only Life. Life is eternal. If you can believe that, then you know that your loved ones are still "here" essentially. Death does not extinguish them. Your loved ones have simply transitioned to the other side of the Veil and have disappeared from physical view. They have started functioning in another dimension of reality, but still as part of the One Life. Their soul purpose in this life was complete and their physical body was no longer an adequate instrument for their soul to function through. At this juncture, which we typically call "death" but which I prefer to call "transition," the physical body falls away in order that the soul might fly free on its journey of evolution.

According to Ernest Holmes, the founder of the Science of Mind, we are constantly growing spiritually to reveal more and more of our Essential Self. The process of shedding our outer layers of personality or our masks, continues after we leave our physical body so we are constantly becoming lighter and more refined.

The Reality in which the spiritual body lives is not visible to everyone on earth—only to some who have ESP i.e. "extra" or "extended" sensory perception. Perhaps your loved ones are next to you right now, in their spirit-body and only a heart-beat away as you read these words and think about them. Thought connects all Life in the One Mind of the Divine. There are no final endings only shifts from one state to another.

My Story

As I mentioned earlier, my father was an alcoholic. He was also a chain smoker. He also over-ate. Like most addicts, he was cross-addicted. After my mother left him, he turned to the bottle, to cigarettes and to food full-time.

Despite many of the problems that typically prevail in the family of an alcoholic, my father and I had a kinship that improved with age like a fine wine.... We shared the same spiritual passion and sensitivity. We also shared the same disease of alcoholism.

In November, 1999, when I flew from the U.S.A. to the U.K. en route to South Africa to start my ministry, I saw my father again for the first time in the seven years since he had attended my ministerial graduation at Santa Anita in 1992. Since then, alcohol had done more damage to his organs; his liver, heart and lungs were all very weak. He had the onset of diabetes. His feet had gone gangrenous—they were rotting from the toes up and had to be dressed every morning by a visiting nurse so that he could still walk. The next "step" would have been to amputate his legs to halt the progression of the gangrene but, thankfully for him, it did not come to that.

While I was in America, dad had been rushed to hospital twice with heart and lung failure. Each time he had had an NDE (Near-Death Experience) during which he went to the Other Side of the Veil and was told that it was not his time to leave his body and he was sent back to the earth plane. After the second NDE, he got the message and finally stopped drinking with the help of Anti-Booze.

When we met up again in the U.K. in November, 1999, I found out that dad did not have a proper will. If he had died intestate, his entire estate would have been shared equally between his next of kin, his six brothers and two sisters. Without resisting, he allowed me to lead him to a W.H. Smith's bookstore where we picked up a *Write your own Will* packet and he duly filled it out, signed it and lodged it with the solicitors.

The next time I saw my dad was in February, 2000, for his mother's funeral in Brighton, England, and then again fifteen months later in May, 2001. Personally, I had no plans to fly to the U.K. in May, 2001. Growing my ministry in South Africa was a full-time exhilarating occupation and there was nowhere else I wanted to be. So why did I go to England? Well, in April, 2001, I led my first long-awaited pilgrimage to Egypt with a group of congregants from my church in South Africa. We flew with Egypt Air from Johannesburg to Cairo and for a few extra South African rands it was possible to book an extra leg from Cairo to London. So I did it, only because the price was so ridiculously cheap but looking back, I can see that it was Spirit-driven.

Whilst in Egypt, my group and I had climbed Mount Sinai with hundreds of other pilgrims to witness the sunrise. It is said that Moses received the Ten Commandments upon this very mountain. I knew dad would have loved that experience, fascinated as he was by ancient history, archaeology and religion, and I picked up a small alabaster rock to take to him in the U.K. as I was making my way back down the mountain.

At the base of Mount Sinai, we visited St. Catherine's monastery where the Burning Bush is located. *(And the angel of the Lord appeared to him in a flame of fire out of the midst of a bush; and he looked, and behold, the bush was on fire and the bush was not consumed. Ref.: Exodus 3:2.)* Given dad's wry sense of humour, he would have chuckled along with me when we shuffled, with a horde of other tourists, past the unassuming, not-even-slightly-smouldering Bush. On the wall nearby there was a sign saying "No matches allowed" plus a fire extinguisher in case any religious tourists with pyromaniac tendencies disobediently tried to replicate Moses' experience.

Thanks to the disease of alcoholism, and the wreckage that it causes, dad's home had not been very visitor-friendly for years so, while in the U.K., I generally stayed with an old school friend in Epsom, about five miles from dad's home in Ewell. On the day after my arrival, dad and I met up in his favourite café in Epsom where he went for breakfast every morning. It was a Christian café and he had become an active member of that particular church community since giving up the booze.

Well, dad and I hardly talked about Egypt and I completely forgot to give him the alabaster rock that I had put in my coat pocket especially for him. There was more pressing business at hand and my visit had clearly been orchestrated for this very purpose....
How do you tell your father that you want to help him plan his funeral? I felt he did not have long left in his body and I only had a few days in the U.K. So I leapt in and told him that I would enjoy the privilege of leading his Funeral Service and that I wanted to design and facilitate it as he would have wanted it with his favourite music, poems, readings etc. Thankfully, dad humbly surrendered, accepting that he would not live forever, and he participated willingly in the planning of his farewell service.

That same day, we took a trip to Ewell, to his local undertakers where he ordered and paid for a coffin, all of the funeral services, the cremation and a plot for his ashes. The undertakers agreed to keep the body on ice for up to three weeks after his death to give me time to arrange to leave my ministry in South Africa and fly back to the U.K. to lead the service.
Dad wanted to hold the reception after the Service at his favourite local pub which was just across the road from the undertakers and he took care of the costs with a large advance payment. The owners of the pub, Ken and Marlene, had always been very kind to him and, much as they did not want to see him go, they felt honoured to be assigned the task of hosting his farewell reception.

The day before I left the U.K., we met in Epsom again and had our farewell breakfast at his favourite café. Dad usually got the bus home from Epsom but, on this particular day, his feet were in a lot of pain and he called for a taxi. He offered me a ride to the other end of town where I had to do some shopping. So there we were sitting together in the back seat of the taxi and it did not occur to me, or the taxi-driver, that this could be the last time that I ever saw my father. I was in child-mode, comfortable in the knowledge that my parents would live forever. The taxi driver said he would gladly drop me off but then he could not find a legal place to park or even stop to let me out. The traffic lights were turning red. The driver stopped the taxi and hurriedly told me to jump out while I had the chance! Startled, I said a hasty "Goodbye," to dad and kissed him on the cheek.

After I got out of the taxi and watched it speed away, I thought: "Oh no! That could have been the last time I will ever see my father—and we didn't say goodbye properly."
The alabaster rock from Mount Sinai was still in my pocket.
Then I heard the Voice inside me say:
"You will see him one more time."
I felt reassured, believing that the Voice meant my dad would be alive for the next few months, or at least until my next trip to the U.K., although I had no plans to return and no flights had been booked.

The next morning, I booked my taxi to pick me up and take me to Heathrow Airport. I was busy doing my last-minute packing when I suddenly remembered the rock. Immediately, I called the café where my dad usually went for breakfast in Epsom. Most days he was in by 9:00 a.m. and out again by 10:00 a.m. By then it was about 10:30 a.m. and I assumed that he would have already gone home. I told the waitress over the phone that I was Mike's daughter and that I wanted to leave the Egyptian rock with the staff at the café to give to my dad the following day. She said that would be fine but she omitted to tell me that dad had not been in that day. I then sped down to the town and into the café, anxious because my taxi was due to pick me up and I had not finished packing.

I saw one of the waitresses whom I knew and asked her to give the rock to my father. She said he had not been in for breakfast that day, which was unusual. We looked at each other and said nothing but we were both thinking the worst:
Had he even woken up that morning...?
"Maybe he is just late?" she mused, seemingly undisturbed.

I wished that I had had her careless detachment. My head was filled with a thousand thoughts around what I would need to do if he had, indeed, made his transition during the night. My belly was full of hollow emptiness as the awareness dawned that I would never see him again. I was so lost in dark imagination that I did not see the restaurant door open.

"Oh, here he is now!" said the calm and faithful waitress.

The bell on the door jangled and my father walked in. Relief!
Dad explained that he was late because the nurse, who dressed his feet every morning, had been stuck in heavy traffic on the way to his maisonette. I gave him the rock. He was visibly moved and accepted it happily. We hugged goodbye. I knew it would be the last hug. Somehow, he knew it too. There was no time for long drawn-out farewells. It was perfect that way. What do you say to a parent when you know that these words will be the last ones that pass between you in the physical?
Dad smiled at me and said:
"We're alright, aren't we, mate?"
"Yes," I said.
There was peace between us and it was fine for him to leave. Nothing more needed to be said.

A few months later, my sister called me in South Africa to let me know that dad was in Epsom District hospital with pneumonia. I called him right away. Dad already knew he would not be going home—well, not home to his maisonette anyway. There was no motivation for him. It was cold and miserable and lonely and there was no-one to take care of him there. Since his two NDEs, he had no fear of death and he was ready to go to the Other Side. The pneumonia had left him too weak to talk for longer than a minute. He apologized and hung up quite abruptly. Soon afterwards, he was in Intensive Care on a life support machine.

On 28th November, 2001, I drove home from teaching an evening Science of Mind class in Johannesburg with my dear friend and student, Russell, following behind me in his car. I had asked him to stay over because my housemate had gone out of town with her two guard dogs. The house was empty, there was no security or electric fences, and we had had three attempted burglaries in the previous four weeks!

I called the nurse in ICU at Epsom Hospital just before midnight. She said that dad was being kept alive on the life support. I asked her to tell him that I loved him and to let him know that it was fine to leave. I wished him well on his journey to the Other Side.

I went back into the dining room to talk to Russell. Then we heard a strange noise. There were double sliding doors leading from the hall into the lounge. They must have been very slightly opened and my house-mate's cat had decided to push them open with her body so that she could get into the lounge. The doors clanked as they were roughly pushed back on their runners by the determined and resourceful cat. It was a sign. I knew my father had left in that moment. His Spirit had pushed out of his body through the sacred doorway into the eternal realm of Light. I called the hospital. Indeed, they had pulled the plug and dad had shuffled off the mortal coil. It was 12:05 a.m. on 29th November.

That night when I lay bed and tuned into my dad's spirit, I sensed he was peaceful and happy as if he were in Paradise – the state he had always tried to simulate with alcohol. I knew he was fine.

As planned, I flew back to the U.K. and led his farewell service. The little chapel was surprising full of all the people whom dad had befriended and served in the last few years of his life when he was not drinking.

Having raised our glasses to dad at the pub after the service, my sister and I began the work of clearing out his maisonette. The first thing I saw when I opened the dining room cupboard was the alabaster rock. Humbled, I thanked the Egyptian gods who had

- organised the ridiculously cheap flight on Egypt Air from Cairo to London seven months before dad's transition;
- given me the power to coax my dad into writing his will, planning his funeral service, his cremation, the burial plot for his ashes and the farewell reception at the pub;
- forced me out of the taxi at the red traffic lights, forgetting to give the rock to my father;
- made me aware of the rock in my pocket while I was packing to leave;
- delayed the nurse in the traffic so that dad would arrive at the café late on the day of my departure;
- timed my trip to the café in accordance with dad's arrival so that I could give him the rock and say "Good-bye."

Four years after dad's transition, in 2005, I was in Egypt again, this time climbing a mountain in the Valley of the Kings with my Egyptian friend, Ahmed. As I reached a plateau and looked out across the huge silent expanse of the valley below, the ancient burial grounds of the Egyptian Pharaohs, I thought to myself:

"I wish I could share this with dad. He would love it here."

Then I corrected myself:

"Dad is probably here with me already since he is not limited anymore by time or space."

My silent thoughts were interrupted by a Cockney sounding voice behind me.

"Alright, mate?"

What?!!
I turned around, half-scared, half-excited, expecting to see a ghostly image of my father—even though I had never seen any ghosts but often felt them. It was only Ahmed, grinning at me.

"Where did you learn that expression?" I asked. "I have never heard you say that before. And you had a Cockney accent too! You sounded just like my father."

He shrugged: "I met some Australian tourists a while back. They said it all the time and I picked it up from them."

Thanks, dad.
Glad to know you're alright, mate.

Chapter 22

Spiritual Journeywoman

*34. Then the King will say to those at his right,
Come, you blessed of my Father, inherit the
kingdom which has been prepared for you from the
foundation of the world.
35. For I was hungry, and you gave me food; I
was thirsty, and you gave me drink; I was a
stranger and you took me in;
36. I was naked, and you clothed me; I was sick,
and you visited me; I was in prison, and you came
to me.
37. Then the righteous will say to him, Our Lord,
when did we see you hungry, and feed you? or
thirsty and gave you drink?
38. And when did we see you a stranger, and took
you in? Or that you were naked and clothed you?
39. And when did we see you sick or in prison, and
came to you?
40. The king then will answer, saying to them,
Truly I tell you, Inasmuch as you have done it to
one of the least of these my brethren, you did it to
me.*

Matthew 25:34-40

Interpretation

This verse would seem to speak about expressing love for our fellow human beings and it is – on one level. Yet if we look at it from the metaphysical perspective and remember that it addresses our consciousness, we can interpret it to be a teaching about our relationship with ourselves.

The Inner Christ within each of us is that which feeds, clothes, visits and cares for the parts of ourselves that are operating from a false sense of separation. In that state of separation, there is always thirst, hunger, and a craving to be reconnected with the Indwelling Source. This Inner Source frees us from a false sense of imprisonment, illness and alienation. The I AM Presence is the answer to *all* human needs and problems.

To give true spiritual service to another means that you and I are firmly established in the knowledge that we are one with our Divine Source as well as being one with all our fellow human beings, regardless of the disguises they are wearing. Simply put, when we serve others, we serve the Christ, the Spiritual Core in all humanity, which includes ourselves. Everyone is lifted up and the gifts that are given are transformed into food that satisfies a spiritual hunger, liquid that quenches a spiritual thirst and clothing that befits a god.

My Story

Even though we, in the Science of Mind teaching, do not believe in evangelising, one of my big passions has always been to travel in groups with others of like mind, conscious that we are on a spiritual mission to serve the planet and to uplift global awareness. And while we travel on an outer physical journey, we know that we are essentially on an inner spiritual journey of growth and development.

Primarily, I had always seen myself as a teacher but was amazed to find that I loved every other aspect of my work as a minister too – both the ecclesiastical and the organisational. Somehow I felt that "for this I had been born" and I did my work with joy (except the filing). I did not see myself as particularly gifted in the area of hands-on, charitable community projects. I found the aching, clawing African social issues of poverty, hunger, crime and the pandemic of AIDS overwhelming. For the highest good of the whole, I decided to focus on my strengths of teaching, speaking and writing. Well, that was until one Saturday night when, while preparing my Sunday service, I got a cry for help from a friend, Clarissa, from the Northcliff Spiritualist Church. She sometimes booked me as the guest speaker on Sunday evenings before the professional clairvoyant came onto the platform.

Lesotho Project

Clarissa was calling on behalf of some ex-pat friends of hers who had a farm in the tiny mountain kingdom of Lesotho and who wanted to assist their local African community. The winter was fast-approaching and the local tribes-people were going to suffer from the freezing temperatures and a shortage of food. Clarissa asked if we could we help by gathering and sending food, clothes, shoes and blankets.

Clarissa's plea touched my heart and I decided to invite my community to give to the Lesotho Project during our Sacred Gathering the following day. Fortuitously, my topic that Sunday was *Divine Abundance* so it was a natural segue to give a very practical call to action at the end of my talk. I encouraged my community to give generously so that they could experience their already-present Inner Storehouse of Abundance. After the regular love-offering, I took an extra collection for the Lesotho tribes-people. With those funds I was able to purchase 21 emergency blankets from a refugee organisation in Johannesburg.

Something galvanised within the hearts and minds of my congregation and the outpouring of generosity was truly abundant on that following Sunday. I will never forget seeing the "altar" table in the centre of our sacred space, piled high with food and clothing, instead of the usual flowers and sacred objects.

One of my congregants offered to organise a truck to deliver the goods to Lesotho the following Saturday. He and his brother would drive the four hours down to Lesotho together. In the end there were so many items of food and clothing that they had to take a truck each! The following Sunday, they reported back that in Lesotho they were welcomed like celebrities amid much gratitude and celebration.

My congregation continued to collect the much needed items and a couple of weeks later, I also accompanied a small team of volunteers on a delivery mission. We were greeted by the family who ran the farm, Helen and John and their 10-year old son. They were doing their best to provide work and income for the local villagers but were stretched to the limits themselves and could not employ everyone who needed a job. In addition, they noticed that the locals were stealing supplies from the farm buildings, especially firewood.

You see, according to African culture, if one person in the community has an abundance of any resource, he or she naturally shares it with the other members (it is the concept of *Ubuntu)* so other members feel free to simply help themselves.

My friend, Diana Arthur in Johannesburg, was particularly generous towards her African staff. They never lacked for anything to eat, they received a good salary and Di paid their children's school fees too. Yet, Diana caught her maid "stealing" cabbages from her vegetable garden. When confronted, the maid answered,

"But Madam, you have so many cabbages – more than you can eat – so I have been taking them to feed my family."

No guilt. No shame.

You cannot argue with logic like that, can you?

The Lesotho tribes-people had prepared a wonderful experience for us in order to show their gratitude. We were given a guided tour of the village and shown the various self-sustaining projects they were engaged in; weaving mats and hats from long dried grass, beadwork for jewellery, household items and souvenir gifts as well as vegetable growing.

What made the biggest impact on me was the local school. It was a large round mud hut with a thatched roof. The floor and the walls were daubed with cow dung. Yes, rural Africans have an intelligent way of creating a sturdy, odour-free, cost-effective floor covering out of dung. The walls served as "black-boards;" the teacher could write clearly in chalk on the smooth, dark brown surface. The children sat on the floor, all in the one room, no matter what grade they were in. For their maths lessons, they learnt to count using Castle beer bottle tops, the only items in plentiful supply. Sadly though, these tops also represented precious funds that had been "leaked" away since many of the men in the tribe had turned to alcohol as an escape from the pain of poverty, cold and hunger and the shame of not being able to work and provide for their families.

Helen and John really appreciated our support and had invited us to stay as their guests overnight. Some of us were given a bed in the main farmhouse and others in the various rondavels on the property for guests and tourists.
A rondavel is a small round hut, usually with a thatched roof; very common on the rural African landscape. Typically an entire extended African family lives in a one-roomed rondavel. There is a fire pit in the centre and the smoke escapes through the hole at the apex of the conical roof. In a westernised rondavel, there might be electric heaters in place of a fire pit but, consistent with African tradition, the loos ("long drops") are set apart from the main hut; in our case they were in a separate building outside. Not fun on a wintry night but very authentically African.

By the time dusk settled in, we were hungry and weary. We had left Johannesburg before 6:00 a.m. and it had been a long day of being moved, humbled and inspired by many unforgettable impressions and heartfelt interactions with the local people.
Helen and John had prepared a "braai" (South African for "barbeque") for us that evening and invited some friends from the local, ex-pat farming community. It was all very informal; no-one had to dress for dinner so I was still wearing the clothes I had been in all day; my old trainers, my black leggings and a long black T-shirt with the words *Relax. God is in charge* emblazoned on the front. My hair was looking maniacally windswept, my make-up had worn off and my nose was sunburnt. Okay, I did not look like a stereotypical minister but I do not think I looked particularly demonic either. The guests had their doubts though, as I was about to find out....

Helen was busy mingling and serving food and she introduced me, as the leader of the team from the Johannesburg church, to a tall, middle-aged, beer-bellied, ex-pat, South African man. After some polite social niceties and slightly flirtatious overtures, the man made it clear that he was a traditional Christian.
Unlike me.
Obviously.
As he spoke, he stared pointedly at my large ankh, nestled between my breasts. (Reader, do not be alarmed. This was not a bare-cleavage-moment; my T-shirt chastely covered me up to my neck.) He then asked me, in a tone which had very little to do with the spirit of inquiry and much more to do with the "ass" of assumption, a tone which suggested that he was fundamentally appalled but could still be broadminded and deign to have sex with me:
"So you are a Satan worshipper, are you?"
What?!
My ego-identity was severely rattled. How could anyone think that of me? Well, apparently, they do as I have no control over what people think. His comment took me off-guard and I leapt to

the defence of the ancient Egyptian spiritual symbol around my neck. He was not interested. He was a "good Christian" and he had made up his mind that I was Devil-Spawn. I expect you are wondering if he was spiritually "upright" enough to save my soul with sex? I never gave him the opportunity to find out. After all, he was not nearly as attractive as my fellow passenger from Chapter 16.
In hindsight though, I wish I had responded to his assertion with, "Yes, well-spotted. Satan is my lover!" and then convinced him that I came from that small, discreet, branch of Satan worshippers who, in their spare time:

- preach in church on Sundays;
- bless the new-borns;
- bury the dead (Christian or otherwise);
- pray for the suffering;
- minister to the sick;
- visit the incarcerated;
- donate to the needy, and
- organise charitable projects to feed and clothe poverty-stricken, starving tribes-people....

But that would have been a bit childish, wouldn't it?

Russia

2003 was a year of spiritual peaks and valleys. The peaks included two Global Heart journeys, one to Russia and the other to Mexico. The valleys I will tell you about later.

The Global Heart team was a group of Religious Science ministers, practitioners, students and congregants based in the U.S.A., who gave support to member churches outside America. The Global Heart Journeys were often led by my dear friend, Rev. Kathy Hearn, who was the President of the United Church of Religious Science (which later changed its name to Centers for Spiritual Living or CSL) worldwide from 2002 until 2012. These journeys were a method of implementing the organisation's global vision of "a world that works for everyone" by giving spiritually inspiring talks and workshops to the Science of Mind communities around the world. They also contributed to local charitable projects, such as redecorating orphanages.

Towards the middle of 2003, I entered the valley of burn out. It became necessary to take a few weeks' break to regain my strength. On 15th June, 2003, I held my last Sacred Gathering for a while, in which I explained to my community that I would be away for six weeks because I needed to rest. On the next day, 16th June, my birthday, I got an email from the United Church of Religious Science (UCRS) Head Office asking me if I would speak at the annual Science of Mind conference in Izhevsk, Russia, with all expenses paid. Goddess bless Rev. Kathy Hearn. She knew that I spoke Russian and would be able to get around in Russia without an interpreter, if necessary. So she had put my name forward to the Global Heart committee to be considered as a speaker.

Of course I accepted and extended my time away from South Africa and Soul Home to take advantage of this opportunity. UCRS was going to fund me for two weeks but I booked to stay on for an extra three weeks, so that I would be able to travel through Russia afterwards and go where the Spirit led me.

Even though I had expected to be the only speaker at the conference from outside Russia, a small group of Global Heart visionaries from San Diego's UCRS communities, decided to participate at the last minute, most of them had been on our Global Heart journey to the Ukraine in 2002. We bonded well as a team and together we created an eight-day programme of lectures, workshops and entertainment for the Russian Science of Mind students. They had come from far and wide for this annual highlight in their spiritual development.

Accommodation was in a dilapidated Soviet pioneer camp, an hour outside the city of Izhevsk. The plumbing was ancient and sometimes there was only cold water in the showers. At other times there was no water at all. The floor of the toilets was flooded regularly. The curtains were too small for the bedroom window so the early morning light poured in relentlessly to make sleep impossible. The rusty bed springs creaked at the slightest movement. The food in the canteen was less than appetising. But above and beyond all the physical deprivations and the lack of creature comforts, was the Great Russian Soul, that all-pervading warmth and love, generous hospitality, heart to heart telepathic communication, joy, vibrancy, and sincere appreciation towards the international UCRS team who had come all the way to this far flung, rustic camp on the border of Siberia, to teach the Science of Mind.

That journey to Russia restored my soul, not just because I felt at home in the former Soviet Union, even after a 20-year absence, and not because I was greeted so warmly by the Russian Science of Mind students. The primary reason was that I was in my element travelling and teaching metaphysics. After about three weeks there, I had absorbed enough of the language by listening to my interpreters at the Science of Mind conference to enable me to even give metaphysics lectures in Russian! There was something so redeeming about using my language skills to spread the Word. Divine Orchestration had clearly been at work and my four-year degree in German and Russian that had felt so pointless when I left University in 1981, suddenly took on purpose and meaning 22 years later in Izhevsk, Russia.

Once I returned to South Africa, it was through Rev. Kathy and the Global Heart group from San Diego that I learnt about the next Global Heart journey, which had been planned to Mexico City in late October. My heart leapt. I wanted more of this travelling, teaching, serving and basking in the rich, joy-filled, consciousness of the American ministers and practitioners.

Mexico City

Once I had made the decision to go to Mexico and preparation was underway, I remembered that a few months earlier, in February, 2003, I had gone to the movies in Johannesburg with a friend to see *Frida* – the film about the Mexican artist, Frida Kahlo, and her relationship with her fellow artist, Diego Riviera. The movie was totally inspirational and, as I watched it, I thought, "I would love to visit Frida's house in Mexico City" but let the thought go entirely....
Have you noticed in your life that those flippant thoughts with no attachment are the ones that often manifest so powerfully?

I contacted my old friend from Ministerial School at Agape, Rev. Rebeka Pina, who had founded a Science of Mind ministry in Mexico City. Goddess bless her, she offered to host me for a few days before the Global Heart group joined us so that I would have time to acclimatise and recover from jetlag.

Rebeka was doing an amazing job. Like me, she was living in a densely populated city, where there was extreme poverty and crime. Her biggest obstacle was Catholicism. New Thought was frowned upon in the country. She was considered a heretic and she had to operate in disguise, which made marketing very difficult. But her students bravely spread the word and her church was thriving with enthusiastic, albeit mostly poor, members.

In addition to the stresses and strains of beginning her own ministry from scratch, Rebeka also had to translate all the class material from English into Spanish. Spanish was her mother tongue and she was fully bilingual, having lived in Canada for many years, but nevertheless, she was stretched to her limit and had little time for relaxation. So I was surprised when she suggested that we go for coffee in the city centre before the Global Heart group arrived. I was even more surprised when we sat in the coffee shop and she said,

"Frida Kahlo's house is just round the corner from here. Would you like to visit it and then we can get the bus back to my home?" She was so casual, as locals generally are when they live next door to a national monument and pass it every day on their way to work. I was ecstatic!
"Yes, please!"
So there I was in Frida's domain, surrounded by her bold, unique, paintings, her ubiquitous plants, the strong, bright Mexican colours of the walls so unlike any other house in that street, remembering my casual wish in the movie theatre in Johannesburg only eight months previously.

But it got even better than that.... Rev. Rebeka had organised a public conference for the UCRS team, to introduce the local people to the Science of Mind philosophy. My talk was supposed to be a short one but I got into my flow and told my story of how I hated imperialism, colonialism, racism, sexism and my mother, and had fought against them all as a young woman in the UK. I had then landed in South Africa in 1985, where all of these evils were running rampant and where the Voice told me to stay and get on with "the work". And that is when I met Rev. Gladys Harrison and started my journey with the Science of Mind. The audience was laughing at my antics, my human blunders on my spiritual path. Rev. FranCione, an African-American member of the UCRS team, was laughing too but, at the same time, her heart was beating out of her chest. She was being impressed by the Spirit to share something personal, which she had not planned to do, as her introduction to the Global Prayer for Peace which she had consented to deliver. And this is what she shared....

In 1988, Rev. FranCione taught a 30-week class in the San Francisco Bay area called *Practising the Presence*. One of the three 10-week terms was focused on *Loving those who are hard to love*. The task which she set for herself and her students was to identify someone who was hard to love and to learn to forgive and love them.

Rev. FranCione knew there was a Religious Science church in South Africa and she found it hard to believe that a Science of Mind teacher could be teaching the philosophy of Oneness yet still be involved in Apartheid. How incongruous! Rev. FranCione's sister was actively involved in the struggle against Apartheid in the Bay area of Northern California and her relatives were also deeply engaged in the fight against racism and injustice for any who were oppressed. Rev. FranCione was an avid student of the Science of Mind. She wanted to practise what our founder, Ernest Holmes, taught, i.e. we have to be for something not against something so she did not want to fight racism, nor did she want to be against the evil of Apartheid but she nevertheless selected Rev. Gladys Harrison, my first Science of Mind teacher in Johannesburg, as her target whom she would learn to love during the 10-week class.

One day, as she was driving to work, the Voice of Spirit asked her, "Why are you trying to love someone so far away? You will never meet her!"

Rev. FranCione realised then that she had not set herself a real challenge. Nevertheless, as Spirit would have it, before the 10-week class was over, she found herself at the UCRS Convention in Long Beach, Southern California. In the opening session, Rev. FranCione got quite a shock because none other than Rev. Gladys Harrison of UCRS in Johannesburg was being introduced to the crowds of ministers and practitioners. She had come all the way from South Africa for her Ordination in the U.S.A.

Rev. FranCione knew that she could not avoid Life's invitation to "embrace the one who was hard to love" so she bravely went up to Rev. Gladys and asked if they could meet and talk. Rev. Gladys suggested breakfast the next morning. Well, unexpectedly, breakfast lasted three hours during which time these two wonderful ministers, the black and the white, spoke about their differences and judgements and fell in love with each other. Much of the time they disagreed but FranCione came out of that session realising that she was uninformed about the very complex South African situation and had a lot to learn from Rev. Gladys.

In order to continue their conversation and to allow Rev. FranCione to experience South Africa first hand, Rev. Gladys invited her to stay in her home during the upcoming INTA Convention in January 1989. (That was the event described in Chapter 9 where I met Dr. Margaret Stevens and was interviewed for a place at the Santa Anita Ministerial School.) Much as she wanted to go to South Africa, Rev. FranCione declined for personal financial reasons.

During her talk in Mexico City, Rev. FranCione told a story, written by Olive Schreiner, the South African author. It is about a group of adventurers seeking to build a path through a mountain which was inhibiting passage to the other side. They set about hacking out a tunnel with their axes. They cut for days, months and even years. Gradually they all died, except for one. Just when the last one was about to die, he began to hear the sound of hacking on the other side of the mountain rock at the end of the tunnel. Unbeknown to him, another group of adventurers had been building a tunnel from the opposite side of the mountain. The sound of their axes was the confirmation that they were connected, even though they never actually met, and that their work had not been in vain. The dying man knew that the tunnel would be completed after he had gone. God had come to meet him half way. As a result of her intention to learn to love, Rev. FranCione saw God coming to meet her in the form of Rev. Gladys in Longbeach in 1988. By opening up to love another person who she had judged and rejected, she was healing a part of herself and part of our collective humanity. Then, fifteen years later, Rev. FranCione and I met in Mexico City. The African-American and the Caucasian had always been moving towards each other, drawn together by the Law of Attraction without knowing it but sharing the same intention to practise and teach the Science of Mind philosophy as a vehicle for the healing of racism.

When all is said and done, there is only One of us here.

Chapter 23

Many Mansions

In my Father's house are many mansions:
if it were not so,
I would have told you.
I go to prepare a place for you.

John 14:2

Interpretation

Think about a "mansion" as a "dimension in consciousness" rather than a grand palatial home. Some of these dimensions are visible to us on earth and some are not. In the spiritual domain, there are many dimensions of consciousness. There is a "mansion" for all of us because we all inhabit our own dimension of consciousness based on our beliefs, attitudes, words and mental habits.

Our spiritual beingness is not time-bound. It is always everywhere present. It seems to go ahead of us to prepare the way but actually It inhabits a dimension beyond the body.

A change of physical dwelling during our earthly incarnation usually means that there has been an internal shift in consciousness—either expansion or contraction—and, therefore, the previous home is no longer an accurate reflection of the internal state and cannot sustain itself. We are either inspired to move or we have to move, seemingly being forced out by external powers like landlords or earthquakes. The new space that we move into has, meanwhile, been prepared by the consciousness of the previous inhabitant to make way for us, and whatever it is spiritually that we bring to it.

A place is forever being prepared for us to dwell within spiritually, whether we are in the body or not and whether that place has a physical structure or not.

My Story

As you know, during my first few weeks back in Johannesburg in early 2000, I set about the business of getting in touch with many of my old friends from the past, one of them being Peter Armstrong. He was delighted to reconnect. Many of my South African friends thought they would never see me again. They could not imagine why anyone would want to leave America to return to South Africa.

Pete invited me over to his flat in Sandown, in the wealthy, white, northern suburbs, where he both lived and ran his own business as an NLP (Neuro Linguistic Programming) practitioner.
I loved Pete's townhouse from the instant I walked into it. It was on the second floor and looked out over the park in Sandton, giving it a feeling of rural spaciousness even though it was in the middle of the new international Central Business District. Pete showed me the lounge area where he ran group meetings and training sessions. He pointed out the desk in the corner where his part-time secretary sat. As soon as he did that, I had the thought:
"This would be the perfect place to run my ministry from! I could have a part-time secretary too!"
Then Pete showed me the third bedroom that he had turned into a NLP practice and the second bedroom that was his private office. There were plenty of spare parking spaces for guests and a security guard at the entrance gate to screen visitors. There was even a swimming pool. Lucky Pete!

My first home in Johannesburg after moving out of my sister's house was a tiny cottage on a property around the corner from the Masonic Hall where I ran my Sacred Gatherings on Sundays. It was a charming little place—and freezing cold!
One night, after I had been living there a few weeks, I was preparing a memorial service script for a ceremony the following day while listening to a beautiful new CD of angelic voices singing requiem music. This was going to be a particularly poignant service in honour of Quinn Wagner, a beautiful angelic child who died of leukaemia at the age of seven. Quinn's mother, Renee, had called me "by accident" to perform the service whilst trying to contact another Rev. Stephanie. She and her husband were in shock and in deep grief. To serve them in the most profound way

possible, I was opening up to Divine Inspiration to make the event as spiritually uplifting and comforting as it could be.

At about 11 p.m., the tranquillity was shattered by a loud scream. It sounded like it came from the cottage behind mine where the landlady's domestic servants lived. Was the maid being raped by her boyfriend? I was afraid that if I went to check it out, I might have been raped or murdered myself, so I sat and prayed.

Just then, I heard a tapping on the windowpane of my front door. Should I open up? Who or what would I be letting in? I heard my name being called feebly. Through the glass of the front door I saw a blurry image of my landlady. Quickly, I let her in. She was covered in blood and her front teeth were missing. Quaking with fear, she explained that her ex-gardener, a Zimbabwean whom she had fired for stealing thousands of rands the previous week, had jumped over the wall with three of his buddies, and attacked her and her boyfriend while they were in the kitchen making dinner. One of the gang-members had a gun. The men had forced my landlady and her boyfriend to hand over their mobile phones and then carefully cut all the phone wires in her house so that the police could not be contacted. My landlady's boyfriend had screamed at her to run for help. I was the first person she could think of and the closest. She was terrified that the gang members would all follow her to my cottage after they had killed her boyfriend. We called the police and asked them to come as fast as possible.

Just then there was another knock on my front door. We looked at each other terrified. The police could not have arrived so fast, could they? There was no back door to my cottage. No escape. Should we be quiet and hide in the bathroom? They could easily bust down the door and kill us. Or should we open the front door?

In a faint voice, someone outside said: "Let me in. It's Stephen!" Relief. It was the landlady's boyfriend.

Stephen was alive, but covered in blood and rapidly losing more blood from his wrists where he had broken free from the wire with which the gang had tied him up. He threw the gun, that he had managed to wrest away from one of his attackers, on to the floor and then he sank to the floor himself, completely weakened by the loss of blood, shock and exhaustion.

Where were the four men? They had fled. My landlady had managed to press the silent panic button above her nightstand right before one of the attackers had pinned her to the bed with his hands about her throat, intent on strangling her. His buddy, however, had cautioned him not to kill her. Burglary and theft they could easily get away with by bribing the judge. A murder charge would be a more difficult issue to evade and might involve a prison sentence. The panic button had silently alerted the local security company and the gang had made a run for it when they heard the sirens approaching.

My landlady and I found some clean tea towels and tried to wrap up Stephen's wrists to prevent more blood loss. I called my boyfriend and asked him to come over which he did about 20 minutes later. Nearly an hour after our emergency phone call, the police showed up at my cottage and took a statement from my landlady, her boyfriend and myself. When the police left, my boyfriend took me back to his place for the next three nights. After that incident, I could never settle in my cottage again. As the gang ran off, they had threatened that they would be back to finish the job. Any slight noise after dark was terrifying and triggered memories of the screams, and the image of the little black gun and the pools of deep red blood on my white tiled floor.

My next "mansion" was at the home of Dr. Philip Sherwin and Amanda Uys. Amanda was the daughter of Rev. Johanna Meiring who had so generously supported me before I left for ministerial school in the U.S.A. When I came back to South Africa, I tried to contact Rev. Johanna to let her know that I was now qualified and starting my own church. Her daughter, Amanda, informed me that her mother was in the final stages of Alzheimers, completely bedridden, and would not recognize me so it was best not to visit. However, Amanda was excited to hear about my new ministry and asked to be on my mailing list.

To my great delight, Amanda and her partner Philip began attending my Sunday Gatherings and my classes on *Conversations with God*. When Rev. Johanna finally made her transition in June, 2000, Amanda asked me to facilitate the memorial service. This was my first memorial in South Africa and a great honour since I was the new kid on the block in amongst some veritable heavyweights, albeit aging heavyweights, who were the female ministers in the South African metaphysical movement.

Amanda and I met to prepare the ceremony together. I did not have a white ministerial robe and I did not want to wear my black one. I asked Amanda if I should just wear a business suit but she remembered that her mother had a white robe. She offered to find it and have it cleaned and pressed for me before the service.

The service was held in Amanda's living room which she had transformed into a chapel. Before the service began and the guests started arriving, Amanda bustled me into the kitchen and there she held out the white robe. As she placed it around my shoulders, I teared up. I felt truly honoured. It was as if Rev. Johanna had "passed the mantle" to me from the Other Side of the Veil. *(So he departed thence and found Elisha the son of Shaphat, who was plowing, and twelve ploughs were ahead of him and he was one of the twelve; and Elijah came up to him and cast his mantle upon him. Ref.: 1 Kings 19:19.)* She had covered me with her blessings of power and protection.

The service was a joyous celebration of Rev. Johanna's life. No mourning or depression—just as she would have wanted it. We drank champagne and toasted her. We released balloons and waved her goodbye as they disappeared behind the distant clouds.

Three days later, when the violent incident occurred at my cottage, it was the night before my second Memorial Service as a new minister in South Africa. The following weekend, when Amanda and Philip found out through a mutual friend that I wanted to move because of the trauma I had experienced in my cottage, they offered me the flat above their house. There was only one snag: the flat belonged to Amanda's daughter who was away in Israel and, therefore, I would have to move out when she came home. However, the daughter was in love and wanted to stay in Israel forever, so it looked like a good, long-term prospect. I decided to take the risk and moved in.

After four months of harmony and laughter and wonderful friendship with Phillip and Amanda, Amanda's daughter announced she was now out of love and coming home. Where would my next "mansion" be?

Sad Footnote:
Amanda Uys made her transition on April 26, 2016. It was unexpected. Within 6 weeks of the cancer diagnosis, she left her body. I was on the Baltic coast in Poland at the time, doing research for my next book on the Amber Road. Amanda had been with me every step of the way from the conception of the book idea in late 2014 to my trip to the Amber Coastline where I collected my first pieces of amber. I felt her presence so close to me that day, little knowing that she had made her transition a few hours before. I could not wait to tell her about all my Amber

Road miracles and imagined sharing the experience with her on my next trip to the Baltic. Only when I got to my accommodation that evening, did I learn in an email that she had passed away early that morning. Amanda had asked her family to contact me to lead her Memorial Service and, of course, I flew back to South Africa as soon as I could. The gods were with me and before I left for Heathrow Airport, I managed to locate Rev. Johanna's white robe in amongst all the boxes in my storage locker in the U.K.
Before the service at the Johannesburg Country Club, I met Amanda's daughter, Tania, for the first time – the one whose flat I had stayed in without her knowing.
A few days after the memorial, I was visiting my friend Lucille Kent Lueckhoff who was up from Cape Town staying with her daughter, Jackie, and her granddaughter in Johannesburg. I learned then that Amanda had sent Tania to boarding school in Cape Town – the same school that Jackie attended. Jackie and Tania became best friends and Tania invited Jackie up to Johannesburg to come and stay with her at Amanda and Philip's house for a long weekend. Can you believe that Jackie actually stayed with Tania in that very same upstairs flat that I moved into a few years later?!

I was not worried about finding another place to live, so sure was I that something would show up. Nine days before my move-out date, the "something" still had not shown up! Oops, time to pray a little more seriously.

The answer to prayer showed up through a friend of a friend, who had a cottage on her property which she was almost finished renovating. Gratefully, I moved in but this cottage was tiny and the ministry was expanding. I needed something bigger where I could teach my evening classes from home. In post-Apartheid South Africa, I felt extremely vulnerable driving home alone late at night. The police had made it clear that driving through a red traffic light was no longer illegal if the driver felt s/he was being followed or might run the risk of being car-jacked while stopped at the lights. However, despite that, it was common knowledge that most car-jackings and burglaries took place while drivers were entering their properties and waiting the few seconds for their remote controlled garage door or entrance gates to open. I did not have a remote for my garage door so I had to get out of my car, unlock the padlock, lift the rusty squeaky door, drive in, get out of the car again and then close the door behind me. This process would have allowed ample time for a car-jacking if anyone had been waiting for me in the bushes on that eerie unlit street. I used to pray intensely and I was certainly protected because no harm came nigh me *(There shall no evil befall you, neither shall any plague come near your dwelling. For he shall give his angels charge over you to keep you in all your ways. Ref.: Psalms 91:10-11)* but I needed to move. Enter Tina.

Tina was the daughter of one of my mum's closest friends, Anna, who happened to be an exorcist. When I first arrived in South Africa in 1985, Anna was very supportive towards me on my spiritual path and drove me down to Margate to visit the Dutch yoga teacher, Nellie. And when I wanted to go to Cape Town while I was still on my two-month holiday in early 1986, her daughter, Tina, had driven me down with her on her way to start the new semester at Cape Town University. We had an argument in the car. For most of the way she did not speak to me. Years later, she wrote me a note to apologise for her bad behaviour. And suddenly there I was becoming her housemate and tenant. Life can be weird.

Tina was very accommodating and allowed me to use most of the house for my ministry. Prayer was answered in the form of a large dining room, complete with huge wooden dining room table, comfortably seating 14 people and perfect for my classes. I had my own bedroom with bathroom en-suite and an extra room for my office. There was a long driveway where we could safely park about eight cars off-street on class nights. For the cars that had to park on the street outside, I hired a security guard.

The only problem was that Tina had no electric fencing. Sure, she had high walls around the property, but they were easily scaled by agile burglars. She had guard dogs and a contract with a local security company. She felt safe in her skin. I still didn't. The Alexandra township was a short distance away, not as big as Soweto but equally as impoverished. It was normal for me to hear gunshots in the neighbourhood on Saturday nights while I was preparing my sermons for Sunday. Someone close by was being burgled or raped or murdered or all three. All I could do was pray.

Tina and I lived side by side in the same house, hardly seeing each other for over a year, and then Tiffany came to stay.

Tiffany was the answer to prayer. I needed help. The ministry was growing. I had no practitioners to assist me with the ecclesiastical duties nor was I in a position to hire an administration assistant. So apart from some sporadic help from volunteers in my office, I was running the whole show single-handed in a very stressful environment.

Tiffany was a Religious Science Practitioner who had also studied at Agape. We had been introduced a couple of times by our mutual friend, Rev. Harriet Hawkins, in the late nineties. Tiffany was studying Religion and Economics in Massachusetts, U.S.A. She wanted two months experience, between semesters, working alongside a New Thought minister, to see if the ministry was right for her as a life path. Our mutual friend, Rev. Harriet, did the liaison. Where was Tiffany going to sleep though?

I told Tina about my dilemma. She kindly let me clean out the spare room where she stored all her junk and she increased the rent slightly so that I could provide a home for Tiffany. A couple of congregants, Thembi and Miriam, helped me clean and then choose some new bedding. Lo, we had created a beautiful guest room the day before Tiffany's arrival!

Tiffany was in her late twenties, very bright, very committed and she had a very, very healthy prosperity consciousness. She collected registration fees from my students and had them all pay up on time, joyfully too! She began praying for me, for a prosperous home, for myself and my ministry.

One day, soon after her arrival, Tiffany and I were driving through Sandton. We happened to be on the street where my friend, Peter Armstrong, lived in the townhouse that I had admired so much when I first arrived back in Johannesburg. Tiffany commented:

"I like this area. It is very prosperous. This is where you should be living."

"Yes, but I could never afford it," I thought silently to myself.

A few days later, I was prompted to call my friend, Pete, because I knew he owned other properties and I wanted to ask him for some suggestions as to where I might rent a place that was central, with lots of safe parking and a spare room for guests. He answered:

"Funny you should call right now because I am trying to rent out my home in Sandown. I have just heard from a very interested potential tenant who has signed the documents but not come up with the deposit. So, if he does not pay by the end of today, you can have it if you want it.'

Yippee! It was twice as much as I had been paying to live at Tina's, but my inheritance had just come through from my father's estate and so I could afford it. I moved in on June 13, 2002. Tiffany helped me move and, while I was doing my best to keep on top of all the ministerial work, she unpacked all the boxes and found orderly homes for all my things. In complete awe, I could not help but notice that she was playing out the role of my part-time secretary just as I had visualised two and a half years previously when my friend Pete had first shown me his home!

After I had lived in this beautiful townhouse for a year, happy and contented, Pete informed me that he wanted to sell the place and buy another property. Was I interested in buying it off him? Was I interested?! I loved that place and never wanted to leave it in my whole life! I bought it and then left it 18 months later and moved back to Europe.
But that is another story....

Chapter 24

All Good Things Come to an End (except God)

There is no Bible quote for the last chapter.

My Story

Some readers of previous editions of this book were disappointed by the end (see last page of Chapter 23), which left them hanging on the edge of a literary cliff, with a bunch of unanswered questions.

You may be also be asking:

"Why did she leave her ministry, her family, her friends, the land and the people she loved so much?

Why did she abandon the Divine Vision that had been propelling her forward since 1987?

Why did she leave the South African sunshine to go back to miserable, rainy old Europe?"

Yes... why indeed?

So, in deference to my previous readers and now, to you, my current Reader, here is the untold story.

For a long time, the whole painful unfolding was far too raw for me to write about so I simply avoided it. You see, in 2003 a breakdown occurred, which I experienced as completely devastating. In Ministerial School we had been warned that most new ministers burn out in their first three to five years of ministry and I remember thinking at the time, "Yes, but that won't happen to *me.*" Oops, clear case of feeling "special and different!" Burnout did happen to me, exactly three and a half years into my ministry. Unfortunately I did not recognise the signs until it was almost too late.

By nature I am a pioneer and very self-sufficient yet carrying the responsibility of a new ministry alone for three years was definitely taking its toll. I had co-dependently exhausted myself through doing all the things I thought a minister was "supposed" to do, based on my perception of the traditional Christian church. In a Christian church, the minister is financially supported by his or her organisation but in UCRS churches, that was not the case. In spite of this, I threw myself whole-heartedly into building the community and I made myself super-available to my students and congregants. I never asked for recompense, which eventually left me greatly depleted emotionally, spiritually and financially.

At the same time, most of the members of my congregation were operating on the same false premise that my ministerial work was a calling, my gifts came from God and, therefore, they were not obliged to contribute financially. "The Lord will provide," they said....

Of course, I was paid for teaching classes, counselling clients and facilitating ceremonies but not for anything else. And the "anything else" was a relentless and full-time business. Phone calls from desperate students and congregants came through at all times of the night and day:

"My granddaughter has just been bitten by a poisonous snake and rushed to hospital. Can you pray for her?" I never replied, "Well, actually, it is Monday and this is my only day off in the week so let the medical team handle it."

"I have a job interview tomorrow morning and am really anxious about it. Can you pray for me?" I never replied, "Look, it is 11 p.m. and even ministers have to sleep. Call me tomorrow to make a counselling appointment between the hours of 10.00 a.m.-4.00 p.m."

"My brother has just been murdered."
"My son has disappeared."
"My husband has left me."
"I am about to throw myself off the 10th floor balcony."

I could not ignore these cries for help nor did I want to. I felt so privileged to be living inside my Divine Purpose in this lifetime and I loved it all. I was living a life of meaning and usefulness.

In February, 2013, I was selected to present a workshop based on my book, *Down Dirty and Divine* at the CSL (former UCRS) Convention in Vancouver, Canada. A former colleague, Rev. Mark Anthony Lord, presented a workshop on church growth to ministers. It was at this workshop that I almost did not attend, that I came to understand the two major reasons for my breakdown. The first was co-dependency. The second was a simple lack of knowledge about a successful method of growing a church while maintaining a balanced personal life. Things might have been very different if I had been familiar with Rev. Mark Anthony Lord's concept for church growth when I was a new minister. I was not and so I tried to take care of the whole growing congregation on my own and to build the community at the same time. Imagine being a mother with fifty children.... Burnout was inevitable. AND, in hindsight, it was all perfect and had to be the way it was for me and all those who chose to walk the path with me.

In addition to my personal crisis, Soul Home was going through its own painful growing phase. The honeymoon was over and the dark side of the spiritual community was emerging in the form of power struggles, anger and resentment, particularly over money. It was classic, it happens in most churches. Theoretically, I knew there was a way through this, which would help us become a stronger more bonded community but I did not have the inner resources to deal with the situation effectively at that time.

Unexpectedly, I was approached by a national television producer and asked for permission to run a feature on Soul Home. Our vibrant spiritual community had come to the attention of the media via the Law of Attraction and suddenly, we were on the brink of national visibility and with that, a massive growth spurt. You would think that I would have been flattered and excited after my dedicated efforts to spread the Science of Mind teachings and to build a New Thought spiritual community but I turned the producer down. I was running on empty and was as white as a sheet – definitely not a good ad for a metaphysical minister. At the same time, Soul Home was falling apart. The way I saw it, I did not know if it would even exist as a community by the time the feature appeared on TV a few months into the future.

In desperation, I flew down to the South Coast to seek help and advice from my friend, Nine Merrington, the intuitive. Right away she predicted that I had only three months left to live if I kept going at the same superhuman pace that I was operating at. At the time, her words sounded unbelievable. Until then, I had been oblivious to the almost fatal urgency of my situation. Once I became aware of it, I knew that I had to pull back and so I did, on 15h June 2003. And a day later, on my birthday, I received the offer from UCRS Home Office to teach Science of Mind in Russia for a few weeks. That turned out to be my saving grace.

After I returned from Russia in September 2003, Soul Home was never the same. The vision I had nurtured since the late 1980s seemed to be crumbling. The community split in two and so did my heart. From then on, I scaled back considerably and focused my energies on teaching classes rather than on community building and outreach. Life became more manageable without the pressure I had been putting on myself to build a mega spiritual community. I now had more time to travel and do spiritual work outside South Africa.

From the early days of my ministry in 2000, I had always had the prophetic knowledge that there would be a big shift at the end of 2004. I saw myself on a long sabbatical from the ministry, pursuing my passions of writing and travelling, but not in South Africa. I sensed I would be back in Europe while another minister, perhaps an American, anchored the Soul Home energy in Johannesburg.

While I was in Russia, the ex-boyfriend from Chapter 3, Tim, contacted me again "out of the blue." We had not communicated for many years when his email suddenly popped into my inbox while I was sitting in an internet café in Moscow. He initiated a conversation about resuming our relationship. I was open to considering that option but knew I would not be free to pursue that track until the end of 2004. Why? I had committed to my four practitioner students that we would complete their four-year curriculum in December 2004. I was not about to abandon them.

In June 2004, I consulted some naturopaths who suggested I go on a vegan diet to detoxify my system. As soon as I started becoming conscious of what I was putting into my body and watched the excess mass begin to dissolve off my frame, I got mentally far clearer too. I knew my time in South Africa as the minister of Soul Home was done and I would head back to Europe to seek my fortune.

England, the country of my birth, was to be my destination. There I would have the legal right to live and to work. When I prayed for the right work in the U.K., the advertisement for the one-month intensive CELTA training (Certificate for English Language Teaching to Adults) at International House in Braamfontein, Johannesburg, kept flashing across my computer screen, irrespective of whether I had clicked on that particular website link or not! Clearly it was a sign from Upstairs. I signed up, absolutely loved the programme and qualified as a TEFL teacher (Teaching English as a Foreign Language) in December 2004.

I am proud to say that the three students who hung in until the end of their practitioner training completed their studies in December 2004 and graduated in 2005. These were Gerd

Pontow, Penelope Gottlieb and Anka Daly. Many heartfelt thanks to Revs. Bob and Barbara Grabowski, Pam Wilson RScP and John Merutka RScP who came to South Africa from San Diego in January 2005 to take my students through their oral panels.

6th February, 2005, was the date of my last Sacred Gathering. It was a beautiful coming together of all the Soul Home members who had been part of the community until mid-2003. The American team was there too and together, we honoured the new practitioner graduates. There was a sense of reconciliation and celebration in the air and also of completion. Even my mum and stepfather attended!

All three of the new practitioners took over the leadership of Soul Home when I left South Africa in March 2005. They rose to the occasion spiritually and did an amazing job of anchoring the consciousness. Gerd Pontow, my successor, who I had appointed to head up the Soul Home leadership team, stepped into the breach seamlessly, as if he had been preparing for the role over lifetimes, which indeed he had. He completed the new online ministerial training in 2015, a long distance learning programme designed for international ministerial students. In 2016, Gerd became a licensed Spiritual Director of Religious Science and is giving wonderful service in the CSL global outreach programme, along with running Soul Home full time. I never imagined that Soul Home would be sustained and maintained in my absence by my own home-grown students but I am delighted with the way it all turned out.

After leaving South Africa in March 2005, I spent two months living in Egypt (that is another story for another book) and then flew to the U.K. My dream for my new life in England was that I would be based in or near London, where I would be able to take advantage of the inexpensive short-hop flights to Europe. I particularly longed to explore Eastern Europe after the fall of

Communism, as I had been away from Europe since 1985, when I first went to South Africa.

After my first summer teaching English at Summer School in Bath and Canterbury, I prayed for short-term English teaching contracts in Europe, which would include hotel accommodation and airfares. A week later I manifested exactly that; a TEFL job which had me flying back and forth to central Europe, to Austria for the most part. I did that for a couple of years and then became a Marketing and Sales Officer for the same company, *English in Action Ltd*, which involved spending a few weeks a year in Russia, Slovenia, the Czech Republic and Hungary as well as Austria, Germany, Italy and Holland. You can read more about my adventures and miracles in Europe in my upcoming book: *Tears of the Goddess: Isis and the Amber Road* (scheduled for publication in 2018.)

My English teaching work also took me to Japan, the fulfilment of a long-term dream since age 20. Yet, despite all the travelling and all the amazing experiences I have had, the Church Lady in me has always been homesick for Soul Home and South Africa.
I thought I might be coming home in 2007 but it was a false alarm. In 2006, my friend, Rev. John Oliver, the Anglican minister of St. Mark's church in District Six in Cape Town, asked me if I would come back to South Africa and work alongside him to help him run the Western Cape Interfaith Programme and eventually take it over from him so that he could retire. Yes, I would. There was no hesitation. However, I was turned down for the position by the Board because of my skin colour and the fact that I did not speak any African languages. I can appreciate the Board's decision but was still very disappointed.

Every Christmas and New Year, when I few back to South Africa for the holidays, I would feel "wrong" getting on the plane to head back to Europe. But as you will see in the next story, we are always in the right place at the right time, engaged in the Divine Right Activity and it all had to unfold in exactly the way it did.

On 4th December, 2013, I checked in to the Hotel National in Bern, the capital of Switzerland, for my annual three-day marketing trip to my Swiss territory. On the morning of Mandela's transition, 5th December, 2013, I was sitting at breakfast when I saw a coloured and a black woman at the next table. I felt they were South Africans and sure enough, when I asked, I found out that they were performing artists from Cape Town participating in "South Africa Week" in Bern. They invited me to come to their concert at a local grammar school that afternoon. It was a private concert for the schoolchildren but I arranged my work schedule around the concert and trusted that I would find a way in.

I walked into the school, looking as if I knew what I was doing and followed the sound of the singing. Unnoticed, I was able to creep into the back of the theatre and there I sat with tears in my eyes, blessing Mandela for all he had given to the Beloved Country. On the stage I witnessed blacks, whites and coloureds, Brits and Afrikaners, gay and straight people – the Rainbow Nation in microcosm, sharing their creative musical gifts with the world. Without Mandela, this would never have been possible.
That evening, I had dinner with my Swiss agent and fell into bed exhausted.

The next morning, the first piece of news I read on my Blackberry was that Mandela had gone beyond the Veil. In shock, I fell back onto my bed and cried. Even though he had been ill for ages, it was still unfathomable that this living legend had passed on. It felt like the end of the world. What was I doing in that stupid hotel room in Switzerland? I should have been in South Africa with my friends and family and my spiritual community, crying together and grieving the loss of Madiba.

Despite my loss of appetite, I went down to breakfast to get some coffee before setting off to work and, in the restaurant I saw two coloured women. Intuitively, I knew they were from the same group of South African performers I had encountered before. I approached them and said,
"I just heard the news."
Their eyes were already red from crying. We all burst into tears together. They invited me to sit with them and we talked over breakfast. Within five minutes, my prayer to grieve in community had been answered.

In July, 2013, a good friend of mine had asked me to come back to Cape Town in December, 2013, to perform her wedding ceremony. I had booked my ticket for 12 December. What an absolute miracle! Within a week, I would be at home. I told the two women that I would be staying in Cape Town with my good friend, Lucille Kent Lückhoff of Ivydene. Did they happen to know her? Yes!! One of the women, a beautiful poet and storyteller, Diana Ferrus, was also a good friend of Lucille's and we arranged to meet at Ivydene towards the end of December.

Diana told me about the South African concert to be held that night in the Petruskirche in Bern. The focus would, of course, be a tribute to Mandela. She hoped I would be able to get a ticket. I declined. I had planned to spend the weekend with friends in Germany and had already booked my weekend hotel, three hours drive north of Bern.

But as I travelled back to the city centre from my first client of the day, the Voice said,
"Offer to do the opening prayer at the concert. You can stay an extra night in Bern and go to Germany tomorrow."
"Yes," I thought. "Of course!!"

I raced back to the hotel as I had to pick up some materials for my next client. Who should I see as I walked into the foyer of the

Hotel National but Jo-nette LeKay, the first coloured woman I had met in the South African group. I ran my idea by her. She thought it was fantastic and gave me the phone number of their producer and the organiser of the concert, Sherlock. Jo-nette only happened to be in the foyer for that brief three-minute period of time because she had toothache and was waiting for an interpreter to pick her up and take her to the dentist. The interpreter arrived and she left.

Quickly I sent a text message to Sherlock and offered to do the opening prayer. He wrote back right away and said "Yes" without knowing anything about me. He asked me to be there at 7.00 p.m. for a 7.30 p.m. start. Immediately I cancelled my hotel booking in Germany for that night and booked an extra night at the Hotel National.

But what would I wear? No ceremonial robes, nothing vaguely ministerial in my suitcase of clothes for a marketing trip. Only a beige mini-dress with funky beige and black zigzag patterned leggings and black suede over-the-knee boots. At least I had a large black and beige pashmina over my shoulders but that did not look like a ministerial stole by any stretch of the imagination. That evening, I completed my hooker image with vibrant red lipstick and set off for church in the icy cold Swiss night. I was so happy to be paying tribute to Mandela with a talented group of South African artists whom I had met so "randomly."

Sherlock greeted me warmly and introduced me to the media manager for the group who was going to welcome everyone and introduce me on the stage. She was a typical Afrikaans "Tannie" (auntie or middle-aged lady), warm at first but quickly becoming cold and suspicious when she took in my red lipstick, my dyed long red hair, cut in an asymmetrical style, my mini-dress and my black over-the-knee boots. She felt compelled to ask questions about my religion. Did I believe that Jesus died to save me from sin? She did not like my answer:

"I believe that Jesus existed and articulated universal truth principles in his teachings. However, I don't believe that I am a sinner and, therefore, I don't need to be saved."
Hrmph. As an Afrikaner from the Dutch Reformed Church, she was horrified and disgusted with my answer. How could I dress like a hooker and tell her I was not a sinner? The incongruity had her flummoxed.
"I will pray for you," she said and abruptly turned away from me to speak to someone else.
"Thank you," I replied, feeling compassion for her confusion and snippiness.

When we got on to the stage together, my new Afrikaans saviour simply introduced me as "Stephanie," rather than "Reverend Stephanie." There was no time to introduce myself and let the audience know about my background as a metaphysical minister and the founder of the first New Thought multiracial ministry in South Africa. I could have done all that in German and then start praying in English but I had been allotted exactly two minutes of stage time so I approached the microphone, closed my eyes and began to pray. But, wait a minute... What a strange experience! I could not focus my attention. Where was all the static coming from? Was there something wrong with the microphone or the sound system? What was that noise? And then it dawned on me that my saviour had not left my side. She was loudly whispering her Christian prayers over my New Thought prayer so that the audience would not be contaminated by my sin-soaked words. As soon as I had grasped where the disturbance was coming from, I could continue with my prayer and let my saviour do what she had to do in the background.

At the end of a beautiful concert and tribute to Mandela, Sherlock was effusive with his thanks for my prayer. So many people had come up to him - Muslims, Jews, gays - and said how surprisingly included they felt by my words. He wanted to stay in contact and to work together again, should the occasion arise.

I went downstairs to help the singers pack up their wardrobe. As Jo-nette and I were leaving the church and walking towards my car, we heard singing. South African singing. Where was it coming from? We followed the sound to an upstairs landing outside the minister's office. The entire troupe (except my saviour) had erupted into a spontaneous celebration of Mandela, dancing in a circle and singing famous South African songs. It could not have been a more joyful, more satisfying, more unexpected way to grieve for Mandela, surrounded as I was by South Africans of all colours on a freezing winter's night in the middle of Switzerland.

In August 2014, I came home to South Africa for my mother's 80th birthday. It was only then that I saw firsthand how difficult her life had become as the primary care-giver for my stepfather, who had advancing Alzheimer's and is also stone-deaf and lame. Mum felt that she was going insane too. The love of her life was disappearing before her very eyes and she was powerless to stop it. She was living with the constant threat of his violent attacks on her. He would shout at her in his frustration and use his walking stick as a weapon to hit her. I knew I would not be able to live with myself if she were to decline, or even transition while I was chasing the next sale for my employer in Europe, so I made a decision to leave my job and come back to South Africa to support her. Another year passed while I made my plans to take the leap back into being an unemployed alien in South Africa. However, I quit my job in July 2015, and returned home a month later.

You will be pleased to learn that my relationship with my mother has gone through many revolutions, since Chapter 13 on Forgiveness. My intention to lift from her the burden of caring for my stepfather was fulfilled in September 2015 when my three step-siblings finally agreed to place their father in full-time residential care in the Alzheimer's unit close to his home. Her loss, loneliness and grief has been of a peculiar nature for my mother as her husband is still alive in his body. I believe it is pure Grace that I am able to be a companion to her and to be of service to her. I am giving back some of the love and care that she has given to me throughout my life, whether I was being kind to her or not. We have a beautifully harmonious co-existence, which no-one could have predicted based on the evidence of the first 44 years of my life. It took me a long time to stop being a teenager....

The spiritual community, Soul Home, is still alive and well under the excellent leadership of Rev. Gerd Pontow. I had always envisaged a multiracial community, 50% black and 50% white. However, the vision continues to unfold in its own holy way and under Rev. Gerd, the ratio of blacks to whites has changed completely. There is now a mix of approximately 90% blacks and 10% whites. This is a far better representation of the current population ratio of South Africa. On most Sundays Rev. Gerd gives me the floor as the guest speaker, which fills me with joy.

My two other Practitioner students, who held the heavenly fort with Gerd for ten years – Anka Daly RScP and Penelope Gottlieb, RScP, recently went through a major change in their circumstances and in July 2016, we held a ceremony at Soul Home to celebrate these shifts.
Penelope has moved down to Cape Town for professional reasons where she is anchoring our Cape Town branch of Soul Home.
Anka has moved to Retired status as a Religious Science Practitioner, still a deep well of consciousness but no longer as active in the community as before.

Having read about my spiritual journeys with the Global Heart team from UCRS/CSL in the Ukraine, Russia and Mexico, you may have sensed how much I love travelling, particularly with spiritual groups who are on a conscious journey together. An old dream that I did not fulfil during my first half century on the planet, was to become a tourist guide. Another ambition, which I had when I was 30, was to move down to Cape Town but Ministerial School beckoned and instead I moved to America. Sooo.... when I knew I would return to South Africa, I registered in August 2015 to train as a tourist guide in Cape Town.

One of our assignments on the course was to design a three-day tour and I created a themed tour called *From Slavery to Freedom*. It traces the journey from the old days of colonialism in South Africa to Apartheid and then to the new democracy which was birthed by Mandela and his fellow inmates in the prison on Robben Island. This tour is, of course, primarily an inner journey but is designed to unfold against the backdrop of the fascinating history and breathtaking scenery of the Cape.

When I finished my training course in Cape Town and got into my taxi to Cape Town airport for my flight back to Johannesburg, I started chatting to the driver about his life. It turned out he was a prison guard for a few years. In fact, he
Worked on Robben Island. In fact, he was Nelson Mandela's warden and used to play chess with him! Not only that, but he now has a business driving tourists around the Cape in his mini-bus. You can see Something formulating itself, can't you?

I AM home now, living in the sunshine, happy to be reunited with my biological family as well as with my spiritual family of Soul Home. The vision I had of racial integration in South Africa all those years ago, continues to unfold in a dynamic way as a blessing to all.

Looking forward to the next chapter of Miss-Adventures, Miss-Stories and Miss-Demeanours as the Scroll of Life unfurls.

EPILOGUE

Thank you, Beloved Reader, for following me around the planet on my mad, passionate dash after Truth, Love, Freedom, Justice, Joy, Wisdom and all the other qualities of the Divine that have already been bestowed upon each one of us in infinite measure and which are within us now, waiting for a chance to be revealed. No one has to go running around for this Divine Essence, but I chose this option to make my journey more interesting.

Thank you too, Reader, for being my witness on this grand rollercoaster of incarnation. If it had not been for you, calling this book forth from within me, I would never have had the compulsion to write it. It is your consciousness that desired to witness my journey and personal expression, your consciousness that desired to observe how this individual soul, called Stephanie, learned how to work with the Law and learned how to love. (Note: this is called "growing up".)

You wanted to read this book and I wanted to write it. "When two or more are gathered (in agreement) there I AM," said the Christ. You and I gave birth to this and, let me tell you, it is not what I expected. No, I had different plans—a bad habit of mine that I am sure you are familiar with by now!

Yep, this was going to be a humorous collection of vignettes illustrating the Bible quotes and the metaphysical interpretations. It was going to be light-hearted entertainment with a spiritual punch. It was going to make me look good. It was *not* going to be autobiographical. It was *not* going to be self-revelatory. I certainly was *not* going to get naked with you and let you into my interior world on our first date. But now that I have, let me ask you:

Was it good for you too?

www.TimelessTransitions.net

ABOUT THE AUTHOR

Rev. Stephanie Clarke was born and raised in London, graduated from Bradford University with a degree in German and Russian then moved to Amsterdam to become a hippy. While visiting her mother in South Africa in 1985, Stephanie discovered the Johannesburg United Church of Religious Science and the Science of Mind teaching and decided to emigrate! There she had a vision of starting a multi-racial spiritual community as a forerunner to the healing of Apartheid.

This vision for South Africa led Stephanie to the U.S.A. in 1989 where she completed her New Thought Ministerial Training under the auspices of Dr. Rev. Michael Beckwith (of *The Secret* fame) at the Agape International Center of Truth in Los Angeles, California.

Returning to Johannesburg, South Africa in January, 2000, Stephanie successfully founded a vibrant, multi-racial, metaphysical community known as Soul Home. Her greatest passion was teaching her students how to pray, the affirmative way, creating sacred ceremonies (weddings, memorials and baby blessings) and leading groups to Egypt on pilgrimages. She was a guest speaker at international Science of Mind conferences in Russia, the Ukraine, Mexico and Egypt. She was also interviewed on South African national radio and TV.

Passing the baton to her qualified practitioner students in 2005, Stephanie returned "home" to the UK where her new CELTA qualification afforded her the opportunity to travel widely and to teach English in Europe and Japan.

In 2015, Stephanie returned "home" to South Africa to take care of her elderly parents and to continue serving the vision of Soul Home. The multi-racial spiritual community is alive and well under the excellent leadership of Stephanie's former student, Rev. Gerd Pontow.

Currently, Stephanie is writing her 3rd book *Tears of the Goddess: Isis and the Amber Road.* It is about her miracles and adventures in Europe. (Due for publication in 2018.) She is a metaphysical speaker, a Law of Attraction Life Coach, a spiritual tourist guide and a Ceremony Facilitator, helping mourners and celebrators to create their own sacred ceremonies.

Please go to Rev. Steph's website www.TimelessTransitions.net and click on the link for your free e-book: ***7 Steps to Creating a Healing Memorial Service for a Loved One***

CONTACT REV. STEPH

Thank you for coming with me on this metaphysical ride through the Bible. If you would like more, my new blog "Miracles, Miss-Stories and Metaphysical Musings" can be found here: www.miraclesandmissstories.wordpress.com

I hope you will communicate with me on Facebook (Rev. Stephanie Clarke) or via my website. My fleshly form can be found mostly in South Africa but also in the U.K. and Europe.

Go to the Website: www.TimelessTransitions.net
For more information about Rev. Steph's first book
Down, Dirty and Divine: a spiritual ride through London's underground
Plus more information about Rev. Steph's CD
Uncommon Prayer.
Please contact Rev. Steph here to book her as **Speaker** for your next event or to make an appointment for a private **Counselling Session**.

Here you can also book Rev. Steph for **Sacred Ceremonies:** weddings, baby blessings, memorials and other special occasions or get help creating your own special ceremony.

AVAILABLE NOW!

BOOKS

Down, Dirty & Divine: a spiritual ride through London's underground

Rev. Stephanie Clarke's first book, published in July 2012. It was written based upon instructions she received in a dream on September 25, 2011. Could London really be the New Jerusalem, the centre of reconciliation, harmony and peace on the planet? First, we must heal its shadow as well as our own. And we access the shadow of humanity by going underground...

Publisher: Matador, UK ISBN: 978 1 78088 299 4

Available for order on Amazon.com

Praise for *Down Dirty and Divine*

"This is a brilliant, holy book that needs to be read by all visitors and lovers of London! Rev. Stephanie Clarke's words and vision heal us by opening our hearts to the hidden parts of ourselves, as well as London, recognizing we are one and the same. She is tender and fearless in this fascinating, never-before-told, exploration of London's history and destiny. You will be forever grateful and blessed by every moment you spend reading this extraordinary book!!"

Rev. Harriet Hawkins, Lighthouse Center for Spiritual Living, Livermore Valley, California, USA

"Rev. Stephanie Clarke has written an extraordinary book - one of profound wisdom and vision. Skilfully, she helps us to heal the wounds in our own hearts while shining the light of awareness on the dark shadow of underground London. Her gifts of writing, speaking, and teaching spiritual principles are expressed so graciously, touching every soul who comes into her presence. She is truly a blessing to the world!"

Rev. Savanna Riker, Centers for Spiritual Living, Oakland, California, USA

RECORDINGS

Uncommon Prayer

A CD by Rev. Stephanie Clarke

10 affirmative prayers, spoken spontaneously for you, with classical music in the background, to inspire, motivate and uplift.

Publisher: Ministry of Light Expressions.

ISBN 978-0-9567716-1-2

To order: please go to www.TimelessTransitions.net

Praise for *Uncommon Prayer*

"This wonderful CD, *Uncommon Prayer*, is my constant companion. It reminds me of who I truly am and of the endless possibilities in this magical Universe. Listening to it keeps me present and focused, joyful and light. Thank you, Steph!"
Diana Arthur, Reiki Master, UK

"Stephanie is a very inspirational and warm speaker whose voice I miss and so I listen to her CD, *Uncommon Prayer*, whenever I feel down. ..."
Yuuki Hio - Physical Therapist, Kanagawa-ken, Japan

Many thanks to **Russell Stirling** for composing the beautiful classical music behind Rev. Steph's voice in "Uncommon Prayer". To contact Russell, please email him at: russells@ananzi.co.za

SACRED TOURS

1. *The London sites in **Down, Dirty & Divine***
2. ***From Slavery to Freedom** – a spiritual journey in Cape Town and the Western Cape tracing the history from slavery, colonialism and Apartheid to the new democracy of the Rainbow Nation*
3. ***The Amber Road** – a spiritual journey for women on the trail of the Goddess Isis in Roman Europe*

Please contact Rev. Steph if you want to be on her mailing list for the upcoming ***Amber Road Tour***.
www.TimelessTransitions.net

Rev. Steph's upcoming book: ***Tears of the Goddess: Isis and the Amber Road*** is due for publication in 2018.

"Travelling through Egypt with Stephanie as our tour leader was a magical, spiritual experience that brought the majesty of Ancient Egypt to life for me."
Penelope Gottlieb, Communication Specialist & Spiritual Practitioner, Johannesburg, South Africa

SACRED CEREMONIES

Please contact Rev. Steph if you would like help in facilitating a sacred ceremony such as

- ***Weddings***
- ***Memorials***
- ***Baby Blessings***
- ***House Blessings***

or indeed any transition in your life journey which you would like to mark in a sacred way.

Or go to the website www.TimelessTransitions.net to pick up your **FREE** copy of Rev. Steph's e-book:

7 Steps to Creating a Healing Memorial Service for a Loved One.

PRIVATE SESSIONS

Rev. Steph offers the following individual sessions:

- ***Spiritual Counselling***
- ***Law of Attraction Life Coaching***
- ***Akashic Readings***
- ***Psychic Channelling (to assist with the death of a loved one)***

If you would like a Skype session with Rev. Steph, please contact her to set up an appointment at www.TimelessTransitions.net

Testimonials

"Rev. Stephanie Clarke offered expertise that exceeded my years of therapy...profoundly specific insights and inspired prayer made all the difference in my world view, singing career, and self-esteem."

Cheryl Kain, singer, journalist, Massachusetts, USA

"Rev. Stephanie Clarke radiates love and joy in her teaching, speaking, counselling and writing."

Rev. Dr. Joan Steadman, Spiritual leader, Oakland, CA, USA

"The best friend anyone could have. Whether up or down, Steph is always willing to share with soup or that amazing laugh - a woman who has found the true meaning of life and I've been privileged to share a part of it."

Jacqueline Louise Miller, Senior Academic Coordinator, Canterbury, UK

Printed in Poland
by Amazon Fulfillment
Poland Sp. z o.o., Wrocław